RESEARCH AND EVALUATION IN RECREATION, PARKS, AND LEISURE STUDIES

RESEARCH AND EVALUATION IN RECREATION, PARKS, AND LEISURE STUDIES

153777120

Richard Kraus

Temple University
Philadelphia, Pennsylvania

Lawrence Allen

University of Illinois
Champaign-Urbana, Illinois

Publishing Horizons
Columbus, Ohio

Printed in the United States.

1 2 3 4 〽 7 6 5 4

Library of Congress Cataloging-in-Publication Data

Kraus, Richard G.
   Research and evaluation in recreation, parks, and leisure studies.

   1. Recreation—Research. 2. Recreation—Evaluation. 3. Leisure—Research. 4. Leisure—Evaluation. I. Allen, Lawrence R. II. Title. GV14.5.K72 1987   790'.072   87-12913
ISBN 0-942280-39-3

CONTENTS

and Evaluation. Emphasis on Accountability and Documentation. Two Research Orientations: Applied and Pure. Examples of Applied Research. Examples of Pure Research. Need for Middle Ground in Research Emphasis. Obtrusive and Nonobtrusive Research. Research Settings: Field or Laboratory. Quantifiable or Nonquantifiable Data. Time Frame of Research: Past, Present, and Future. Summary. Endnotes and Assignments.

PART II

Guidelines for Interviewing. Observational Study
Methods. Reliability. Other Issues of Experimental
Validity. Summary. Endnotes and Assignments.

Correlation. Limits of Quantification. Summary.
Endnotes and Assignments.

PART III

gram Evaluation in National Youth Sports Camp.
Examples of Goal-Achievement Model in Program
Evaluation. Identification of Specific Performance
Measures. Other Approaches to Program Evaluation.
Participation/Attendance/Income Model. Staff Rat-
ings and Participant-Satisfaction Approach. Systems-
Based Evaluation. Transaction-Observation Model.
Summary. Endnotes and Assignments.

INTRODUCTION

During the past several years, research and evaluation have emerged as increasingly important areas of concern for professionals and educators within the field of recreation, parks, and leisure services. Many managers have become heavily dependent on data-based planning and marketing processes in public departments, voluntary agencies, the military, commercial and other types of leisure-service agencies. With increased pressure to justify their existence, document their outcomes, and improve productivity, many recreation and park managers have undertaken widely expanded research and evaluation functions. Much of this has been interdisciplinary, with skilled research and evaluation teams in colleges and universities joining in collaborative efforts with community recreation organizations to conduct research, planning, and needs-assessment studies.

Linked to this has been the need to strengthen the professional image of the field of recreation and leisure by developing a body of specialized knowledge based on sound research. More and more university leisure-service curricula today offer specialized courses in research and evaluation, and national professional organizations regularly sponsor research symposia and assist in the publication of scholarly research journals. Federal and state agencies have sponsored numerous studies, particularly in areas related to outdoor recreation and environmental needs and therapeutic recreation service.

However, few specialized textbooks have appeared in this field. Two books dealing exclusively with evaluation have been published during the past several years; in terms of research, recreation and park educators have been forced to rely on books dealing generally with social, psychological, or educational research.

Our purpose therefore is to provide a specially designed text which focuses directly on recreation and leisure, and which presents both research and evaluation as closely integrated elements of the process of scientific inquiry. In doing so, we have included a wealth of basic information about the research process and the scientific method, as well as detailed guidelines for conducting research and evaluation studies on an applied level. While it is recognized that many college and university curricula offer *separate* courses in research and evaluation, they often include overlapping materials and functions. Evaluation *is* a form of research, and requires sound conceptual frameworks and data-gathering and analytical procedures if it is to be effective. We have therefore combined both elements in this text—with the understanding that an instructor might choose to emphasize one aspect of the book more than another, depending on student needs and course descriptions.

ORGANIZATION OF THE TEXT

This book has been divided into three sections. The opening group of chapters presents an introduction to the field, by defining the processes of research and evaluation and showing their relevance to the field of recreation, parks, and leisure services. It gives examples of numerous recreation studies which have been carried out in recent years and presents key concepts and terminology of research. It also describes several major categories of research design, including historical, descriptive, and experimental methods, with evaluation characterized as a specialized type of applied research.

The second section of the book deals with the process of designing and carrying out studies. It begins with the task of identifying appropriate research problems and refining problem statements and questions. It then describes the task of developing research proposals, using examples related to recreation and leisure-service needs. Sampling methods and instrumentation are examined, along with the need for validity and reliability in the study process. Two chapters deal with data analysis, including an overview of descriptive and inferential statistical methods. These chapters are *not* intended to substitute for a full-fledged course in statistics; instead, their purpose is to provide a beginning understanding of key concepts and processes in statistics, and to help students become more comfortable in reading the research literature. Instructors should feel free to use this material flexibly, depending on the level of their students and the stated purpose of the course. Chapter Nine is likely to be too advanced for most undergraduate and many graduate courses, and instructors should feel free not to make use of this chapter. The section concludes with a chapter on the preparation of research reports, ranging from academic or scholarly dissertations to less-academic, practitioner-oriented reports.

The third section of the text contains a discussion of several specialized aspects of research. It includes three detailed chapters on evaluation, which show its essential purposes and methodology. Examples of evaluation instruments and procedures used in agency and program appraisal are presented, with the last chapter in this group describing the assessment of participants' needs and behavioral outcomes, and methods of personnel evaluation. The final chapter deals with planning and marketing aspects of recreation and park management, as elements of integrated management-information systems.

Throughout, the text steers a middle course between a highly conceptual approach to the subject which is primarily concerned with theoretical aspects of recreation and leisure, and a much more practically oriented approach to recreation management needs. Thus, while it contains numerous references to the writings of Kerlinger, Selltiz, Suchman, and other authorities on social or educational research in general, it also includes numerous specific examples of studies and research methods in applied aspects of the recreation and park field.

APPLIED LEARNING ACTIVITIES

It is difficult to learn about research simply by reading about it. This text therefore suggests a number of questions, exercises, and assignments which are designed to promote an experiential and participative approach to exploring its contents.

At the end of each chapter are a number of suggested learning activities. Depending on the content of the chapter, they may include any of the following: (1) suggested questions for class discussions or examinations; (2) problem-solving assignments to be undertaken by small groups of students within the classroom setting; and (3) other assignments or tasks to be undertaken outside of the classroom and reported back to the class itself. Taken all together, they comprise an ongoing workshop in the process of planning and carrying out research and evaluation studies, and may include both hypothetical or simulated tasks or actual preparation of instruments or conducting small-scale surveys or other investigations in the field.

While there are too many such assignments for all students to be involved in all types of learning activities directly, it would be feasible to have each student undertake approximately three such tasks during the course of a semester within a small-group structure that reports back to the overall class. Other students may view their presentations and discuss them, or analyze their research designs and instruments, and so share in the learning process.

USE OF VARIED SOURCES

In preparing this text, the authors have combed the professional literature thoroughly, using citations or other materials drawn from publications in the United States and Canada. They have also drawn on the reports of research symposia and the views of numerous authorities in the recreation, parks, and leisure-studies field.

However, they have also relied heavily on their own experience as educators and researchers in the field. Between them, they have had in-depth experience as graduate students, faculty members, and research advisors in eight colleges and universities. They also have conducted approximately twenty-five research, evaluation, and planning studies as part of team projects over the past two decades.

These studies have included both highly practical needs assessments or operational analyses and evaluation reports, and more-theoretical research investigations. One of the key tenets presented in this text is that the widely held position that research must be classified as either *applied* (practical) or *pure* is somewhat arbitrary. Such a rigid division accounts in part for the gap that exists between researchers and practitioners today, and for the lack of communication or collaborative effort in many settings. This text takes the position that even highly conceptual studies may have important practical implications, and that even applied studies may be based on sound theory and may contribute significantly to an understanding of the field.

As indicated, in preparing this text the authors have drawn on the writings and ideas of numerous authorities in the field, including such individuals as John Bullaro, Peg Connolly, John Crompton, Julia Dunn, Christopher Edginton, Patricia Farrell, Seymour Gold, Scout Lee Gunn, Dennis Howard, Christine Howe, Benjamin Hunnicutt, W. B. Kinney, Roger Lancaster, Joseph Levy, Herberta Lundegren, Tony Mobley, Nancy Navar, Carol Ann Peterson, J. Robert Rossman, Stuart Schleien, Chrystos Siderelis, Daniel Sharpless, Stephen Smith, Ted Tedrick, William Theobald, Glen Van Andel, Betty van der Smissen, Andrew Weiner, and Peter Witt. It has not been possible to credit all such sources in detail. However, the authors express their deep gratitude to them and to other educators and researchers who have contributed to the development of scientific inquiry in recreation, parks, and leisure studies, and to its applied offshoots.

The final product, of course, is our own. We hope that it is one that meets the approval of faculty members, students, and practitioners throughout the field, and that it proves useful to them in the years ahead.

NATURE OF RESEARCH AND EVALUATION

Research is best understood as an extension of the scientific method which provides a more rigorous approach to seeking solutions to specific problems. The scientific method is not the private domain of the scientist or the researcher...In assessment, evaluation, and decision making, research is the only way to make rational choices between alternative practices, to validate improvements, and to build a stable foundation of effective practices as a safeguard against faddish but inferior innovations. This type of research is an activity in which every future-oriented (leisure-service) professional should engage . . .[1]

INTRODUCTION

This text is concerned with the related processes of research and evaluation in the field of recreation, parks, and leisure studies. It is designed to achieve the following specific purposes:

1. To familiarize students with the meaning of research and evaluation, and to describe their professional applications to the overall leisure-service field.

2. To present and discuss the basic concepts of scientific inquiry that underly all forms of research and evaluation.

3. To describe in detail several different types of research methodology, including historical, descriptive, experimental, and evaluative designs, and to show how they may be used in recreation, parks, and leisure studies.

4. To present basic guidelines for carrying out research and evaluation, and to develop competence in the following steps of scientific inquiry: (a) framing appropriate research questions or hypotheses; (b) preparation of research proposals; (c) implementing the research, making use of suitable sampling methods, instruments, and needed controls; (d) analyzing and interpreting the data; and (e) preparing a final report of the research.

5. To help students: (a) gain the skills needed to read and understand research reports in professional journals and (b) recognize the value of research and evaluation as important professional tools, and learn to rely on them to improve their own professional performance.

Chapter One begins by defining research and evaluation and showing their relationship to the planning process. It describes the growing need for fuller documentation and accountability in the leisure-service field. It provides a brief overview of the development of research and evaluation in recreation, parks, and leisure studies, and concludes with a statement of desired outcomes for students taking courses in this field.

DEFINITION OF TERMS

The two terms "research" and "evaluation" are closely connected and often describe similar processes. Both are forms of *systematic inquiry*. In contrast to casual or haphazard observation, or the use of scattered evidence to draw conclusions or make judgments, research and evaluation must be purposeful and carefully directed. They employ scientifically designed data-gathering methods, along with controls and data-analysis techniques that ensure valid and trustworthy results. However, there *are* certain differences between research and evaluation, as the following section demonstrates.

RESEARCH

There are many different conceptions of the meaning of the term "research." If you were to ask a dozen different scholars or scientists to define it, you might well receive a dozen different replies— some lofty and complex, others more casual and down-to-earth. One approach is to use the definition found in an authoritative literary source. *Research* is defined in Webster's *International Dictionary* as:

Studious inquiry or examination; . . . critical and exhaustive investigation or experimentation having for its aim the discovery of new facts and their correct interpretation, the revision of accepted conclusions, theories, or laws, in the light of newly discovered facts, or the practical applications of such new or revised conclusions.[2]

Kerlinger sharpens this definition by stating:

Scientific research is systematic, controlled, empirical, and critical investigation of natural phenomena guided by theory and hypotheses about the presumed relations among such phenomena.[3]

Research may be extremely varied in its purposes and the forms it takes. It may involve observational studies, mailed surveys, historical investigations, laboratory experiments, and numerous other types of designs or data-gathering procedures. As this text will show, it may be highly theoretical, dealing with abstract issues or concepts, or may have extremely practical and utilitarian purposes.

At one level, research may simply observe and report *what is,* in an organized way. At another level, it may be concerned with developing theories that explain the *how* and *why* of things, or that show the relationships among various phenomena. Research may deal with the past, the present, or the future, and may be carried out in real or in artificial settings. It may involve an unobtrusive, "hands-off" approach in which the researcher seeks to be as invisible as possible, or may introduce various factors or environmental conditions which affect the behavior of participants.

Whatever its dimensions, the ultimate purpose of research in recreation, parks, and leisure studies is to provide a solid base of knowledge and theory, both to the field at large and to individual practitioners.

EVALUATION

The term *evaluation* is defined in Webster as the "process or result of evaluating." The verb *evaluate* means "To ascertain the value or amount of; to appraise carefully; to express numerically."[4]

Evaluation has commonly been thought of as a means of documenting an agency's worth, by providing evidence of its positive contribution to society, or other desirable outcomes it has achieved. Suchman points out that, increasingly, the public has become unwilling to accept the legitimacy of social institutions through faith, and instead demands facts, or tangible "proofs" of value.[5]

Within varied types of community organizations, evaluation is used to determine the success of programs in meeting their stated objectives. It may also seek to assess the quality of agencies or programs, based on professionally accepted standards or criteria used to judge such agencies. In addition to examining overall agencies or programs, evaluation may also measure the effectiveness or quality of component elements, such as administrative policies and practices, personnel, or facilities. Particularly in specialized fields like therapeutic recreation service, evaluation may focus heavily on participants and on behavioral change brought about through program involvement.

RELATIONSHIP BETWEEN RESEARCH AND EVALUATION

Evaluation is actually a form of research, in the sense that it relies on the use of valid, carefully designed data-gathering instruments and procedures to arrive at conclusions. It differs from research in terms of its scope and purposes. Evaluation is always concerned with practical or applied purposes. It always uses empirical evidence—meaning data that can be directly observed and measured. It deals with real situations or conditions in the present or recent past. It is always concerned with the effectiveness or professional quality of agencies, programs, personnel, procedures, or similar subjects.

In contrast, research is extremely broad in its purposes and methods. It deals with both theoretical and practical concerns; while evaluation is always intended to gather useful information, research may seek to test theories or hypotheses that have no obvious practical implications beyond their contribution to scholarly knowledge in the field of recreation, parks, and leisure studies.

CONTRIBUTION OF RESEARCH AND EVALUATION TO LEISURE SERVICES

Any social institution or field of human service that seeks to gain public respect or to be regarded as a legitimate profession must advance its body of specialized knowledge through scientifically valid research and evaluation. These procedures serve both to document the actual benefits and outcomes derived from the field, and to develop more effective policies and procedures. They also provide a theoretical base for the field, by formulating basic principles or concepts that support professional practices.

In the field of medicine, for example, research is constantly being conducted to identify the causes of disease and to develop new solutions in terms of environmental controls, medicines, or other treatment procedures to combat illness and maintain individual and community health and well-being.

In the business world, research and evaluation lead to new products or improved methods of marketing them, to fuller understanding of consumer needs and attitudes, or to more effective personnel management or financial investment strategies.

Psychologists conduct extensive research studies which explore the nature of personality, psychopathology and mental health, learning processes, and family relationships. Sociologists, anthropologists, and other social scientists systematically examine human institutions and cultural practices, individual and group behavior, and similar aspects of modern living.

The basic point is that recreation, park, and leisure-service professionals *must* conduct meaningful research and evaluation studies if they are to justify *their* efforts, document *their* outcomes, and compete within the total spectrum of governmental and human-service programs today.

OVERVIEW OF PAST RESEARCH PRACTICES

In the past, it was frequently stated that the recreation and leisure-studies field lacked a body of significant research literature. However, there has been a steady increase in the number and variety of studies in this field and in the publication of research journals and reports. The following section offers a brief chronology of research trends in recreation, parks, and leisure studies.

EARLY STUDIES OF PLAY

During the nineteenth century, a number of authorities examined the nature of play activities in both animal and human societies. Including such writers as Karl Groos, Herbert Spencer, and G. Stanley Hall, they formulated several theories of play behavior.[6] These theories were based on the systematic observation of play and constituted an early form of empirical research in this field. For the first time, play and recreation were perceived as significant aspects of life that deserved careful scholarly attention.

VEBLEN'S ANALYSIS OF LEISURE

In the late nineteenth century, the Danish scholar Thorstein Veblen carried out an extensive historical and sociological study of leisure in the lives of the wealthy. He developed a conceptual model of the so-called "leisure class" that profoundly influenced our understanding of the relationship of leisure and social class.[7]

EARLY TWENTIETH-CENTURY STUDIES OF RECREATION AND LEISURE

During the first three decades of the twentieth century, several forms of research into recreation, play, and leisure were initiated: (a) With the establishment of community recreation and park systems throughout the United States, there were a number of nationwide studies of facilities, programs, and personnel which documented progress in this field; (b) a number of psychologists examined the role of play in the lives of children, and documented its value; and (c) with growing concern about leisure as a social problem, many cities and social welfare organizations conducted surveys that focused on the problem of poorly utilized free time, including juvenile delinquency and gang activity, as a means of gaining support for organized recreation programs for youth in American communities.[8]

DEPRESSION AND POST-WORLD WAR II PERIOD

During the 1930s and 1940s, more comprehensive and solidly based studies of recreation, parks, and leisure services began to appear. Lebert H. Weir, for example, did an extensive, detailed survey of recreation and park systems in European nations.[9] George Lundberg, Mirra Komarovsky, and other social scientists carried out studies of the leisure behaviors and values of different age groups, occupational groups, and social classes.[10] Studies carried out by the National Recreation Association provided a continuing profile of the expanding recreation and park agencies in American communities. Some social scientists, such as Gunnar Myrdal, examined the role of recreation in the lives of American blacks.[11] Other sociologists included leisure as an important element in community life, in their studies of prototypical American cities like "Elmtown" and "Middletown."

RESEARCH IN OUTDOOR RECREATION: THE ORRRC REPORT

In 1962, the twenty-seven-volume report of the Outdoor Recreation Resources Review Commission provided a comprehensive picture of the nation's forests, wilderness, and water-based resources, and overall park and open-space needs.[12] This study stimulated a wave of national concern in this field, and led to legislation that assisted open-space acquisition, the protection or restoration of wild rivers and trails, and substantial funding of outdoor recreation planning studies by federal and state agencies.

EXPANSION OF HIGHER EDUCATION IN RECREATION AND PARKS

The prominence given to the ORRRC Report and the merging of the recreation and park field (illustrated by the establishment of the National Recreation and Park Association), combined with rapidly expanding spending and employment in recreation, led to the dramatic growth of higher education curricula in recreation, parks, and leisure studies during the late 1960s and 1970s.

Many of these new departments began to develop independent courses in research and evaluation. Graduate curricula on the master's and doctoral levels produced growing numbers of theses and dissertations, and encouraged a number of national and regional conferences on research needs and methods in recreation and leisure, during the mid-1960s.[13] With funding support given by the federal and state governments to research in outdoor recreation and the needs of special populations, professional conferences began to sponsor symposia reporting research studies and findings. In addition, several new research journals were established, and other professional publications regularly reported research findings.

As a result of these developments, research in recreation, parks, and leisure studies has become far more extensive and sophisticated in recent years. Today, many social and behavioral scientists are exploring various aspects of the psychology of play and sport, the sociology of leisure, and the economics of recreation programming and participation. Political scientists have examined recreation as a governmental function and other researchers in fields such as urban studies, environmental planning, and management are conducting studies, often on an interdisciplinary basis.

SOPHISTICATION OF CURRENT RESEARCH APPROACHES

To illustrate the advanced nature of research today, Finsterbusch and Wolf list over twenty-five types of research designs that are being used to assess the social and environmental impacts of government projects, including highly technical and specialized data-gathering methods.[14] Within the leisure-service field, such

complex and scholarly studies often deal with issues that have little relevance for practitioners concerned with the realistic task of
providing facilities and programs to meet public needs. As a
result, Mobley suggests that a significant gap has developed
between researchers and professionals in recreation and park
agencies.[15] Too often, he states, college and university professors
carry out studies that use agencies and participants as sources of
data, without giving practitioners the opportunity to become
meaningfully involved in the process. Often their reports are not
intelligible to readers who lack research expertise, and are rarely
read by practitioners.

To bridge this gap, Mobley argues that it is essential to develop a
broader base of support for research that will include both theoretical and applied forms of investigation, and that will provide
needed information to support professional planning and program
practices. He writes:

> The practitioner needs to communicate to the researcher the specific
> nature of the problems encountered in operating park and recreation
> agencies. The researcher needs to be more articulate in interpreting
> the research results as well as applying the results to specific prob-
> lems faced by the practitioner.

Extending this argument, students, who are the professionals of
tomorrow, need to become literate with respect to research and
evaluation principles and methods—not only for the sake of fur-
thering their own careers, but also to strengthen the field. Such
expertise is critically important for professional-level personnel in
all types of government, business, educational, and social agencies
today. Isaac and Michael identify eight kinds of audiences who
should acquire literacy in research and evaluation, including:

1. The busy project director.
2. The "occasional" researcher.
3. The proposal writer.
4. The evaluator.
5. The reviewer and consumer of research.
6. The undergraduate student in the beginning courses.
7. The graduate student preparing for theses, dissertations, and
   examinations.
8. Members of research staffs or project teams.[16]

Even for those who are not planning to become researchers as
such, it is essential to gain a basic knowledge of simple research

designs and skills, or of the most useful models of evaluation. In terms of being able to read research findings intelligently and critically, in the modern era we are all "consumers" of research results and must be able to judge the adequacy of the methods by which they have been obtained. As students, you may find that many of the "facts" presented in courses are based on the results of research. However, the findings of one study may differ widely from those of others. Both as students and as professionals-to-be, you will need to be able to judge the adequacy of research methodology, by asking such questions as:

> How do the investigators define their terms? Are they really both talking about the same things, or have they used the same words for different phenomena? Was the evidence they gathered relevant to the problem? Were there any obvious sources of bias in the way the data were gathered?[17]

The ability to apply such criteria is a valuable asset for practitioners within any profession or field of public service. For those planning to enter the field of recreation, parks, and leisure services, the following outcomes should be gained from a course in research and evaluation.

DESIRED OUTCOMES FOR STUDENTS

1. Students should gain a feeling of *enthusiasm* about research and evaluation, and a degree of confidence in terms of using them as professional tools. While they *cannot* become expert researchers by taking a single course, they *can* gain a beginning understanding of research concepts and methodology, and develop skill in formating research problems and proposals. They can also learn to develop evaluation instruments and to analyze descriptive data.

2. They should develop the habit of *reading the current literature* in recreation, parks, and leisure studies. This means that they can identify useful journals, and can understand research articles at an appropriate level of complexity. They should also be exposed to literature retrieval methods and techniques for carrying out computer searches, using available reference sources and similar tools.

3. They should recognize and respect the potential *contribution of research and evaluation* in terms of: (*a*) developing the field's status by providing a body of scholarly knowledge and theory and (*b*) improving their own job performances and enhancing their

own career development by gaining useful professional skills in this area.

4. They should develop the capacity for *critical thinking,* through which they view research findings cautiously and accept claims or statements of outcomes only on the basis of sound evidence. One of the key purposes of research and evaluation is to dispel unrealistic claims and platitudes that are carelessly used to support and justify the field. These strategies must be replaced by accountability and solid documentation that command respect from other professionals, public officials, and members of the public at large.

SUMMARY

This chapter defines the terms "research" and "evaluation," showing their similarities and differences, and their relationship to planning as a professional function. It stresses the fact that all forms of human enterprises or societal organizations rely heavily on research to advance knowledge and improve professional practice.

The chapter presents a chronological overview of the past development of scientific inquiry in the recreation, parks, and leisure-studies field, and reemphasizes their importance in the preparation of capable practitioners. In conclusion, it should be stressed that research and evaluation are *not* mystical, abstruse, or dull areas of practice. Instead, they can and should be highly interesting and challenging areas of personal and professional growth, which can lead to increased competence, productivity, and career success.

ENDNOTES

1. Tony A. Mobley, "Practitioner, Researcher—A Team," *Parks and Recreation* (April 1980): 40.
2. *Webster's New International Dictionary* (Springfield, Mass.: G. and C. Merriam Co., 1956): 2118.
3. Fred N. Kerlinger, *Foundations of Behavioral Research* (New York: Holt, Rinehart and Winston, 1973): 10.
4. *Webster's New International Dictionary, op. cit.,* 883.
5. Edward Suchman, *Evaluative Research: Principles and Practices in Public Service and Social Action Programs* (New York: Russell Sage Foundation, 1971): 2.
6. For a summary of these, see: Richard Kraus, *Recreation and Leisure in Modern Society* (Glenview, Ill.: Scott, Foresman and Co., 1984): 21–23.

7. Thorstein Veblen, *The Theory of the Leisure Class* (New York: Viking Press, 1899).

8. Kraus, *op cit.,* 99–112.

9. Lebert H. Weir, *Europe at Play: A Study of Recreation and Leisure* (New York: A.S. Barnes, 1937).

10. See: Eric Larrabee and Rolf Meyersohn, *Mass Leisure* (Glencoe, Ill.: Free Press, 1958).

11. Gunnar Myrdal, *The American Dilemma* (New York: Harper and Row, 1944).

12. "Outdoor Recreation for America," *Report to the President and Congress by the Outdoor Recreation Resources Review Commission* (Washington, D.C.: U.S. Government Printing Office, 1962): 95–117.

13. See for example: *Recreation Research: Report of a National Conference* (Washington, D.C.: American Association for Health, Physical Education and Recreation, and National Recreation and Park Association, 1966).

14. Kurt Finsterbusch and C.P. Wolf, eds., *Methodology of Social Impact Assessment* (Stroudsberg, Pa.: Dowden, Hutchinson and Ross, 1977).

15. Mobley, *op. cit.,* 41, 72.

16. Stephen Isaac and William B. Michael, *Handbook in Research and Evaluation* (San Diego, Cal.: EdITS Publishers, 1971, 1980): iii.

17. Claire Selltiz, Lawrence S. Wrightsman, and Stuart W. Cook, *Research Methods in Social Relations* (New York: Holt, Rinehart and Winston, 1976): 11.

QUESTIONS FOR CLASS
REVIEW AND DISCUSSION

1. Compare research and evaluation. Define each term and show their similarities and differences, as presented in this chapter.

2. Why is it essential for a field such as recreation, parks, and leisure services to have a body of specialized knowledge that is based on carefully designed research studies?

3. Mobley describes the gap that has developed between professional practitioners and scholarly researchers in the recreation, park, and leisure-service field. What is the cause of this gap, and what are its implications? What can be done about it?

PROFESSIONAL APPLICATIONS OF RESEARCH AND EVALUATION

Research underpins all of these criteria (of professionalism) . . . A body of validated knowledge on which the profession is based requires codification of research findings from a variety of sources as well as research results from studies geared to recreation programs or leadership problems. This last criterion calls for a social policy concern on the part of the profession which again requires research methods for an explanation of the causes and consequences of such social problems. Research then becomes a major vehicle in professionalizing recreation.[1]

INTRODUCTION

This chapter begins by discussing the general role of research and evaluation within the recreation, park, and leisure-service field, with emphasis on the current pressure for documentation and accountability in agency management. It then categorizes and illustrates a number of recent specific kinds of studies that are of an applied or practical nature; similar examples are given of research studies that are "pure" or theoretical in focus. The chapter concludes with a discussion of unique values of both types of approaches and with a summary of several other contrasting models of research as they relate to the leisure-service field.

GENERAL ROLE OF SCIENTIFIC INQUIRY IN THE LEISURE-SERVICE FIELD

The most important contribution of research and evaluation to the overall field of recreation, parks, and leisure studies is that they provide a body of contemporary scholarship based on scientific investigation. This is essential if the field is to be recognized as a significant professional discipline, comparable to other specialized areas of human service or social management.

SPECIFIC FUNCTIONS OF RESEARCH AND EVALUATION

There are a number of specific needs in the field of recreation, parks, and leisure services that can be met through systematic, carefully designed research and evaluation studies. They include the following:

1. The need to improve, test, or apply new professional techniques and practices, in order to upgrade leadership and management operations in various areas of leisure service, including programming, facilities development, and fiscal management.

2. The need to understand the leisure experience, its motivations, structure, and consequences. Linked to this is the need to identify and measure the leisure needs and wishes of clients, patients, or other population groups in institutions or communities, as a basis for developing policies and programs designed to serve them more effectively.

3. The need to be able to measure the specific outcomes and values of organized recreation and park service and experiences, to provide convincing documentation and support for the field. Related to this is the need to measure the quality of agencies or programs, to provide an intelligent basis for decision making or policy formulation.

In a sense, each of the preceding functions is related to the overall task of planning, managing, and marketing recreation programs and services. Beyond these values, research may also contribute to society's understanding of recreation and leisure as important aspects of community life and personal well-being. In addition, it may provide insight into changing social conditions or factors which influence recreation behaviors.

EMPHASIS ON ACCOUNTABILITY AND DOCUMENTATION

Of the preceding functions of research and evaluation, one of the most critical is the need to document the value and effectiveness of recreation agencies and programs. For the past decade, we have experienced an era of budget-cutting and increased demand for accountability, particularly for leisure-service agencies that depend heavily on tax allocations or voluntary contributions for financial support. Woo and Farley state:

> Ongoing evaluation of past policies and commitments is critical because public funding is shrinking and the era of cutback management has arrived. Evaluation provides information that documents, supports, and makes public programs accountable to their constituency.[2]

Supporting this position, Ellis and Witt point out that, in the past, evaluation of recreation programs tended to be "biased, self-serving, and ultimately misleading." Today, they argue, such "evidence" will not suffice. Instead:

> . . . evaluation by design is a necessity. No longer will intuitive judgments suffice. The best proof possible is needed so that what is said to be done is really being done. There is a need for ammunition to fight to save park, recreation, and leisure services from the tax cutter's axe. It is also essential to fulfill the responsibility to spend tax dollars in the most efficient and effective way possible.[3]

Similarly, Connolly makes the point that the limited resources that are available today for the support of human services make it necessary for accountability to be convincingly demonstrated in the competition for funding support:

> Accountability is a relative term that describes the capability of a service delivery system to justify or explain the activities and services it provides. Program accountability reflects the extent to which program expenditures, activities, and processes effectively and efficiently accomplish (their) purposes. Evaluation methods are employed to determine program accomplishments. . . .[4]

RESEARCH AND EVALUATION MUST BE UNBIASED

It should be stressed that research and evaluation must *not* be expected to provide automatic justifications for one's program. They must be carried out in an objective, unbiased, and totally honest fashion; when they are, they may well yield negative findings, rather than positive outcomes. Like all forms of research, evaluation does not seek to "prove" a case. Instead, it gathers evidence and makes judgments as objectively as possible—not only to determine whether programs have been successful, but also to improve them as they are being carried on, or in future planning and implementation.

TWO RESEARCH ORIENTATIONS: APPLIED AND PURE

The preceding section dealt with a number of practical functions of research, which are directly useful in improving agency performance and enhancing the overall leisure-service profession. Such studies are usually referred to as "applied" forms of research. Customarily, they deal with the "how" and "why" of practical programming or management tasks, and are intended to yield immediately useful findings. In contrast, a second type of research is referred to as "pure" or "theoretical," meaning that its primary purpose is to gather knowledge for its own sake—usually of a conceptual nature—rather than because of its direct usefulness. It attempts to identify and explain phenomena and the relationships among them, in order to develop a stronger theoretical base for leisure-service delivery.

EXAMPLES OF APPLIED RESEARCH

The following section presents examples of applied research and evaluation studies in the field of recreation and leisure services. Four areas of concern are identified: (*a*) recreation programs and services and their outcomes; (*b*) professional development in recreation and parks; (*c*) design, development, and maintenance of areas and facilities; and (*d*) management functions, problems, and trends. In each case, several typical research topics are presented, followed by listings of several recently published research reports that illustrate the category.

1. Recreation Programs, Services, and Outcomes
   a. Surveys of program practices and trends, within a community or region, a given type of agency, or other setting. Such

studies might deal with program activities, participation levels, economic factors, areas and facilities, or other elements.

b. Feasibility studies, which are intended to determine whether it is necessary to develop a particular type of facility or program, and whether it can be economically justified; these studies may examine the potential audience or market for the project; competitive facilities or programs in the area; potential revenues to be derived; possible environmental impacts; and similar elements.

c. Participant needs assessments are studies which measure the felt or expressed leisure needs and interests of individuals or groups and other factors related to time, cost, and levels of participation. Needs assessment may also be carried out in a prescriptive manner, in which the programmer makes his or her independent assessment of the individual's needs based on observation of functional performance and other background information.

d. Studies of program outcomes or benefits, either in general terms or by measuring success in achieving stated objectives. These studies may be conducted in several ways: (1) through self-reported satisfactions and reported benefits; (2) through observation of performance and behavioral change; or (3) through measurement of other factors, such as changes in absenteeism or the accident rate, in a company-sponsored recreation program.

e. Examination of a program or agency based on published performance guidelines or standards, or accreditation standards and criteria.

Examples of research studies reported in the literature or at professional meetings which deal with such topics include the following; they are drawn from both research journals and more general professional publications.

T. David Botterill and John L. Crompton, "Daycare: Is an Opportunity Being Missed?" *Journal of Park and Recreation Administration* Vol. 2, No. 2 (April 1984): 37–45.

Mary F. Chenery, "Effects of Summer Camp on Child Development and Contributions of Counselors to Those Effects," *Journal of Leisure Research* (3rd Quarter, 1981): 195–207.

Stuart J. Schleien, Karen D. Olson, Nancy C. Rogers and Margaret E. McLafferty, "Integrating Children with Severe Handicaps into Recreation and Physical Education Programs," *Journal of Park and*

Recreation Administration Vol. 3, No. 1 (1st Quarter, 1985): 50–66.

Leonard M. Wankel, "Personal and Situational Factors Affecting Exercise Involvement: The Importance of Enjoyment," *Research Quarterly for Exercise and Sport,* Vol. 56, No. 3 (1985): 275–282.

2. Professionalism in Leisure Service
   a. Surveys of personnel at work in the field; for example, surveys of numbers of professional employees in public recreation and park agencies in a given state; their salaries, job titles, and descriptions; working conditions and qualifications or standards for employment.
   b. Competency-based studies, which systematically analyze the specific job skills needed for successful performance in a given type of position or area of professional service.
   c. Studies of college and university curricula in recreation, parks, and leisure studies, including degree options and curriculum trends, number and background of faculty members, enrollment statistics, and accreditation processes.
   d. Role of professional societies in promoting public awareness of the leisure-service field, improving professional performance, unifying the field, supporting needed legislation, sponsoring research, and similar functions.
   e. Research into staff productivity, using systematic cost-benefit analysis or other techniques to evaluate performance.

Glen D. Alexander, "Evaluate Your Personnel Services for Greater Productivity," *Parks and Recreation* (October 1978): 30–31.

Melinda Conway, "Performance Appraisal System for Therapeutic Recreation," *Therapeutic Recreation Journal* Vol. 18, No. 1 (1st Quarter 1985): 44–49.

David Culkin and Dennis R. Howard, "Collective Bargaining and Recreation and Park Operations," *Parks and Recreation* (October 1982): 58–65.

Karla A. Henderson, "Continuing Education Needs of Therapeutic Recreation Professionals," *Therapeutic Recreation Journal* (1st Quarter 1981): 4–10.

Ted Tedrick, "Personnel Evaluation: In Search of Valid Performance Standards" *Journal of Park and Recreation Administration* Vol. 1, No. 3 (July 1983): 35–42.

3. Recreation and Park Areas and Facilities
   a. Planning studies which include inventories of parks; playgrounds; aquatic, sport, and other specialized facilities.

Might include classification of facilities as to type and purpose, linked to projections of future needs and short- and
long-range priority ratings for acquisition and development.

b. Experimentation with different types of facilities to determine their effectiveness in attracting participants, promoting specific types of play, or minimizing accidents or other
undesirable incidents.

c. Studies of the environmental impact of recreation on forest
areas or other outdoor resources. Examples might include the
effect of off-road vehicles on vegetation and wildlife, or boating and related water activities on reservoir water quality.

d. Studies concerned with access to recreation facilities for the
disabled, including both indoor and outdoor settings. May
deal with application of guidelines for ramps, doorways, lav-
atories, and other modified facility elements, or with the
design of special types of facilities to encourage participation
by the disabled.

Franklin E. Boteler, "Carrying Capacity as a Framework for Managing Whitewater Use," *Journal of Park and Recreation Administration,*
Vol. 2, No. 2 (April 1984): 26–36.

A. J. Haley, "Municipal Recreation and Park Standards in the United
States: Central Cities and Suburbs," *Leisure Sciences,* Vol. 2, No. 3/4
(1979): 277–289.

W. F. LaPage, "Recreation Resource Management for Visitor Satisfaction," *Journal of Park and Recreation Administration,* Vol. 1, No. 2
(April 1983): 37–44.

Leonard E. Phillips, Jr., "Computerized Tree Inventory," *Journal of
Park and Recreation Administration,* Vol. 3, No. 3 (Fall 1985): 43–47.

Chrystos D. Siderelis, "Park Maintenance Management Systems:
Past and Present," *Journal of Park and Recreation Administration,*
Vol. 3, No. 3 (Fall 1985): 29–36.

---

4. Management Problems and Trends

a. Research in fiscal practices, including trends in budgetary
allocations, use of fees and charges, leasing and concession
arrangements, use of gift catalogs, grants and subsidies, subcontracting of recreation functions, and similar topics.

b. Studies of vandalism, crime, and related management problems in recreation and park settings, including methods used
to deal with them. Linked to this area, studies related to risk
management, accident prevention, health, and safety.

   c. Analysis of community relations and cosponsorship practice involving synergetic relationships with other community agencies or businesses.

   d. Examination of new or emerging managerial approaches, including marketing methods, systems-planning techniques, participative management emphases, and similar topics.

James E. Fletcher, "Assessing the Impact of Actual and Perceived Safety and Security Problems in Park Use and Enjoyment," *Journal of Park and Recreation Administration,* Vol. 1, No. 2 (April 1983): 21–36.

Christine Z. Howe, "Description of an On-Line Information and Referral Service," *Therapeutic Recreation Journal,* Vol. 20, No. 2 (2nd Quarter 1986): 19–23.

Brian J. Mihalik, "Practitioner-Identified Technical Assistance Needs for Community Leisure Service Agencies," *Journal of Park and Recreation Administration,* Vol. 2, No. 1 (January 1984): 52–63.

Richard J. Schroth and Daniel R. Sharpless, "Development and Design of a Computer Supported Management Information System," *Journal of Park and Recreation Administration,* Vol. 1, No. 3 (July 1983): 23–34.

Rodney B. Warnick and Dennis R. Howard, "Market Share Analysis of Selected Leisure Services from 1979 to 1982," *Journal of Park and Recreation Administration,* Vol. 3, No. 4 (Winter 1985): 64–76.

At the simplest level, such studies may simply provide a descriptive report of the factual findings of the research. When this is done, using tables and charts or other convenient forms of summarization, the process represents a somewhat superficial or mechanical form of research. At a more advanced level, applied research studies may seek to test hypotheses and build theories or models that explain relationships and cause-and-effect sequences. In either case, the intention of the researcher is to gather information or arrive at conclusions that will be directly useful to practitioners. Such results will obviously be more valuable if they have broad applications to the overall leisure-service field, rather then just to the agency that conducted the study, or the specific setting that was examined.

EXAMPLES OF PURE RESEARCH

In sharp contrast to applied research studies are so-called pure or "basic" research studies. Such investigations are usually concerned with developing or testing concepts and theories, and tend to make use of investigative and analytical techniques that are found in the social and behavioral sciences, such as psychology, sociology, anthropology, or economics. Their purpose essentially is to examine recreation and leisure as social phenomena, to clarify their meanings and implied values, and to relate them to the broader societal context.

Twelve examples of the kinds of subjects dealt with under this broad heading follow. The list is by no means exhaustive; many other theoretical research subjects are discussed each year at national research symposiums.

1. Philosophical or conceptual analyses of play, recreation, and leisure in society; typically, they might involve defining the term or concept, examining its historical roots, and suggesting contemporary applications or changes in public perceptions of it.

2. Examination of the influence of such socioeconomic or demographic variables as social class, racial or ethnic identification, occupation, or educational background on leisure attitudes and behavior.

3. Studies of personality patterns in relation to recreational interests and involvement.

4. Historical studies of specific types of leisure activity (sports, performing arts, gambling, etc.) in different eras, or of changing attitudes toward recreation and leisure.

5. Anthropological analysis of play and ritual in primitive societies, or of the social impact of tourism on undeveloped countries.

6. Esthetic or critical examinations of creative/cultural forms of expression, such as the fine and performing arts, as examples of leisure activity.

7. Relationship between sex or gender and one's leisure values and choices; study of recreational involvement as an aspect of family life or marriage.

8. Measurement of quality and beauty of outdoor environments as factors in wilderness-related planning and management policies.

9. Analysis of changing professional roles; for example, extension of therapeutic recreation specialists' functions into advocacy, community education, counseling, facilitating and referring clients, and similar responsibilities.

10. Typologies of leisure behaviors in relation to fundamental patterns of motivation and psychosocial needs of participants.

11. Leisure behavior patterns of special populations, such as the physically or mentally disabled, aging, alcoholics, or drug abusers.

12. Differences in values and positions with respect to public policy between different groups or recreation participants; for exam-

ple, contrasting environmental attitudes of cross-country skiers and snowmobile club members.

Examples of research studies reported in the professional literature which deal with primarily conceptual or theoretical concerns include the following:

Lawrence R. Allen and Mary Ann Donnelly, "An Analysis of the Social Unit of Participation and the Perceived Psychological Outcomes Associated with Most Enjoyable Recreation Activities," *Leisure Sciences,* Vol. 7, No. 4 (1984): 421–441.

Erik Cohen, "The Tourist Guide: The Origins, Structure and Dynamics of a Role," *Annals of Tourism Research,* Vol. 12 (1985): 5–29.

Edgar L. Jackson and Robert A. G. Wong, "Perceived Conflict Between Urban Cross Country Skiers and Snowmobilers in Alberta," *Journal of Leisure Research* (1st Quarter, 1982): 47–60.

Allan S. Mills, "Participation Motivations for Outdoor Recreation: A Test of Maslow's Theory," *Journal of Leisure Research* (3rd Quarter, 1985): 184–199.

Jussi Simpura, "Drinking: An Ignored Leisure Activity," *Journal of Leisure Research,* (3rd Quarter, 1985): 200–211.

Elmer Spreitzer and Eldon E. Snyder, "Correlates of Participation in Adult Recreational Sports," *Journal of Leisure Research* (1st Quarter, 1983): 27–38.

NEED FOR MIDDLE GROUND IN RESEARCH EMPHASIS

Applied studies tend to be sponsored by leisure-service agencies, government departments, or professional societies. They are usually reported in professional newsletters, magazines that have a broad appeal in the field, or separately published research monographs or reports. When statistics are reported, they are usually fairly simple, and presented through charts or tables that are readily comprehensible to a lay audience.

In contrast, theoretical research is more complex in the questions that it asks and the investigative methods used. Often it is carried out by scholars who are specialists in such fields as psychology, sociology, or economics—or by recreation and park educators who have had training in these disciplines. Usually, the research reports are technical and are presented in scholarly journals with limited readerships.

As Chapter 1 indicated, there tends to be a gap between professional researchers and recreation practitioners. Professional researchers regard the kind of research done by practitioners as mechanical and lacking in scholarly significance. On the other hand, practitioners are usually disinterested in theoretical research studies, and tend to view them as "ivory-tower" preoccupations that do not get at the concrete issues or real problems that need to be solved.

To deal constructively with this situation, one may argue that research is not necessarily divided into mutually exclusive "applied" and "pure" categories. Instead, many studies that are primarily conceptual in nature may have important practical implications for practitioners. For example, analysis of motivations for participation may lead to the more effective design of recreation programs. Similarly, studies that have a strong practical purpose may also yield findings that help to build a theoretical framework for the analysis of leisure behavior or trends. Therefore, it makes sense to visualize a continuum which ranges from very simple, nonscholarly but practical studies at one end of the spectrum, to more complex, scholarly studies at the other end.

In the middle of this range, there is a substantial amount of research that is mixed in both purpose and method. Such studies have both practical and theoretical value. What is important is that they are carefully designed and carried out with true scientific rigor. To conduct such research, it is essential that practitioners and research specialists work closely together in jointly conducted studies. Therefore, fuller emphasis should be given to research studies that occupy the middle ground and are both academically respectable and clearly relevant to the concerns of recreation agencies and practitioners.

CONTRASTING METHODS IN RESEARCH APPROACHES

In addition to the "applied-pure" dichotomy, research studies may take sharply contrasting forms, in the following ways:

OBTRUSIVE AND NONOBTRUSIVE RESEARCH

In one approach to research, the investigator actually manipulates study subjects, environments, or other variables, and thus affects their behavior. This is called *obtrusive research*. Any experimental study in which the researcher deliberately introduces conditions or environmental stimuli which influence participants is an example of such manipulation. For example, a research study in which three styles of leadership are used with groups, to determine their effects, would be a form of obtrusive research.

Studies that are carefully designed to record only what is happening in a natural way, and that seek to avoid influencing subjects in the slightest way, are considered forms of *nonobtrusive* research. In such investigations, the researchers should not be seen, or should be as inconspicuous as possible; he or she must also avoid altering environmental conditions that might influence the behavior of study subjects.

RESEARCH SETTINGS: FIELD OR LABORATORY

A similar contrast may be drawn with respect to the settings in which research is conducted. In so-called *field* studies, the research is done in actual, established settings, such as existing agencies, leisure settings, classrooms, or other places that are not deliberately formed for purposes of research.

Laboratory research refers to studies that are carried out in an artificial or specially created environment. For example, special facilities may be used to explore the influence of different types of toys, equipment, or other factors on children's play. Often, such artificial settings are designed so that they appear to be real to the participants; however, they may contain special viewing facilities, hidden recording devices, or other equipment that would not be available in a natural, field setting.

QUANTIFIABLE OR NONQUANTIFIABLE DATA

Research designs may be of either a quantifiable or a nonquantifiable nature. *Quantifiable* research is concerned with gathering data that can be precisely measured and expressed in terms of numbers, such as amounts, frequencies, speed, weight, height, costs, or scores on tests.

In contrast, *nonquantifiable* research—which also has been described as *qualitative* research—deals with elements that cannot readily be put into numerical terms. Examples might include behavioral styles, esthetic qualities, personality traits or feelings, philosophical theories, or social movements.

Both forms of research represent important and valid approaches. However, there is a widely held view that the most significant kinds of research studies are those that are based on quantitative analysis, and that science must rely on actual measurement of scientific data. As a result, researchers tend to use quantitative measures wherever possible. For example, many historians (who had formerly used narrative approaches to documentation) are using statistical analysis of numerical data, such as annual shipping volumes, health statistics, immigration totals, and similar data, as the basis for hypothesis testing.

Nonquantifiable or qualitative research is less easily described, in terms of its methodology. Howe points out that it typically depends on words, rather than numbers, but that for this reason it may be "imprecise, ambiguous, or open to multiple interpretation."[5] Typically, it involves a search for meanings or explanations, based on careful observation and logical interpretation of verbal or visual data. Although this approach is less widely accepted than the typical quantitative method, a strong case can be made that, in such an individualistic and diversified field as recreation and leisure, there ought to be a place for research of a more intuitive or descriptive nature. Such studies may be of a philosophical or conceptual nature, and should not have to rely on numerical data for documentation. Hunnicutt argues strongly that without such research approaches, we cannot fully understand the subtle role of recreation and play, or of leisure itself within complex human societies.[6]

The quantitative/nonquantitative dichotomy in research approaches is closely linked to the contrast between *empirical* and *rational* research. Empirical research, which makes use of factual evidence gained through actual observation, tends to be quantifiable, while rational research, which makes use of analytical thought processes, tends to be nonquantifiable.

TIME FRAME OF RESEARCH: PAST, PRESENT, AND FUTURE

Research may be carried on within varied time frames. Obviously, it may explore and interpret the past, as in historical studies of colonial life or the establishment of the recreation and park movement. Most research deals with the present or recent past, as we examine the nature of present-day recreation participation or the operation of contemporary leisure-service agencies and programs.

Research may also be used to predict the future, based on projections of past or present trends, or on the use of Delphi planning techniques, in which groups of experts go through a sequence of blending their perceptions of the future. Research may be fixed in time, in the sense that it analyzes what is happening at a given moment, or it may extend over a lengthy period of time through longitudinal studies that examine programs or other subjects at fixed intervals. In contrast, evaluation studies usually deal only with the present or the very recent past.

VARIED RESEARCH METHODOLOGIES

In addition to these alternative approaches to designing research studies, it should be stressed that research may employ a wide range of data-gathering techniques—often of an unusual or even bizarre nature. For example, each of the following examples of research methodologies has recently been reported in the press: (1) regular collection and searches of garbage put out by selected homes within a community, to learn about the dietary or consumption habits of residents; (2) use of toilet-flushing in a political poll in a small community, where residents are asked to flush at given times if they are leaning toward one candidate or another and the water displacement effects on the town's central water tank are immediately measured; (3) setting up fictitious research studies or other "fake" happenings within a community setting to determine how subjects will respond to commands, emergency situations, or other experimental variables; and (4) testing visual or other sensory responses to stimuli, in order to measure personal reactions to environmental conditions.

The professional applications of research to the field of leisure services and studies and the varying characteristics of research are illustrated more fully in the chapters that follow. They describe in detail the basic concepts and terminology of scientific inquiry and the major types of research design that are used.

SUMMARY

This chapter identifies the chief purposes of research and evaluation in recreation, parks, and leisure studies, including the need to build a body of scientific theory to support professional practice and to measure and document the outcomes of recreation programs. Examples are given of both applied and pure research studies in the field, and it is suggested that much research today belongs in a middle ground on a continuum of research approaches—with both theoretical and practical purposes and methods. In conclusion, several examples of the varying methods used in research are discussed, including: (*a*) obtrusive and non-obtrusive research; (*b*) field and laboratory settings for research; (*c*) uses of quantitative and nonquantitative data and methods of analysis; (*d*) varying time frames for research and evaluation; and (*e*) the use of innovative or unusual data-gathering methods.

ENDNOTES

1. Genevieve W. Carter, "The Challenge of Research in Today's Society," in *Recreation Research: Report of A National Conference* (Washington, D.C.: American Association for Health, Physical Education and Recreation, and National Recreation and Park Association, 1966): p. 2.
2. Judith Woo and Michael Farley, "Portland's Program Planning and Evaluation Model," *Parks and Recreation* (April 1982): 50.
3. Gary Ellis and Peter A. Witt, "Evaluation by Design," *Parks and Recreation* (February 1982): 40.
4. Peg Connolly, "Evaluation's Critical Role in Agency Accountability," *Parks and Recreation* (February 1982): 34.
5. Christine Z. Howe, "Possibilities for Using a Qualitative Approach in the Sociological Study of Leisure," *Journal of Leisure Research* (July 1985): 219.
6. Benjamin K. Hunnicutt, "The Freudian and Neo-Freudian Views of Adult Play and their Implications for Leisure Research and Therapeutic Service Delivery," *Journal of Therapeutic Recreation* (2nd Quarter 1979): 3–13.

QUESTIONS FOR CLASS REVIEW AND DISCUSSION

4. Identify and discuss the four major areas presented in this chapter, in which the applied concerns of recreation and park programming and management are described. Of these areas, which do you feel are most critical as subjects for ongoing research?

5. In what ways can essentially "pure" or "theoretical" forms of research be designed so that they may have applied or practical outcomes? Using the examples cited in this chapter, or similar ones found in research journals, show what some of the potential applied findings of such studies might be. If necessary, show how a given study might be redesigned or given an additional focus.

INDIVIDUAL OR SMALL-GROUP ASSIGNMENTS TO BE PREPARED AND PRESENTED TO CLASS

6. Select several articles in recreation, park, and leisure-studies journals which summarize research studies in this field. Show how each study may be classified based on the contrasting approaches described in this chapter, including:

   a. Applied or pure.
   b. Field or laboratory.
   c. Quantitative or nonquantitative.
   d. Empirical or rational.
   e. Nature of time frame (past, present, or future).

3

BASIC CONCEPTS OF RESEARCH AND EVALUATION: THE SCIENTIFIC METHOD

... a parsimonious definition of *science* is that it is the systematic development and organization of a body of knowledge. The material is organized to provide structure by which phenomena can be explained. By phenomena, we mean facts or events which can be observed. Thus, Sir Isaac Newton ... was able to integrate observations (about falling objects) into a universal explanation in the form of a mathematical relationship ... a good example of the content of the physical sciences. The behavioral and social sciences have not yet been able to develop explanatory relationships that are quite so elegant in their simplicity.[1]

INTRODUCTION

This chapter clarifies some of the fundamental assumptions and processes which underlie both research and evaluation. Since both are forms of systematic inquiry, intended to gather meaningful knowledge, it begins by discussing the nature and sources of knowledge, and the ways in which we can accurately perceive and understand reality.

It then describes the scientific method in terms of its intention and its component steps, including the use of inductive and deductive reasoning. The chapter concludes by defining a number of terms which are commonly used in research studies, and which will be found again and again throughout this text, such as concept, theory, hypothesis, parameters, and variables.

THE NATURE OF SYSTEMATIC INQUIRY

Typically, most of us ask many questions each day, and seek answers to them. As part of this inquiry, we may carry out random observations and collect information—usually on a casual basis. Often we make judgments about the meaning of what we have observed on the basis of "common sense," or what appears to be the case to us. While this does represent an informal sort of research, it is not an example of systematic inquiry.

Instead, systematic inquiry—as exemplified in the scientific method—implies that there must be a deliberate, purposeful, and organized effort to gain knowledge. The purposes of the investigation are clearly stated and understood, and the sources of information are selected so that the data they yield will be representative and accurate. The data-gathering instrument or procedure is carefully designed and applied to ensure that the findings are as correct as possible. The researcher must not arrive at conclusions on the basis of inadequate evidence or possibly biased sources.

Beyond these points, systematic inquiry in the form of research and evaluation often seeks information that provides more than just a superficial description of what exists. Instead, it is often concerned with understanding *why* things occur as they do, what the *relationship* is between various factors or study elements, and whether given behaviors or outcomes can be accurately predicted, given certain circumstances. When carried out on this level, research can be used to develop fundamental principles or theories that provide fuller understanding of human or societal processes and that can be used to improve agency functions.

WAYS OF KNOWING

The term *knowing* refers to the cognitive process and to intellectual or mental awareness of a fact or condition. Typically, we are apt to say, "I *know* this is the case," or "I *know* how to carry out a particular activity." But how *do* we come to know something, or *think* we know it? There are several sources of knowledge that we may draw on, including the following:

TRADITION

This describes the kind of knowledge or belief that may have been handed down from past generations, or that has been an accepted custom or behavioral practice. For example, we tend to hold a number of beliefs because our parents or other older relatives believed them—often through superstition, folk lore, or other inherited attitudes. While they may have a degree of validity, as in the case of much folk medicine or herbal remedies, often they are inaccurate or misleading.

Similarly, many of our customs in society tend to be based on handed-down tradition. For example, Mason and Bramble point out that in the United States most children begin formal education at the age of six. When this practice is questioned, they write:

> . . . the response is usually that six has always been regarded as the best age to begin formal education. When traditions are valid, they are dependable sources of knowledge. However, traditions based on false beliefs will result in faulty knowledge.[2]

Tradition exerts an extremely powerful influence on our thinking. Indeed, Kerlinger describes it under the heading of *tenacity*, writing:

> Here men hold firmly to the truth, the truth that they know to be true because they hold firmly to it, because they have always known it to be true. Frequent repetition of such "truths" seems to enhance their validity. People often cling to their beliefs in the face of clearly conflicting facts.[3]

AUTHORITY

Another common source of accepted knowledge is the advice or judgment of so-called experts, who are recognized authorities in a given field. For example, people who have had an advanced level of technical training in a relevant area often are called as expert witnesses to give testimony in civil or criminal trials.

Despite their expertise, however, such experts may disagree; it is not at all unusual to have one psychiatrist or psychologist claim that a defendant is seriously mentally ill, while another authority claims that this is not the case. Such disagreement may occur because authorities use different sources of data or interpret them differently. They may also be influenced by different belief systems, or by a conscious or unconscious bias in favor of the side they represent. Thus, authorities are not necessarily a source of the truth; their advice or judgments may also be influenced by their personal judgments.

PERSONAL EXPERIENCE

One's own personal experience, or knowledge based on direct observation, would appear to be an excellent source of knowledge. However, this can be misleading, if it is based on partial evidence or incomplete sources of information. For example, it would not be uncommon to hear the comment, "I really don't believe that smoking causes lung cancer, because my grandfather smoked all his life, and lived until he was 90." Often racial or ethnic stereotypes are based on very limited kinds of knowledge or contact with individuals of a particular ethnic background. Personal experience is also fallible, in that, for purely physical reasons or environmental factors that distort our perceptions, we may not interpret correctly what we see or hear. Beyond this, we often tend to screen out input that does not agree with our existing biases or value systems.

Linked to personal experience is the notion that "common sense" is a valid source of knowledge or understanding. The method of "intuition" or "a priori" reasoning relies on the belief that people will, through free communication and interchange of views, arrive at the truth, because it just "stands to reason." Often, however, such logical inferences may not yield true understanding or information, particularly within the complex realm of human behavior.

DOCUMENTATION

Another frequently used source of knowledge is documentation, or use of the extensive information that society amasses each year and stores in economic reports, court records, census statistics, and similar sources. While documentation is valuable in many areas of public activity, it is only as good as the methods used to obtain it. Selective reporting or inadequate controls over data-gathering methods may lead to misleading information. For example, for a number of years a national sports organization published figures that portrayed the number of children, youth, and adults who took part regularly in major team or individual sports and games. However, their chief sources for these figures were special-interest organizations or trade associations which were heavily involved in promoting each of these sports activities. Often they either did not know the actual numbers who took part in a given activity because there was no accurate way to find out, or they presented inflated estimates of annual participation because of an understandable desire to make their own activity "look good." In either case, the knowledge that was presented through such documentation was clearly inaccurate. Depending on the sources used, therefore, documentation may or may not represent a valid means of gathering knowledge.

SCIENTIFIC INQUIRY

Clearly, this approach is the most trustworthy source of knowledge that is available to us today. Through it, purposeful and unbiased investigations are carried out to gather information and interpret it accurately. The element of subjective, personal judgment is eliminated, insofar as possible, with a fundamental purpose of the inquiry being to determine the "why" of things, rather than simply the "what." Best writes that scientific research consists of:

> ... the systematic and objective analysis and recording of controlled observations that may lead to the development of generalizations, principles, or theories, resulting in prediction and possibly ultimate control of events.[4]

However, as later sections of this text will show, even scientific inquiry may be limited, in terms of the methods it uses or its ability to analyze data meaningfully. It may also be influenced by political, religious, or other pressures or controls. As an example, Soviet scientists have a distinctly different view of the influence of genetic or environmental factors on human development, or of the nature of mental illness, than Western scientists do. They are required to follow a party line on such matters. Thus, even scientific inquiry may yield distorted findings. However, of the five sources of knowledge cited here, it clearly offers the most valid source of accurate knowledge and understanding.

Within the recreation, park, and leisure-studies field, while we may recognize value in tradition, authority, or other sources of knowledge, we must accept that the most reputable and respected approach to developing a body of valid information is through research based on the scientific method.

THE SCIENTIFIC METHOD

The scientific method has been described as a "controlled extension of common sense," implying that there is nothing magical or mysterious about it. However, it differs from "common sense" in several important respects.

First, science typically makes use of theoretical structures and concepts as a basis for explaining events; it applies them regularly and submits them to repeated tests. This is done through the systematic, controlled testing of theories and hypotheses. Control is exerted by making sure that only the key or critical variables in any process are tested; the rest are prevented from exerting influence on research outcomes. Kerlinger points out that the scientific method has a characteristic that no other approach to gaining knowledge has: self-correction. He writes:

> There are built-in checks all along the way to scientific knowledge. These checks are so conceived and used that they control and verify scientific activities and conclusions to the end of attaining dependable knowledge. Even if a hypothesis seems to be supported in an experiment, the scientist will test alternative plausible hypotheses that, if also supported, may cast doubt on the first hypothesis. Scientists do not accept statements as true, even though the evidence at first looks promising. They insist on testing them.[5]

Another important difference between science and common sense is that, while the layperson is only casually interested in the relationships among different phenomena, the scientific researcher sees them as a primary focus of his or her investigations. Science sees all phenomena as subject to certain basic laws which can be explored and defined. They must adhere to certain underlying assumptions.

ASSUMPTIONS UNDERLYING SCIENTIFIC METHOD

Nature of Reality

This assumption holds that the world is real and knowable, and that all human or social phenomena can be explored and logically explained. Thus, supernatural elements such as magic or other metaphysical explanations cannot be accepted as the cause of such events or conditions.

Related to this assumption is the principle of determinism—that nothing in the world occurs totally by chance or accident, or in a purely spontaneous way. Instead, every phenomenon has a *cause,* although we may not be able at present to explain such unusual happenings as demonstrations of extrasensory perception or other mystical forms of human performance.

Concepts of Natural Kinds or Classes

This assumption holds that all kinds of elements—including people, animals, events, social conditions, communities, or programs—can be classified in appropriate groupings according to their shared characteristics or other common factors.

Thus, instead of having to deal with great numbers of totally dissimilar or random events or subjects, researchers are able to classify the subjects of their investigations into typologies or models. To illustrate, instead of accepting the idea that people have thousands of different reasons for taking part in recreation, the researcher seeks to identify a limited number—perhaps fifteen or twenty—key motivations which would include all possible reasons. Linked to the first principle that events are not purely random and unrelated, but tend to stem from specific causes, this assumption argues that they tend to follow common or typical patterns which may be identified and predicted by researchers.

Principle of Constancy

This assumption holds that conditions in nature or in human society tend to be relatively constant, until their equilibrium is upset by intrusive factors of some sort. These disruptions bring about certain changes or outcomes which can be logically explained; in other words, the principle of *causality,* in which given factors or circumstances tend to cause the same effects consistently.

It should be noted that this principle emerged first within the physical sciences, such as chemistry, biology, or physics, in which all elements or phenomena could be precisely measured and in which causal relationships could be confidently identified as scientific laws. Emile Durkheim, a pioneer sociologist, argued that the same approach could be applied to human behavior and social institutions.

> He said that social phenomena are orderly and can be generalized
> . . . just as physical phenomena follow physical laws. In Durkheim's
> view . . . there was little difference between physical and natural
> science and social science except for subject matter. The logic of
> inquiry was essentially the same.[6]

This approach to inquiry is often called *logical positivism.* It suggests that sociologists or other social scientists should use the methods of natural science, such as experimentation, to examine and explain social phenomena. In contrast, other social scientists have argued that human beings have free will, and that one cannot therefore predict their actions and generalize about them. A later sociologist, Max Weber, took a middle course, writing that the fact that humans had free will did not mean that their actions were necessarily random and unpredictable. Instead, Weber suggested that free will was exercised in a rational way, and that therefore human behavior could be predicted by understanding rational action.[7]

THE SCIENTIFIC ATTITUDE

Beyond these beliefs, scientists typically share a common attitude. In the words of Alfred North Whitehead, a great philosopher of science, they have a "vehement and passionate interest in the relation of general principles to irreducible and stubborn facts."[8] In Whitehead's view, all life is part of a comprehensive "order of things," governed by basic laws and principles. This order must combine carefully gathered or observed facts (the basis of empirical research) with theories based on the "weaving of general principles," which tie the facts together.

The scientific attitude does not claim omniscience. Scientists recognize that error is possible, and that their findings are therefore tentative and subject to possible revision. Scientific theories are refutable and others may challenge them by carrying out similar studies or advancing competitive theories.

INDUCTIVE AND DEDUCTIVE REASONING

Generally, the scientific method is considered to be based on two distinctive types of reasoning and analysis: inductive and deductive.

INDUCTIVE REASONING

This approach moves from the specific to the general, by using logical analysis of individual cases or occurrences to develop a broad explanatory theory. To illustrate, one might use the example of caring for house plants. Based on systematic observation, it might be learned that too little water leads to stunted growth of a plant, too much water to root rot and plant sickness, and the appropriate amount of water to healthy growth. Thus, the examination of plant growth under varied circumstances provides the basis for developing a theory or set of guidelines for effective plant care.

Stated abstractly, inductive reasoning is summed up in the following sentence; "These *specific* forms of behavior which have been seen to occur provide support for the following *general* theory."

DEDUCTIVE REASONING

This approach is exactly the reverse, moving from the general to the specific. It involves using a general theory or model of behavior or casual relationships to develop inferences or predictions about a specific case. Using the illustration of plant care, one might predict the different frequencies and amounts of watering that would lead to the maximum healthy growth of different types of house plants. Applied to a different type of situation, such as personnel management within a leisure-service agency, one might state:

"Based on this *general* theory of personnel management, we will observe the following *specific* examples of job behaviors in employees, in given work situations."

Deduction is basically a matter of logical reasoning. It is illustrated by Aristotle's famous syllogism (a logical scheme or analysis of a formal argument, consisting of three propositions called respectively the *major premise,* the *minor premise,* and the *conclusion*): "If men are mammals, and mammals are mortal, then men are mortal."

Stated as a formula, "If a equals b, and b equals c, then we must deduce that a equals c."

Such reasoning must be carefully applied, and has logical validity only if the premises are correct. Both types of reasoning are found in social and behavioral research. For example, when researchers develop hypotheses that they intend to test through experimentation based on a theory, they are using deductive reasoning. In contrast, when they initially observe natural phenomena, using simple descriptive methods of data gathering to formulate theories, they are using inductive reasoning.

CLASSICAL MODEL OF SCIENTIFIC RESEARCH

Often the scientific method is described as a three-step process which makes use of both inductive and deductive reasoning, as follows.

INDUCTION

This consists of observing natural or social phenomena and then generating a preliminary theory or tentative explanation that is consistent with the observed facts and explains them and their relationship.

DEDUCTION

From this preliminary theory, one "deduces" what the logical consequences or outcomes will be if exactly the same circumstances or conditions prevail in another setting or at another time. Customarily, this is presented in the form of one or more hypotheses, which are definitive statements or predictions of what will be found when the study is completed (see pg. 40).

VERIFICATION

This is the testing stage, in which the hypotheses are tested under controlled conditions to determine whether the presumed consequences do occur or the predicted relationships can be found. Based on this process, the researcher arrives at conclusions that are justified by the evidence and that lead to accepting, rejecting, or modifying the hypothesis. He or she may also continue to develop new theories or hypotheses based on the study findings. Other researchers may also replicate the study in different settings, to determine whether or not the findings are confirmed and whether the study has been a valid one with generalizable conclusions.

If fully accepted, the conclusions may become accepted as actual scientific laws. This is more common in the physical or natural sciences, where it is possible to maintain a high degree of rigor and obtain proof that is very convincing. It is less common in the social or behavioral sciences, where it is extremely difficult to control and predict human behavior, or to control the variables that influence it within the societal setting.

THE LANGUAGE OF RESEARCH

A number of terms have been used in this chapter which may not be fully familiar to the reader. Mason and Bramble write:

> The language of the researcher is specialized; like all technical languages, it involves the use of certain words in the ordinary vocabu-

lary in markedly specific ways, and it includes words created to meet specialized needs. . . .[9]

Although it is not possible to define the full lexicon of research terminology in this text, a number of the most important terms are explained in this chapter; other words are defined in later sections of the book. They include the following: "concepts" and "constructs," "theories," "hypotheses," "models" and "paradigms," "variables," "parameters," and "data."

CONCEPTS

Basically, a concept is an idea. It is an intellectual representation of some aspect of reality but is not tangible or concrete. Instead it is a term or symbol that helps us understand the nature of various phenomena, or describe them in useful ways.

Concepts do not represent material objects as such, but may describe aspects of them. For example, concepts like "liquidity," "weight," or "density" are essentially abstract ideas, although they refer to physical characteristics of objects or substances, and can be measured.

Other concepts like "brotherhood," "patriotism," or "religion," describe social values or behavioral patterns. They can also be measured, although they are clearly abstract. Both "leisure" and "recreation" are concepts in a broad sense, although they may be made more tangible or visible in the form of acts of participation, physical resources for play, or spending patterns, which can all be measured. An important task in research is to *operationalize* abstract concepts, by translating them into concrete phenomena that can be observed and studied descriptively.

Constructs

The term "construct" is used to describe a concept that has been deliberately invented or adopted for scientific or research purposes. For example, Kerlinger points out that the term "intelligence" is normally viewed as a concept, based on the observation of behavior that shows varying degrees of problem-solving or coping ability. However, as a construct, scientists use the idea of intelligence in two ways: (*a*) as a way of explaining or understanding behavior and (*b*) as an element that is so defined and specified that it can be observed and measured. In the latter case, intelligence has become a construct that is useful in scientific research.[10]

THEORIES

A theory is a generalization or series of generalizations on a theme, through which we seek to describe or explain some phenomena in a systematic and logical way. Often it is used to clarify relationships between research elements, or to predict outcomes that will occur.

Selltiz, Wrightsman, and Cook define the term theory as:

> . . . a set of concepts plus the interrelationships that are assumed to exist among those concepts (and the) consequences that we assume logically to follow from the relationships proposed in the theory.[11]

Theories can range from relatively simple generalizations to much more complex formulation of ideas. They help to provide a framework for research by giving a systematic picture of the elements that are being studied, showing how they influence or interact with each other in logical ways. Within the scientific method, the word "theory" may be used in several ways: (a) inductive theory, based on observed facts with essentially an unconfirmed statement; (b) functional theory, or "best guess," which is really a working statement that is a preliminary tool of a research plan that is being developed; or (c) deductive theory, to be confirmed or tested by systematic observation under controlled conditions.

Theories may be used to assist research by identifying or summarizing relevant facts, classifying phenomena into logical groups or classes, formulating explanations of relationships, predicting facts or happenings, and showing the need for further research. When they are based on very impressive, consistent evidence, theories may be described as *laws* or *principles*.

HYPOTHESES

Hypotheses (plural form for the word "hypothesis") are statements or predictions of relationships that are believed to exist between two or more variables. They represent concrete, declarative statements of these anticipated relationships, based on a theory. The key variables in the theory are operationally defined and placed within a research context so that it is possible to measure accurately whether the expected relationship occurs. Kerlinger defined the term hypothesis concisely, as a "conjectural statement of the relation between two or more variables . . . (with) clear implications for testing the stated relations."[12]

Hypothesis statements must therefore contain two or more variables that are measurable or potentially measurable, and they must specify how they are related. Customarily, hypotheses take two forms in research proposals.

Working Hypotheses

These are general, declarative statements of the relationship that is believed to exist and that is to be tested through the study process. They are stated positively, and may also be called "conceptual," "research" or "alternative" hypotheses.

Statistical Hypotheses

These are more precise statements of the working hypotheses, put into operational terms that permit testing and statistical analysis. Usually, statistical hypotheses are stated in the "null" or "negative" form, which indicates that the *opposite* of the working hypotheses will be found and that *no* significant relationship will be proved to exist between the key variables in the study.

If the null hypothesis is accepted or confirmed, the working hypothesis has been rejected. If, on the other hand, the null hypothesis is rejected, the working hypothesis has been proved to be correct.

MODELS AND PARADIGMS

A model is a theoretical abstraction or depiction of a given process or set of relationships. It identifies the major elements of the subject or system under investigation, and shows how they are believed to relate to each other, or how a process occurs over a period of time. Models often take a visual form, and may involve charts or constructions showing the sequence of events occurring in a process. Science teachers may use models of the atom or the solar system to make these phenomena clear to students. In such fields as government or social service, models may be used to show the interplay of community groups, or how social change occurs. Models may either deal with real phenomena, such as the work schedules and productivity of park maintenance personnel, or with more abstract concepts, such as the therapeutic uses of play.

The words "models" and "theories" are sometimes used interchangeably, in the sense that a set of propositions relevant to one section of a field may be expressed as a theory or, in more concrete and operational terms, as a model.

Paradigms

Paradigms are sometimes described as being similar to models, in that they serve as a means of conceptualizing research. Mason and Bramble write:

A paradigm . . . represents the perspective of the researcher toward the problems being studied. A paradigm may be a flow chart or scheme that outlines steps in research or relationships among variables.[13]

In a broader sense, the term *paradigm* refers to a perspective or frame of reference for viewing the social world or some other subject of investigation, consisting of a set of concepts and assumptions held by the researcher. Bailey describes a paradigm as:

. . . the mental window through which the researcher views the world. Generally, what he or she sees in the social world is what is objectively out there, as interpreted by his or her paradigm of concepts, categories, assumptions, and biases.[14]

Often, there may be several different, conflicting paradigms within a scholarly discipline or area of research. Since each paradigm is likely to have its own set of concepts or jargon, and since they may also differ in the research problems they consider important, this may lead to difficulty in carrying out effective and cooperative research efforts within a field.

VARIABLES

A variable is an element or characteristic of the subject being studied through research; it may take different values or forms for different observable units. Examples of variables might include different types of participants or characteristics of participants (such as age, sex, or educational level); different categories of recreational participation; settings for participation; leadership styles or behavioral outcomes. There are basically two types of variables: independent and dependent.

Independent Variables

These are factors or elements in an experiment or other empirical research study which, in the researcher's view, influence other variables or cause certain effects. Although they are called independent, they may be introduced deliberately or manipulated by the researcher, to test their influence.

For example, in an experiment which seeks to determine the best methods of preventing vandalism in a recreation center, if three methods are used (such as expelling youth gangs from the center, hiring guards to supervise the areas, or seeking to work out the problem through group discussion and an attempt to change the values of those responsible), each of these methods represents an independent variable.

Dependent Variables

These are factors or elements in a study which are caused or influenced *by* independent variables. In the example just given, the vandalism rates in the recreation centers where the three methods of preventing vandalism were used constitute the dependent variable. Bailey describes the relationship between independent and dependent variables:

> . . . the variable capable of effecting change in the other variable is called the *independent variable.* The variable whose value is dependent upon the other is called the *dependent variable.* In a casual relationship, the cause is the independent variable and the effect is the dependent variable.[15]

A third type of variable is referred to as *intervening* or *extraneous;* these are elements or factors in a study over which researchers may have little control and which may contaminate or distort the results of a study. For example, fluctuating weather conditions or short-term economic factors might influence the results of a study of recreation participation and be beyond the ability of the researcher to control. As much as possible, researchers should seek to keep the possible influence of intervening variables to a minimum.

Variables may be compared to *constants,* which are study elements which are held constant (kept the same) for all observable units within the study. To illustrate, in an experiment which seeks to measure the effects of fees and charges on recreation program participation, variables might be the different levels of fees and charges (independent) and the actual rate or frequency of participation (dependent). Constants might be the kinds of activities or the sponsoring organizations, which are kept the same for all research units.

PARAMETERS

Parameters are somewhat similar to variables or constants, in that they refer to elements or characteristics of a study. The term has two specific applications:

1. A *parameter* is an element of a study that remains unchanged throughout the course of research. It refers to the important

dimensions or characteristics of the population that is being studied, or the process that is being carried on. For example, quantitative factors, such as the numbers of subjects, their age, or length of involvement, that are descriptive of the entire study population are referred to as parameters of the study.

2. In a related meaning, a *parameter* is a property or characteristic of the entire universe that is determined or measured through research. In contrast, a *statistic* is a piece of information obtained from a *sample* of the population, which therefore represents an estimate of an actual parameter.

DATA

Another commonly used research term is *data*. This is the plural form of the Latin word *datum* and is usually defined as information derived from the observation of one or more variables. It may take the form of numerical or qualitative ratings or descriptions, or other kinds of information about the variables observed. Data are gathered through observation, interviews, the use of survey forms or questionnaires, the perusal of records, psychological or physiological testing, or numerous other procedures.

ROLE OF THE RESEARCHER

The investigator plays a key role in all research studies. It is never the researcher's purpose to *prove* that something is true, although he or she may have a hypothesis that suggests what the study is expected to disclose. Instead, the researcher's purpose is to *test* the hypothesis, and to *determine whether or not* it is accurate. For this to happen in a truly scientific way, the researcher must have the following characteristics.

1. *Expertise.* It is essential that the investigator be knowledgeable within the area being studied. This does not mean that he or she must be a leading authority in it, but rather that he or she has a high level of knowledge and competence in the subject and sufficient command of the methods that will be used to investigate it.

Researchers often improve their expertise while conducting a study and examining other work that has been done in the area. In addition, researchers often do successive studies within a particular area of research and thus gradually gain greater competence and reputation within the area.

2. *Objectivity.* The investigator should be objective, in that he or she lacks bias or preconviction in a given area, and does not seek

to prove a case, to deceive, or to exclude or distort evidence. This is a critical concern, in that researchers obviously stand to gain from successful research, or from findings that benefit their own organizations or professional groups. Too often, the press reports studies that have been manipulated within such areas as medical research, political affairs, or marketing surveys. When such short-cuts or deliberate distortions are discovered, they inevitably damage the public's confidence in scientific research and can destroy the careers of those responsible for presenting inaccurate findings.

3. *Thoroughness and Rigorous Process.* Even when the researcher's intentions are honest, study findings must be questioned when they rely on inadequate or irresponsible investigation, with casual observation or follow-up of subjects, the use of inexact data-gathering instruments, or poor sampling procedures. Studies must be designed so that the entire process is as rigorous as possible.

4. *Ethics and Concern for Subjects.* Apart from the need for honesty and careful research procedures, other ethical considerations today include the need to avoid possible dangers or negative effects for subjects. In the past, many research studies have resulted in harmful outcomes for participants. Today, all study proposals that involve human subjects, particularly in experimental research projects where they may be manipulated to the extent that psychological or physical harm may occur, must normally be reviewed and given clearance by a "human-subjects" review committee. Still other ethical considerations may involve the need for confidentiality in research reporting; usually subjects who participate in surveys, for example, are assured anonymity.

OTHER CHARACTERISTICS OF RESEARCH

When carried out according to high scientific standards, research represents a challenging conceptual task. It also often demands the ability to manage a mix of investigative processes within what is often a complicated administrative operation. The best research also demonstrates solid scholarly ability, imagination, and excellent writing skills.

Research findings often are surprising, and may resist the common wisdom. Typically, research tells us that mental illness rises and falls with the economy; that one's height and weight are likely to influence one's pay on the job; that "good-looking" children or children with familiar, "normal-sounding" names are generally better liked by their teachers; and many other factors about our everyday lives.

Research is often circular, building on what has been explored in earlier studies and leading to new theories, investigations, and findings. It is revealing to trace research in a given field through professional or scholarly journals over a period of years, showing how various theories have been developed and disseminated, and how knowledge proliferates and becomes more refined within separate special areas of the overall field. Often, a number of scholars within a profession may be working on the same general problem, communicating with each other through publication and thus cooperating in the advancement of a professional body of knowledge.

For those who carry out truly innovative or ground-breaking research, the task is almost like reading a complicated mystery or detective novel, with painstaking, patient efforts to gather evidence, test solutions, and finally to come out with the "truth".

VARIED METHODS OF RESEARCH

This chapter has focused primarily on the classical model of scientific research, involving inductive and deductive reasoning and the statistical testing of hypotheses. However, many professionally based, practical research studies do not use hypotheses and are not concerned with building or testing theories. Instead, they involve the kinds of applied purposes described in Chapter 2, and are primarily concerned with gathering useful information with respect to recreation needs and operational effectiveness. For this reason, they do not make use of inductive or deductive processes or statistical analysis of quantitative data.

At the same time, they may use research methods that are broader or more diverse than those traditionally regarded as appropriate scientific techniques. Bailey points out that many social scientists avoid rigorous hypotheses and quantification. Instead, observational researchers like anthropologists or ethnologists tend to rely heavily on verbal descriptions and analyses:

> . . . and are likely to be interested in a more subjective understanding of their research subjects. . . . Some observational and documentary research is structured and quantitative, just as some survey research is unstructured, but these are exceptions to the general rule. . . .[16]

He goes on to point out that such researchers while they regard themselves as scientists, differ sharply from positivists (see pg.

35), in that they do not seek to develop general scientific laws or even general concepts. Instead, they focus on the unqiue situational meaning and interpretation of social phenomena in particular settings. Although most social research is empirical, other ways of gathering knowledge may be useful in dealing with such phenomena as recreation, play, and leisure. Selltiz and associates write:

> Many religions, for example, identify revelation (a special, nonempirical, individual way of finding things out) as a source of knowledge. Intuition, visions, and reflective thought are all nonempirical strategies for acquiring knowledge about the social and physical worlds. . . .[17]

Philosophical and critical research and other forms of conceptual analysis may also be useful in developing a diversified approach to investigations of leisure and its meaning in society. Such techniques will help to enrich our understanding of this total phenomenon in ways that purely empirical, statistically based research cannot. Sydney Harris makes a distinction between "science," which he regards as essential to human advancement, and "scientism," which he describes as:

> . . . a reductionist activity, in which life is seen as "nothing but" an assortment or collection of material substances operating according to "laws" or "functions" that have no meaning beyond themselves.[18]

Indeed, the positivist view which sees human behavior as governed by a set of rigid, immutable laws may be challenged readily by those who see life in terms of free will and individual choice, or who recognize that some natural or social phenomena may occur through chance. In viewing research it is important not to be dogmatic in claiming ultimate superiority for any single type of research and condemning all others. Within the field of recreation, parks, and leisure studies, there is justification for having many different types of research that are capable of exploring varied aspects of this complex subject.

SUMMARY

Research and evaluation are systematic and purposeful efforts to gain knowledge. There are several ways of knowing about any event or condition—through tradition, authority, personal experience, documentation, and scientific inquiry. Of these methods, scientific inquiry is the most trustworthy.

It is based on a number of underlying assumptions which hold that the world is real and knowable, that phenomena are divided into natural kinds or classes, and that conditions in nature or human society are relatively constant, with logical explanations for all shifts in the balance of things. Essentially, the scientific method is based on three steps: (*a*) induction, which means generating preliminary theories based on observed facts; (*b*) deduction, which consists of concluding what the natural consequences of a set of circumstances will be, based on such theories; and (*c*) verification, which involves testing such hypotheses.

Several key terms in the language of research are defined, including "concepts," "theories," "hypotheses," "models and paradigms," "variables," "parameters," and "data." The chapter concludes with a discussion of the role of the scientific investigator and other characteristics of research. It emphasizes that, while the most familiar and accepted form of research involves the traditional scientific method and hypothesis building, other acceptable approaches may use freer and more intuitive approaches or data-gathering and analytical procedures.

ENDNOTES

1. Emanuel J. Mason and William J. Bramble, *Understanding and Conducting Research* (New York: McGraw-Hill Book Co., 1977): 2.
2. Ibid., 4.
3. Fred N. Kerlinger, *Foundations of Behavioral Research* (New York: Holt, Rinehart and Winston, 1973): 6.
4. John W. Best, *Research in Education* (Englewood Cliffs, N.J.: Prentice-Hall, Inc., 1981): 26.
5. Kerlinger, op. cit., 6.
6. Kenneth D. Bailey, *Methods of Social Research* (New York: The Free Press, 1982): 5.
7. Ibid., 6.
8. Alfred North Whitehead, cited in Miriam Lewin, *Understanding Psychological Research* (New York: John Wiley and Sons, 1979): 10–11.
9. Mason and Bramble, op. cit., 51.
10. Kerlinger, op. cit., 27.
11. Claire Selltiz, Lawrence S. Wrightsman, and Stuart W. Cook, *Research Methods in Social Relations* (New York: Holt, Rinehart and Winston, 1976): 16.
12. Kerlinger, op. cit., 11.
13. Mason and Bramble, op. cit., 54.
14. Bailey, op. cit., 24.

15. Ibid., 47.
16. Ibid., 8.
17. Selltiz et al., op. cit., 22.
18. Sydney J. Harris, "Scientism Has Its Limits," *Philadelphia Inquirer,* November 26, 1982, 15-A.

QUESTIONS FOR CLASS REVIEW AND DISCUSSION

7. Identify several "ways of knowing" that are described in the chapter, and show how they may apply to public attitudes or understandings about recreation and leisure. Make the illustrations as concrete as possible.
8. How do the "inductive" and "deductive" approaches to theory building fit into the process of scientific inquiry? Develop several illustrations of possible research questions in recreation, parks, and leisure services and show how they might be approached inductively and deductively.

INDIVIDUAL OR SMALL-GROUP ASSIGNMENTS TO BE PREPARED AND PRESENTED TO CLASS

9. To clarify the meaning of several terms used in this chapter, return to the studies identified in Chapter 2 and select one or more suitable examples that lend themselves to the following:
   a. Identify any basic concepts that are explored or discussed in each study.
   b. Similarly, identify the theory that is advanced, if there is one.
   c. Restate the hypothesis that is presented, if there is one.
   d. Identify the independent and dependent variables in the study.

10. Identify one or more studies that are not empirical but that instead might be described as philosophical, critical, or rational in method. Analyze these reports, showing how they accomplish what empirical or quantitative studies cannot. What are the weaknesses of this method, in terms of developing proofs of outcomes or conclusions?

4

MAJOR TYPES OF RESEARCH DESIGNS

Practically all studies fall under one, or a combination, of these types. 1. *Historical research* describes *what was*. The process involves investigating, recording, analyzing, and interpreting the events of the past. . . . 2. *Descriptive research describes what is*. It involves the description, recording, analysis, and interpretation of conditions that exist. . . . 3. *Experimental research* describes *what will be* when certain variables are carefully controlled or manipulated. . . .[1]

INTRODUCTION

Classifying different types of research that are used in the recreation, parks, and leisure-studies field is a difficult task. Many authors in the overall research field suggest widely varying classification systems. While it is true that research may be broadly described under the three headings suggested above (historical, descriptive, and experimental), this is too restrictive a scheme to cover all of the special approaches used in the leisure-service field.

Instead, this text also identifies and describes several other types of research design under the broad heading of "descriptive" research. These include: (*a*) surveys; (*b*) case studies; (*c*) longitudinal studies; (*d*) cross-sectional and comparative research; (*e*) correlational research; and (*f*) evaluative research. Action research and so-called ex post facto studies are described as modified forms of experimental research. In addition to these major forms of scientific inquiry, a number of other specialized types of data-gathering procedures are described—all of which may be used in the recreation, parks, and leisure-studies field.

HISTORICAL RESEARCH DESIGNS

Historical research is concerned with an examination of the past—either distant or relatively recent. It seeks to develop a meaningful record of human achievement. Too often, history has been taught to schoolchildren in terms of political or military events, with required memorization of dates, the names of conquerors or rulers, and a dry recounting of major explorations and shifts in power. A better sort of approach to the study of history might be described as social history, concerned with the complex lives of people and societies, weaving together the intricate interaction of religion, government, daily living patterns, social customs, economic factors, and similar elements. Best makes the point clearly, in writing:

> History . . . is not merely a list of chronological events, but a truthful integrated account of the relationships between persons, events, times, and places. We use history to understand the past, and to try to understand the present in light of past events and developments.[2]

Within the recreation, parks, and leisure-studies field, historians have examined such subjects as: (a) the past development of various types of leisure pursuits or cultural interests; (b) the role of recreation and leisure in earlier civilizations or historical eras; (c) the development of parks in Europe and the United States; (d) the roots of the recreation movement during the Industrial Revolution; or (e) the development of professionalism in leisure service in the United States. By exploring such themes, historical research has contributed to a fuller understanding of how the present-day recreation and parks field developed. It is difficult to understand our contemporary situation with respect to the public image of the field, widely held attitudes about recreation and leisure, or issues like the place of ethnic or racial minority groups in recreation or the role of women and girls in this field, without full historical understanding.

USES OF PRIMARY AND SECONDARY SOURCES

Historical research makes use of essentially two types of data: primary and secondary.

1. *Primary sources* are eyewitness accounts or first-hand reports of events and social trends, usually reported by actual observers or participants. They may take the form of letters, autobiographies, diaries, newspaper or magazine accounts, transcriptions of oral history, or similar sources. They may also make use of documents such as official records, charters, court decisions, contracts and deeds, films, and research reports, if they are demonstrably authentic in origin.

2. *Secondary Sources.* They are second-hand accounts, in which one person recounts what he or she has heard from others, or in which primary sources have been translated or interpreted so that it is no longer the original information that is being examined. Secondary sources are usually considered to be of limited value in historical research, although they may point out major developments in a field, or help to direct other direct research efforts.

AUTHENTICITY OF DATA

How does the historical researcher determine the accuracy of the data he or she has uncovered? Two methods exist for evaluating historical evidence: external and internal criticism.

External criticism seeks to determine the genuineness of evidence and to establish its authenticity by analyzing such elements as handwriting or language usages; making physical or chemical tests of ink, paper, paint, wood, or other substances; or making sure that the sources are consistent with the knowledge and technology characteristic of the period in which the data were supposed to have originated.

Internal criticism examines the actual content of the document or other source material, to judge whether it appears to be an accurate, unbiased account—based on other relevant evidence, or what may be learned regarding the motives of the writer or individual being quoted. What was the experience of the individuals concerned? Did they have reasons for distorting or suppressing information? Can confirmation be obtained that they actually were on the spot as described and that they were able to make prompt records of the occurrences, or was the information reconstructed after a considerable period had gone by?

STAGES OF HISTORICAL RESEARCH

The key steps in the process of carrying out historical research include the following:

Identify Problem Area

This is usually done by preliminary reading in the field, exploration of easily available sources, and the initial formulation of a research question or possible hypothesis to be explored.

Collect Source Materials

As indicated, these may include a wide range of possible sources, including wherever possible primary sources. Typically, minutes are better than newspaper accounts describing a meeting, and original copies are better than translations. In gathering source materials, every possible repository should be examined, including card catalogs, periodical indexes, encyclopedias, historical guides, visits to key locations, and often detectivelike tracking down of evidence that moves from source to source or person to person.

Evaluate and Analyze Data

Materials should be subjected to critical examination to determine their trustworthiness and importance. Both external and internal criticism should be applied, to determine the authenticity of sources.

Is the material consistent with what has already been written, or with other information that has been gathered in the study? At this stage, the data should be analyzed and placed within a sequential framework, based either on a chronological order, or on a division of the subject into separate topical areas or themes.

Prepare Historical Report

All the material that has been gathered should be synthesized and developed in the form of a historical essay or report, with full citations of all sources used. Knowledge that has been developed at this point should be integrated, and historical explanations or theories may be more fully developed.

Historical research may be used as an introduction to other types of studies, in order to set the stage by providing relevant background information. It may also constitute a separate, independent study in its own right. Typically, when graduate students undertake historical research for theses or dissertations, they tend to suffer from the following weaknesses: (a) developing problems that are too broad; (b) relying excessively on secondary sources; (c) failure to establish the authenticity of data obtained; (d) poor logical analysis, based either on oversimplification of issues or overgeneralizing on the basis of limited evidence; and (e) inappropriate writing style, such as dull or colorless reporting or overly casual or flippant writing. Strong efforts should be made to overcome such weaknesses.

DESCRIPTIVE RESEARCH

Clearly, this represents the most popular and widely found type of research design in recreation, parks, and leisure studies. Best describes descriptive studies in the following terms:

> A descriptive study describes and interprets what is. It is concerned with conditions or relationships that exist, opinions that are held, processes that are going on, effects that are evident, or trends that are developing. It is primarily concerned with the present, although it often considers past events and influences as they relate to current conditions.[3]

Customarily, descriptive research deals with observation of actual practices or behavior in a real setting or with the collection of information from people or agencies. It never attempts to influence the situation being observed or to introduce any elements that might affect behavior. It may use an extremely wide range of data-gathering techniques, including questionnaires, rating scales, checklists, recording devices (such as videotaping or sound recording), observation, interview schedules, tests of physical or mental performance, sociometric devices, documentary analysis, or other means of compiling information. A number of specialized types of descriptive research are described in the pages that follow.

SURVEY RESEARCH

This customarily implies a broad study of normative (typical) conditions within a given population or set of subjects. It may deal with people and their behavior or attitudes, with agencies and their programs and policies, with social conditions, with facilities, with higher education curricula, with professional developments, and numerous other kinds of subjects. It usually gathers data from many subjects or respondents at a given time, and is concerned with drawing a picture of the entire group rather than profiles of individuals. Typically, recreation surveys may include the following:

Public Attitudes and Opinions

Mailed questionnaires or directly administered opinion polls may be used to determine the attitude of members of the public with respect to their leisure needs and interests, their view of present recreation opportunities in the community, their position with respect to policies or problems faced by municipal government, their willingness to pay expanded fees and charges for recreational involvement, and similar concerns. They may also explore participants' motivations or levels of satisfaction derived from recreation.

Patterns of Participation

Numerous surveys are carried out each year which measure the extent of participation in varied activities, such as sports, outdoor recreation, the arts, travel, or similar activities. Such surveys may be done through questionnaires on a local, state, regional, or national level, or may involve studies of representative sites, such as state or national parks, selected cities, or similar settings. They may also examine such issues as the extent of spending on given activities, the nature of family participation, modes of travel used to get to recreation settings, or a comparison of motivations for participation with the satisfactions derived from them.

Surveys of Facilities

Trends in the development of different types of facilities, such as art centers or water play parks may be examined. Whether or not facilities have been made accessible to the physically disabled, the environmental impact of recreation on outdoor settings, where and how people camp in federal or state parks, or safety factors in wilderness or mountainous areas may all be examined.

Surveys may also examine potential public interest in different types of facilities, as part of feasibility studies conducted to determine whether new recreation enterprises would be profitable. Thus, they provide a valuable tool within the overall "marketing" process.

Management Practices

Studies may also deal with management policies and practices, in terms of staffing arrangements, policy development, sources of fiscal support, marketing methods, public and community relations, liability and negligence suits, cosponsorship of programs with other agencies, and similar issues. Recreation and park administrators in varied types of agencies—including private, commercial, armed forces, and therapeutic—may be queried regarding their values and goals; their relations with commissions, boards, and trustees; their philosophies of personnel management; and similar issues.

In the past, surveys were often criticized because they tended to lack careful, systematic procedures or because of the proliferation of studies on relatively trivial and unimportant subjects. However, well-done surveys can meet high professional standards and provide knowledge that cannot be obtained in other ways. Business, political parties, and numerous other social institutions make full use of survey methods, and they represent a useful research technique for recreation, park, and leisure-studies investigators. Often, they may provide the first level of information about a subject that then points the way to later, in-depth analyses.

CASE STUDIES

In contrast to survey research, which examines a broad range of respondents or subjects to get an overall view of a given issue or research question, case studies have a much sharper focus. They usually involve a fuller or more detailed examination of a single entity, such as a person, a family, a neighborhood, an agency, or similar subject. They are concerned with gaining an in-depth picture of the subject within its environment, including all the forces that play on it. Mason and Bramble write:

> Case studies . . . are basically intensive investigations. . . . In a sense, when a physician investigates the condition of a patient he is performing a case study. The same can be said for the work of the psychologist, social worker, marriage counselor, efficiency expert, and school administrator when they investigate a specific person, group, institution, or school.[4]

Case studies are likely to use several methods, including direct observation, interviews, review of records or other documents, testing procedures, and other techniques. In some case studies in which the researcher uses a model found in sociological and anthropological research, he or she may actually become part of a group or organization, or live in a given neighborhood, in order to observe it more fully. Typical subjects of case studies in recreation, parks, and leisure studies might involve the examination of a community center's operations, a juvenile gang's social behavior, or the use of a neighborhood park. Customarily, intensive field studies of this type involve observation over time—so that a leisure setting might be examined during the different seasons of the year, or subject to changing social conditions.

Although case studies usually involve individuals or single clusters of subjects, their findings may be used to develop general theories which have broader applications. For example, Piaget's theories of learning were based on case studies of children observed over a period of years, and Freud's experiences with individual clients led to the formulation of his broader concepts of psychoanalytic theory. Case studies may or may not make use of detailed statistical data and analysis. For example, the study of a large marina operation might include extensive quantitative data concerning use patterns, destinations of boaters, types of craft, income and expenses, and similar factors. Or it might involve a qualitative analysis of boating behavior or social groupings with little numerical content.

LONGITUDINAL STUDIES

These are research studies which are carried out over a designated period of time. Sometimes called "developmental research," they seek to measure change that occurs in a group of subjects— either in a natural, field situation or under controlled conditions.

Such research may be done with people, programs, organizations, or settings for recreation. Often it is done making use of *time-series* observations, which gather data at regular intervals. For example, environmental conditions in a state forest or on an ocean beach might be examined regularly, using the same measuring instruments, with the results correlated to the volume or nature of recreational use over time or with measures that have been taken to protect the environment.

Longitudinal studies are somewhat related to *trends-analysis* research, which seeks to determine key trends in a field over a period of time and to predict future development on the basis of past and current trends.

Trends-analysis research may take a number of forms: (*a*) One common approach is to show several different changes or directions that are likely to occur in the future, contingent on different sets of social, economic, or other circumstances that may occur; (*b*) use of the Delphi method of forecasting, in which experts or consultants develop predictions separately, share their views, revise them, and repeat this process until they have reached an agreement on probable future trends; or (*c*) straight-line forecasting, in which recent and current trends are extended to indicate the probable course of future events.

CROSS-SECTIONAL AND COMPARATIVE RESEARCH

These are two related types of research design which share the common element of making comparisons between two or more sets of subjects.

In *cross-sectional* research, a single large system might be examined, with different elements or component parts within it compared with respect to given variables. For example, participation by different age groups in a community's public recreation program might be studied at one point in time, to gain a picture of each group's current pattern of involvement, needs, special interests, and priority for service. Such studies may be used instead of longitudinal research, since they make it possible to look at given variables for all age groups at once, rather than waiting for years to gather needed data.

In *comparative research,* several agencies or programs might be examined. For example, recreation personnel requirements and practices in several different types of voluntary agencies might be compared. If a study simply gathered the facts and figures of revenue source practices among a large number of departments, it probably would be classified as a survey. If, however, the study did a set of profiles of several different agencies with respect to fees and charges, and then compared them based on a number of criteria or key points, it would be a comparative study.

In recreation, parks, and leisure studies, comparative research may be used either to study theoretical issues or applied, practice-oriented concerns. Several examples of possible research problems follow:

1. Analysis of the use of third-party payments (reimbursement for recreation services by insurance companies or government agencies) in therapeutic recreation agencies, within several different regions of the country.

2. Comparison of the values promoted and coaching methods used in several areas of youth sport (for example: Little League baseball, Biddy Basketball, and youth soccer leagues).

3. Study of attitudes toward leisure or recreation participation patterns among members of four ethnic populations (Caucasian, Black, Asian, and Hispanic) within a particular state or region.

CORRELATIONAL RESEARCH

Correlation is the term used to describe the degree of relationship between two or more sets of variables. For example, height and weight are likely to be *positively* correlated (as one variable increases, so does the other) in a class of junior high school students. This does not mean that the tallest child will always be the heaviest, the next tallest the next heaviest, and so on. However, it does mean that in general, taller children will tend to be heavier, and shorter children lighter. If two sets of variables are inversely correlated (that is, if subjects rank high on one variable they would be low on another and vice versa), their relationship would be described as *negatively* correlated.

Correlational analysis may be part of the data-analysis process in many survey research studies, although not the primary thrust of such surveys. There are also studies which are carried out primarily to discover whether there *are* significant relationships between or among key variables. Examples of the methods used to determine the extent of correlation in either type of situation are found in Chapters 8 and 9.

EVALUATIVE RESEARCH

As described earlier, this consists of research which seeks to measure an agency's success in achieving stated objectives, or the professional quality of an agency, program, or other element within the leisure-service field. Evaluation has become increasingly recognized as an important step in the successful management of many types of organizations. Like correlational studies, it may either be carried out as: (*a*) one element or step in the program-planning process or (*b*) a separate, independent procedure designed to measure a leisure-service agency's quality or accountability.

Evaluation may be applied to total agencies and their overall operations, or to separate divisions or units of an organization. Programs may be evaluated, either in their entirety or as separate program elements. Other aspects of an organization's functioning, such as maintenance service, community relations, or risk-management activities may be evaluated. Emphasis may also be given to the evaluation of personnel, to facilities, or to participants. Specific methods of evaluation and guidelines for carrying it out effectively are discussed in detail in Chapters 11 through 13.

EXPERIMENTAL RESEARCH

Experimentation is generally thought of as the most rigorous and trustworthy type of research, particularly in the physical sciences. It has not been widely used in recreation and leisure studies or in other human service fields, because of the difficulty, in actual field settings, in maintaining the kinds of controls that it requires.

Experiments are essentially a form of action research. They involve *doing,* in the sense that the researcher structures actual situations and introduces or controls certain variables, in order to measure their effect on each other. Simon points out that the crux of the experiment is that the investigator intentionally manipulates one or more of the independent variables:

> . . . . thus exposing various groups of subjects to the different variables (or to different amounts of the independent variables), and then observes the changes in the dependent variables. . . . The experimental groups are usually selected randomly, which further ensures that observed differences among groups really reflect differences in the independent variables.[5]

The essential elements in the classical type of experimental design include the following: (*a*) presentation of a formal hypothesis, in which the investigator states clearly the proposition that the research is intended to test; (*b*) random selection or formation of two or more types of groups of subjects, including "control" and "experimental" groups; (*c*) pretesting of both groups on measures of the quality or performance element that the study is investigating; (*d*) application of one or more experimental procedures or "interventions"; and (*e*) posttesting of both groups.

Although the classical experimental design just described is frequently advocated in recreation research, there are times when it is not possible to achieve it, or when more stringent experimental procedures may be needed. Different experimental designs may vary with respect to their *validity*—that is, the accuracy or truthfulness of their findings, and the extent to which they are generalizable. These two aspects of validity are known as internal and external validity. It is essential to select research designs which give the highest degree of validity of both types, given the realistic limitations that study circumstances may impose.

INTERNAL VALIDITY

There are seven classes of extraneous variables which may affect the truthfulness of study findings, and which can be controlled by the type of experimental design that is chosen. They include:

1. Contemporary History: This refers to events occurring between the pre- and posttesting stages, in addition to experimental treatments or other interventions.

2. Maturation: Subjects actually mature biologically or psychologically, or change in other ways which may affect results, regardless of the effects of the experimental treatment.

3. Pretesting Procedures: These may influence subjects by improving their skills or otherwise affecting their attitude or performance, beyond the effect of the experimental treatment.

4. Instrumentation: Changes in testing instruments, raters, or observers may influence the responses of subjects.

5. Statistical Regression: When subjects are selected who have extreme scores, in subsequent testing there is a natural tendency for them to regress toward the scores of the larger population from which they were selected.

6. Selection: Varying responses by control and treatment groups may be due to inadequate selection procedures.

7. Experimental Mortality: The loss of subjects in experimental and control groups over a period of time may affect the findings of the study.

In addition to these separate factors, it is possible that two or more such conditions may interact with each other to contribute to even greater loss of validity in experimental research findings.

EXTERNAL VALIDITY

The generalizability or representativeness of findings may also be affected by the research design and the rigor with which it is carried out. Four factors affecting generalizability of results are:

1. Interaction effects of selection bias and experimental intervention; the results may be influenced to the degree that findings apply only to the specific study population.

2. Pretesting may cause a reaction to the study's experimental procedures that would not be found in subjects who are not pretested.

3. The presence of raters and/or experimental equipment and an artificial study setting may alter the normal response of subjects, apart from the actual effect of the intervention itself.

4. Multiple treatments may influence the subsequent response of subjects; it may not be possible to eliminate the effect of previous experimental interventions.

LEVELS OF EXPERIMENTAL DESIGN

In addition to such factors, other study circumstances may make it difficult for study investigators to select groups randomly, apply pre- and posttests as needed, and maintain needed controls over independent and extraneous variables. Therefore, researchers may choose to conduct studies at varying levels of experimental design, including the following:

Preexperimental

Sometimes referred to as a one-shot case study, subjects are exposed to an experimental variable, and the effects are measured.

Example: In a playground or community center where there has been a rash of acts of vandalism, the recreation director posts a new set of rules and urges all participants to be on the lookout for vandals. If vandalism declines after several weeks, he or she concludes that this strategy was responsible for it. The data are gathered loosely, with no effort to exclude other variables or identify other possible causes of the change.

This design has virtually no internal or external validity.

One Group Pretest, Posttest

This design is somewhat more structured, in that a single group of subjects is used, with careful measurement being done before applying the experimental treatment and again afterward.

Example: A group of disturbed adolescents in a community mental health center is observed, and a careful record is made of their behavior. New methods of group therapy or behavior-modification techniques are applied, and then the subjects are carefully observed again and their behavior recorded, to determine whether there has been change.

This design has minimal internal validity, controlling only for selection of subjects and experimental mortality. It has no external validity.

Two Groups, Nonrandom Selection, Pretest, Posttest

Here, two groups are used, with one (the control group) receiving no treatment or special considerations, and the other (the experimental group) receiving some type of intervention or special treatment. They are both given pretests and posttests, to determine possible changes. However, the groups have not been randomly selected.

Example: Select two playgrounds for the study. In one, the control playground, provide traditional playground equipment (such as slides, swings, a jungle gym, and a merry-go-round). In the other, the experimental playground, introduce a new set of innovative equipment (such as lumber, ropes, or other materials used in so-called "adventure" playgrounds). Measure the play behaviors of children in both settings, before and after the intervention.

This design has minimal internal validity, primarily because of the lack of random selection. However, it is somewhat better than the previous design because of the control playground. There is no external validity.

Two Groups, Random Selection, Pretest, Posttest

This is similar to the preceding design, except that both control and experimental groups are randomly selected from a larger population so that they are as alike as possible. Thus, any differences that appear in the posttest should be the result of the experimental variable, rather than possible differences between the two groups to start with.

Example: This could involve the teaching of a sports skill with two or more groups of subjects who are randomly selected from a larger group or class of subjects. As a variation of totally random selection, group members might be deliberately paired to match such characteristics as age, sex, height and weight, or previous experience, to ensure that they are as equally matched as possible.

This is the classical type of experimental design and has very good internal validity. The representativeness of the results are somewhat limited because of the possible effect of pretesting. A variation of this approach is found in the following model.

Solomon Four-Group Design

This is a variation of true experimental design, in which four groups are used, but in which only two of them are given a pretest, because it is believed that the pretest may heighten the motivation of subjects or introduce key skills inappropriately, and thus contaminate the study's findings.

Example: In a study of the effects of a leisure education program on recreation interests of physically handicapped young adults, the design is:

Group A: Pre- and posttesting with leisure education intervention.

Group B: Pre- and posttesting without intervention.

Group C: Posttest only with intervention.

Group D: Posttest only without intervention.

This design has very strong internal and external validity, since the effect of pretesting can be accounted for.

SYMBOLS DESIGNATING EXPERIMENTAL DESIGNS

The following symbols are used to represent the elements in experimental research studies:

R   Random selection of subjects.
X   Experimental variable or intervention.
C   Control group.
E   Experimental group.
O   Observation or test.
___ A line between levels indicates matched groups

To illustrate in a study design with matched (randomized) groups and a posttest procedure only, the following formula describes the experiment's structure:

	Pretest	Treatment	Posttest
$E(R)$		X	O
$C(R)$			O

Variations of Classical Experimental Designs

In many forms of social research, it is difficult to select randomized groups or to maintain the kinds of rigorous controls that are necessary in experimental research based on the classical model. For example, Weiner points out that, in many therapeutic recreation settings, researchers would be unable to select groups on a randomized basis.[6] Although guidelines often suggest that there be a minimum number of subjects within population samples—such as 30—therapeutic recreation specialists may not be able to assemble groups of this size, without upsetting institutional routines. In addition, Weiner writes:

> . . . using a control group often implies withholding treatment from one group (or administering a presumably less-effective) treatment, a notion considered by many to be unethical. . . .

> Given the constraints of the institutional environment on the . . . research process, it appears that quasi-experimental designs may have greater applicability to therapeutic recreation settings than traditional experimental designs.

Quasi-Experimental Designs

These are studies carried on in natural or field settings where some, but not all, of the essential elements of experimental design may be maintained. The researcher is able to select the setting and to determine what variables are to be involved; however, it may not be possible to assign subjects randomly, or to control for all of the extraneous variables. While they are not regarded as true experimental studies, such research efforts often represent the only way to investigate a problem area in terms of actually testing hypotheses and observing the effects of given factors.

Ex Post Facto Research

A second variation is found in ex post facto research, which examines events and outcomes that have taken place in the past (the term means "after the fact"). An example of such research was carried out by Brown and Dodson, who examined the possible relationship between Boys' Club programming and juvenile delinquency rates in three areas of Louisville, Kentucky, over several years. The areas were similar in several demographic respects, although they could not be exactly matched, and their populations were obviously not randomly selected. The key finding was that in the one Louisville area where a Boy's Club had been built at an early point in the period that was examined, the juvenile delinquency rate declined steadily over an eight-year period. In the other two areas, the delinquency rate increased over the same period.[7]

While the obvious finding would appear to be that the Boys' Club represented an independent variable that was responsible for lowering the delinquency rate, the fact that the three areas had not been matched in all major respects and that it was not possible to control other social factors meant that the findings could only be tentatively suggested. In such investigations, it is not always possible to identify the exact direction of causality. For example, it is possible that a third factor—such as a stronger sense of civic responsibility or concern about youth, or more stable family structures in the area where the new club was built—was responsible both for the establishment of the Boys' Club and for the decline in delinquency during this period.

STRENGTHS AND WEAKNESSES OF EXPERIMENTAL DESIGNS

The primary *advantages* of experimental studies are the following:

1. Experimental research can be convenient to supervise, since it permits the investigator to control study conditions and operate the study on a time schedule of his or her own choosing. In addition, it is possible to select or impose variables that might not exist in clear-cut form, or at different desired levels, in ordinary life.

2. Experimental research may be less expensive to carry out than large-scale descriptive studies; typically, in other types of research, such as engineering, it is possible to test a small model under experimental stresses, rather than build a full-scale building, boat, or plane.

3. Experiments make it possible to confirm or reject hypotheses through statistical analyses in areas where descriptive methods cannot do this, because the experimenter is able to control the various elements affecting internal and external validity, whereas this cannot be done as easily in surveys or comparative studies.

4. Because experiments are sharply defined in terms of subjects and procedures, it is possible to replicate them exactly in other settings, to determine whether the findings will be exactly the same. When this happens, it shows that the experiment has been valid, and that it has generated theories that are broadly generalizable.

On the other hand, experimental research may have the following weaknesses or *disadvantages:*

1. Despite the statements regarding its relative convenience and inexpensiveness, experimental research may be very costly if it requires special environments, trained observers, or testing procedures.

2. Experimental research may suffer from a lack of reality and external validity, in that it may not be possible to simulate recreational attitudes or behaviors in a laboratory setting, or to establish needed controls in a field setting. To generalize from what happens in an artificial situation (as in the case of children playing in a special play laboratory) may not be applicable in natural settings, such as neighborhood playgrounds.

3. Because experiments are usually done with few subjects, if these individuals are not representative of the larger population findings may be misleading. In addition, because experimental research involves actually doing things to or with people or altering their life circumstances or experiences in some way, there is the risk that it might be regarded as hazardous or harmful from an ethical perspective.

ACTION RESEARCH

A category of research which is often found in human-service fields is known as *action research*. It is somewhat similar to quasi-experimental research, in the sense that it usually involves applying special new measures, or innovative program elements to bring about desired outcomes. However, it is clearly unlike experimental research in that experimental and control variables are not identified, subjects are usually not selected and placed in randomized groups, and there is little attempt to control all the influences that might have an effect on study outcomes.

Action research is sometimes carried on under the rubric of *demonstration projects*. These are programs which seek to test new techniques or methods, or to provide badly needed services in high-priority areas. Usually they receive special funding, and it is expected that they will be evaluated—although not with the degree of rigor found in true experimental studies.

Examples of demonstration projects might include efforts to mobilize volunteers to carry out needed park and playground rehabilitation tasks in their neighborhoods, or the application of special tutoring or substance-abuse programs in youth centers in inner-city neighborhoods. Such projects would rarely concern themselves with developing theoretical models or testing hypotheses, and their results cannot usually be regarded as generalizable to other settings. However, to the extent that they are carefully monitored, with both the methods used and the program outcomes systematically observed and recorded, they may be regarded as legitimate forms of research.

OTHER RESEARCH METHODS

While the preceding types of research designs are the most frequently used in the broad field of social research, including leisure-service studies, a number of other methods may be identified.

DOCUMENTARY RESEARCH

Sometimes called bibliographic research, this method involves careful analysis of the literature, including books, magazine or journal articles, research reports, and other records and documents within a given area. Its purpose may be to identify trends in public or scholarly interest, or to analyze prevalent points of view, or indeed to investigate any scholarly question or issue.

Although it often involves studying a given period in the past, it would not be thought of as historical research, since it does not rely on the use of primary sources. In addition, its intention often is simply to study the literature itself as a reflection of scholarly and educational practices and approaches.

CRITICAL AND ANALYTICAL RESEARCH

This type of research tends to be rather abstract and theoretical in its approach. It is primarily concerned with ideas, and usually does not rely on gathering empirical data. Instead, its purpose may be to examine potential models or to propose new theories based primarily on logical analysis. It may also examine concepts of leisure or recreation based on selected philosophical positions, or from an esthetic perspective.

CRITICAL INCIDENT RESEARCH

This approach to research blends both case study and historical approaches. It usually involves the investigator selecting one or more events which appeared to provide a major stimulus to a field, an important new trend, a shift in public attitudes, or other significant outcomes. The critical incident method usually differs from history in that it avoids drawn-out studies that record events over a long time. Instead, it seeks to study short-term happenings with very intensive and varied methods, in order to reveal the direct causes and effects of such incidents.

In addition to these approaches, other research studies may use a wide range of special techniques for gathering data or testing hypotheses. For example, in some studies which examine interpersonal roles of recreation participants, *sociometric analysis* may be used to show how individuals relate to each other, the roles they play within groups, and how different styles of leadership may affect group involvement and participation. *Projective tests* may be helpful in showing how people relate to concepts related to recreation and leisure. Tests of *physiological response* have been used to measure reactions to natural environments. A technique known as *semantic differential* is used to clarify how people feel about given issues or ideas, and tests of *physical performance* document the outcomes of program experiences in areas such as sports or outdoor recreation.

Numerous other special techniques drawn from scholarly disciplines like psychology, sociology, anthropology, economics, or political science may also be adapted for use in the leisure-studies field.

For example, in marketing studies concerned with determining the present and potential uses of recreation facilities or attractions, a *gravity model* technique drawn from the field of economics and business may be used.

COMBINATION OF METHODS

In addition to using one type of research design exclusively, several different methods may be used in a single study. For example, in a marketing study of leisure needs and interests combined with an analysis of public recreation and park programs and policies in the city of Philadelphia, the authors of this text employed several different techniques: (*a*) mailed questionnaires sent to a sample of adults drawn from voter registration lists; (*b*) interviews with participants of all ages at recreation sites; (*c*) meetings with community groups and recreation administrators; (*d*) surveys of recreation leaders; and (*e*) direct observation of selected playgrounds and centers. In addition, other non-public service providers were interviewed, and a special task force was formed to analyze current programming for the physically and mentally disabled and to develop recommendations in this area. Historical records and annual reports were consulted to provide a background for the study, and census data were systematically analyzed to give a demographic picture of each of the recreation districts of Philadelphia.

Similarly, many other types of studies are likely to include more than one research technique. Not infrequently, a descriptive study may begin with a large-scale survey of individuals or agencies, followed by an in-depth investigation—through observations or interviews—of a sample of respondents to the survey.

SELECTION OF APPROPRIATE RESEARCH APPROACHES

Within all fields of study, researchers have tended to use methods suited to their particular programmatic needs. For example, sociology has typically made use of surveys, field observations, and case studies. Psychology employs varied tests of perception or projective responses, observations of behavior, and both field- and laboratory-based experiments. Anthropology often relies on field studies in which investigators live within the village, neighborhood, or other social group that is being studied. Political scientists may make heavy use of trends analysis, polling techniques, documentary studies, and forecasting methods.

Similarly, in recreation, parks, and leisure studies, the particular focus of a research study normally dictates the methodology used. For example, if the problem was to determine what kinds of recreational services were being offered for the physically or mentally disabled within a state or region, the survey approach would be the most effective means of gathering a picture of normative practices.

If the task was to develop a number of different models of such programs, case studies using varied interview and observational methods probably would be the best choice.

If the issue was to discover which leadership approach was most useful within a particular type of setting or with a specific population, either experimental or evaluative research designs would be indicated.

If the researcher sought to explore the roots of professional development in recreation and parks during a given period, historical research or documentary analysis would be logical methods.

Within all types of research, the tendency in recent years has been to emphasize quantitative research that can be treated by statistical analysis. Too often it is assumed that, because a study has made use of impressive statistical calculations, it therefore represents sound research and should be respected. As Chapters 8 and 9 will make clear, statistical analysis with the help of computers is only as good as the raw data with which it is working. Researchers have a familiar phrase that makes this point: "Garbage in–garbage out," meaning that if you feed sloppy data, gathered with poor study controls, inadequate sampling procedures, or unreliable instruments, into a computer, no matter how sophisticated the statistical analysis, the result will be untrustworthy. It is therefore all the more essential that the research process make use of carefully designed procedures that will yield valid and significant findings.

SUMMARY

Research methods, as presented in this chapter, include the following major design categories: historical, descriptive, survey, case studies, longitudinal, cross-sectional and comparative, correlational, evaluative, experimental, and action research. Each such type is described, with examples given of the component elements of the method and how it may be applied in recreation, parks, and leisure studies. Descriptive and experimental research are described in the fullest detail, including a number of variations or specialized approaches under each broad category.

Other research methods are presented, such as documentary, analytical, or critical incident approaches. The final section of the chapter describes the application of different research study methods, based on the type of problem that is being analyzed or the orientation of the investigator.

ENDNOTES

1. John W. Best, *Research in Education* (Englewood Cliffs, N.J.: Prentice-Hall, 1981): 25.
2. Ibid., 131.
3. Ibid., 93.
4. Emanuel J. Mason and William J. Bramble, *Understanding and Conducting Research* (New York: McGraw-Hill Book Co., 1977): 34.
5. Julian L. Simon, *Basic Research Methods in Social Sciences: The Art of Empirical Investigation* (New York: Random House, 1978): 146–147.
6. Andrew Weiner, "A Quasi-Experimental Approach to Evaluating Recreation Programs: Time Series Analysis," *Therapeutic Recreation Journal* (1st Quarter 1979): 33.
7. Roscoe C. Brown, Jr., and Dan Dodson, "The Effectiveness of a Boys' Club in Reducing Delinquency," *Annals of American Academy of Political Science* (March, 1959): 47–52.

QUESTIONS FOR CLASS REVIEW AND DISCUSSION

11. The most common research method used in recreation, parks, and leisure studies is descriptive research, particularly surveys. Why is this so, and what are its implications as far as the development of a comprehensive body of information and theory for the field is concerned?

12. Discuss the strengths and weaknesses of experimental research as they apply to the leisure-service field, as you understand them. What are some of the difficulties that prevent more experimental research from being done?

INDIVIDUAL OR SMALL-GROUP ASSIGNMENTS TO BE PREPARED AND PRESENTED TO CLASS

13. Select a particular research problem or issue, using the categories of applied and pure research described in Chapter 2, to assist you in doing this. Then, choose any three of the research methods presented in this chapter, such as survey, historical, case study, longitudinal, experimental, or comparative research. Show how each of these methods could be used differently to investigate the problem you have chosen. Present your analysis to the class for review and discussion, making clear the aspect of the study you would be investigating and the possible setting in which the research might be carried on.

5

THE RESEARCH PROCESS: AN EIGHT-STEP MODEL

One of the first tasks in problem distillation is a precise specification of the topic under study. Although this may sound rather redundant, the key term here is "precise." As noted above, the research idea is frequently (presented) in very general terms—often even vague and nebulous. To successfully design and execute an investigation, the researcher must be very clear (and specific) about what is being studied and the nature of the research question.[1]

INTRODUCTION

Developing a research proposal and carrying out an investigation successfully includes a number of major tasks: identifying an appropriate problem area and developing a clear statement of the proposed study's purposes or hypotheses; formulating a detailed study plan or proposal, for approval by a sponsoring committee or funding agency; carrying out the actual investigation; and analyzing the data and preparing a final report.

This chapter begins by considering the possible reasons for undertaking a research study, and examining the different kinds of sponsorship and the settings in which research may be carried on. It deals with the process of identifying suitable problem areas for research, and then outlines the eight-step sequence which is normally followed by investigators. It concludes by suggesting a number of criteria that are useful in examining potential research problems, and with strategies that are helpful in refining problem statements.

MOTIVATIONS FOR DOING RESEARCH

Before undertaking any sort of research investigation, the would-be researcher should take a hard look at his or her own motivations for carrying out a study. Too often, research is done simply in response to a sort of personal challenge, somewhat like the mountaineer who explained his ascent of Mount Everest with the phrase, "Because it's there." Obviously, there should be better reasons for undertaking such a task.

PROFESSIONAL COMMITMENT

A common reason for doing research is that one is required to do so, as in the case of a master's or doctoral student in a university graduate program in recreation, parks, and leisure studies. Similarly, one might be *assigned* to carry out a research assignment as part of one's ongoing work within a leisure-service agency.

INTELLECTUAL CURIOSITY

However, many other individuals undertake research because they are genuinely interested in a subject and seek to explore it in order to make a contribution to the field.

CAREER ADVANCEMENT

Research may do much to enhance one's professional reputation. Individuals—particularly college and university faculty members—who do research are often called upon to address conferences or to be part of special task forces or work groups that carry out investigations or make planning reports. If they write for publication, they become recognized as authorities in a given area, and may be called upon to take consultant assignments. Ultimately, even for generalists in the field, research and evaluation may become an increasing part of their work assignments and they may ultimately hold specialized positions as researchers.

TYPES OF SPONSORSHIP

Research studies may be carried out under several different types of sponsorship arrangements. These include the following:

UNIVERSITY GRADUATE PROGRAMS

As indicated, in graduate programs in recreation, parks, and leisure studies, master's and doctoral candidates are normally required to write theses and dissertations, although in some master's curricula there may be optional choices of doing a project or taking a comprehensive examination.

IN-HOUSE RESEARCH PROJECT

Many leisure-service organizations carry out research as part of their ongoing operations. These tend to be applied forms of research, such as needs assessment studies, feasibility studies to determine whether given programs or facilities should be initiated, personnel evaluation studies, management policy analysis, or similar ventures.

In different types of agencies, such research projects are likely to have different emphases. For example, in therapeutic recreation programs, research is likely to focus on developing diagnostic tools or treatment techniques, or documenting outcomes. In commercial recreation, much of the research emphasis is likely to be on marketing methods. In armed forces recreation, it may be concerned with fitness and morale. Research of this type is usually carried out by personnel employed directly by the agency itself.

SPECIALLY FUNDED STUDIES

Frequently, research projects may receive special funding from an outside source or sponsor. For example, colleges, universities, and professional societies often apply for grants from government agencies or foundations in order to carry out studies within a particular area of interest. Most foundations are known for having special areas of social concern, and typically support grants in these areas. Similarly a number of government agencies fund research; numerous studies related to parks management, outdoor recreation, and related areas have been supported by the U.S. Department of Agriculture and Department of the Interior.

In some cases, government organizations or voluntary agencies may advertise the fact that they intend to commission a research study in an area relevant to them, and may request submissions from individuals or research agencies. Colleges and universities, as well as professional planning firms that respond to such RFPs (Requests for Proposals) must submit detailed proposals outlining their intended procedures, methods of analysis, team qualifications, preliminary budgets, and timetables for doing the research. Such bids are handled competitively, and often must go through a process of negotiation before the assignment is approved and the funding granted.

INDEPENDENT RESEARCH

Some research specialists conduct studies independently, with or without funding, in areas of their own choice. Often they are college or university professors, for whom scholarly productivity and publication represent important priorities. In some cases, they may develop cooperative relationships with professional organizations or societies, which act as formal sponsors for their research.

KEY STEPS IN CARRYING OUT RESEARCH

The following section of this chapter describes eight major steps that are typically followed in carrying out research studies—particularly within a scholarly or academic setting. In general, they would apply also to other types of research sponsors, although less emphasis might be given to exploring the literature or the formulation of theoretical concepts. They are presented as guidelines for those entering the field of research.

IDENTIFY BROAD PROBLEM AREA

Identify the broad problem area through: (a) professional exposure and direct experience; (b) preliminary reading in the professional literature; (c) meetings with other professionals or educators/researchers; and (d) attendance at conferences, seminars, or courses/workshops. Depending on the problem itself and on your own capabilities and purposes, determine whether the basic thrust of the study should be an applied, practical one, or whether it should be directed to more theoretical issues.

Gain fuller understanding of the problem by saturating yourself in the research literature, if it is primarily a theoretical or conceptual study, or by preliminary interviews, meetings with authorities, or field observations, if it is to be a piece of applied research. If it is to be a new area of study for you, make sure that you are thoroughly familiar with what has already been explored by researchers, both in terms of research methods and findings.

DEFINE RESEARCH QUESTIONS AND/OR HYPOTHESES

Based on your preliminary examination of the problem area, the next step is to sharpen the focus of the intended study by identifying one or more specific research questions that are to be answered, or one or more hypotheses that are to be tested. As part of this step, determine the variables that are to be investigated or introduced in the study, as well as the levels at which they are to be employed or measured.

SELECT STUDY DESIGN AND KEY PROCEDURES

Having become familiar with the background of the problem area and made some initial decisions as to the components of the study, it is now necessary to select a study design that will make use of the most appropriate types of data-gathering techniques, and that is suited to the purposes and nature of the investigation. For example, if the purpose is to gather a broad picture of current practices or to identify prevalent leisure behavior patterns, descriptive research such as survey or cross-sectional analysis would be most suitable. If the research is intended to test cause-and-effect relationships, probably an experimental design will be most useful.

At this point, other important decisions must be made with respect to the subjects who will be involved, the population they will be drawn from, and the sampling procedures; the kinds of data-gathering methods that will be used; the most appropriate methods of analysis; and the time frame in which the study would be carried on. In some cases, two or more alternative approaches may be identified, with the final choice of method to depend on an analysis of benefits and costs, or on the feasibility of one plan compared to another.

OPERATIONALIZE RESEARCH METHODOLOGY

Based on the preliminary exploration that has been done, it is necessary to develop the actual instruments and procedures that will be used. This may include: (a) establishing test conditions and making necessary arrangements or gaining permissions or approvals; (b) gathering preliminary data or exploring settings/systems that will be used in data-gathering; (c) operationalizing concepts by transforming each variable into an element that can be observed or tested empirically in the study; (d) developing, pilot-testing, and refining instruments that will be used in the study; and (e) identifying possible obstacles to be encountered or weaknesses in the research design, and planning to overcome or avoid these.

OBTAIN APPROVAL FOR STUDY

At this point, formal approval must be obtained to carry out the study. If it is being done as a scholarly thesis or dissertation, normally a graduate faculty committee is formed to review and approve a detailed proposal or outline of the study. It is probable that the committee would have been formed at an earlier point, and that they would have consulted with and assisted the candidate throughout the earlier steps of the process. However, it is at this stage that they must give official approval to the plan, which then serves as a contract which the researcher must live up to in doing the study.

If the research plan is being submitted as a response to an advertised "request for proposals" (RFP), the individual researcher or team would prepare it according to the requirements or specifications of the organization that is prepared to fund the study. If it is being submitted to a government agency or foundation grants committee, or even if it is being carried out as an "in-house" research study by a recreation and park agency or a professional society, a similar process is normally followed.

In addition, the study may require permissions from those in charge of the setting where the work is to be done. The researcher may also need to obtain permission to proceed from a "human-subjects review" committee and, if the study is to receive support from a professional society or to be cosponsored by other organizations, it will need to be reviewed and approved by them.

CONDUCT RESEARCH

It has sometimes been said that the most difficult and creative task in research is to identify a good subject and to develop a sound proposal, and that the process of actually carrying out the research is relatively simple.

While there is some truth to this, the actual implementation of the study is critical. In gathering data, careful supervision must ensure that all conditions are uniform, that investigators or observers are carefully trained and objective in their work, that research instruments are reliable, that the recording and transmission of data is consistent and accurate, and that possible pitfalls to good research are noted and avoided.

If difficulties are encountered, it may be necessary to change original plans with respect to sampling procedures, timing of research steps, or similar elements. If changes are minor, they can normally be done without obtaining the approval of the advising committee or sponsoring group. If they are more serious, it is best to seek such approval rather than risk later challenges to the procedures followed.

ANALYZE DATA

Even while the data gathering goes on, preliminary analysis of the data may be done. Sometimes questionnaires or other instruments may be changed during the course of a study, as a result of such analysis. When all information has been gathered, the data are fully analyzed. Decisions regarding the research questions and/or hypotheses must be made and the results fully interpreted and discussed in relation to future research needs. This process may vary greatly, ranging from extensive computer analysis of quantitative data to more subjective analysis of qualitative findings.

PREPARE FINAL REPORT

Every research study should conclude with a final report that summarizes its purpose and methodology and presents the findings, both in purely factual terms and also with interpretation of their meaning. Major conclusions are developed and recommendations either for action or further study may be presented. Depending on the sponsorship of the study, the report may be a lengthy and scholarly one—as in a master's thesis or doctoral dissertation—or a brief, factual account for in-house review.

Research findings may also be published in professional journals, general magazines, or even through the major newspaper chains or press associations. Unique or controversial reports are often presented or reviewed through radio or television programs. Researchers may also disseminate their work through conferences and research symposia, lectures at colleges or universities, or other professional society meetings.

GETTING UNDER WAY:
SELECTING A RESEARCH TOPIC

The initial stage of developing a research question is critical to the ultimate success of the effort. Northrop has pointed out:

> Again and again investigators have plunged into a subject matter, sending out questionnaires, gathering a tremendous amount of data, even performing experiments, only to come out at the end wondering what it all proves. . . . Others, noting the success of a given scientific method in one field, have carried this method hastily and uncritically into their own, only to end later in a similar disillusionment. All such experiences are a sign that the initiation of inquiry has been glossed

over too hastily, without any appreciation of its importance or its difficulty.[2]

To ensure that the problem area is a significant one that lends itself to scientific inquiry, the researcher should seek answers to the following questions.

QUESTIONS ABOUT THE PROBLEM AREA

1. Will it be of interest both to the individual researcher, and to some recognized segment of the community (the profession at large, public or nonprofit agencies, those within a specific scholarly discipline, college or university departments, or the public)?

2. Is it likely to be a significant study, in that it will add to existing knowledge or contribute to professional practice in some meaningful way?

3. Will the topic be researchable, in that it requires information that can be discovered or measured empirically, or that can be analyzed by known methods?

4. Will the study be administratively feasible, in that it will be possible to carry it out within a reasonable time frame, and with expenses that the researcher or study team can afford?

5. Will the problem area be one in which the investigator has special expertise and interst, or in which he/she can readily develop the background, testing skills, or other competencies that will be needed?

QUESTIONS THE RESEARCHER SHOULD ASK HIMSELF/HERSELF

In addition to these questions, the researcher should ask himself/herself the following questions:

1. Am I free of bias on this topic that might imperil my objectivity? If I do have some preconceived views—which would be normal in many problem areas—can I be scientifically objective in the design and conduct of the study?

2. Is the problem area one in which research will be helpful to my agency, institution, or program, or of value to other professionals? Will it be helpful to me in my career and professional development?

3. Does the problem meet the scope, significance, or other requirements of the institution I am affiliated with, or the publication to which I would plan to submit a report?

4. Has similar research been done and, if so, is there justification for replicating it (repeating it in another setting or with different subjects, to determine whether the findings will be repeated)? Or

will my research effort extend or enrich the earlier line of investigation?

5. Can I obtain needed administrative support and cooperation to carry out the study successfully? Will access to needed subjects or other resources necessary for the study be available? Will it meet "human subjects protection" guidelines?

6. Can the concepts or variables included in the design that I am considering be made operational, in the sense that they can be identified and measured? Do instruments exist that can be used, or will it be necessary to create, test, and validate them, to carry out the study?

FORMULATING A RESEARCH QUESTION

As the researcher moves from a broad conception of the problem area to a more precisely defined statement of its focus and the related study purposes or hypotheses, such concerns should be raised again and again. They should be dealt with realistically. In many cases, they may lead to a rethinking of the problem area or issue, or to developing appropriate purposes and hypotheses, given the researcher's capabilities and resources. In some cases, they may lead to the realization that the topic is not a suitable one and that a new approach is needed.

At the outset, it should not be too difficult for a would-be researcher to identify a broad area of concern. For example, under the heading of "management problems and trends," a master's degree candidate who has had some professional experience or who has explored the literature might say, "At this point, I can identify several problem areas that I am interested in. These include the following: *participative management techniques,* the *effects of fees and charges,* the *advantages and disadvantages of privatization,* and the *problem of a growing number of lawsuits for accidents in high-risk recreation programs.*"

In reviewing each of these possible research areas, it is possible to identify a number of more specific issues that might represent a significant research question. As the researcher reviews the literature in each area, the following kinds of questions may emerge.

1. *Problem Area:* Participative management techniques.

Possible Research Question: Are participative management techniques effective, in terms of improving the motivation and on-the-job performance of employees?

2. *Problem Area:* The effects of fees and charges.

Possible Research Question: What are the typical effects of fees and charges in recreation agencies?

3. *Problem Area:* The advantages and disadvantages of privatization.

Possible Research Question: Does privatization (that is, the subcontracting of public agency functions to private or commercial firms) lead to greater efficiency and/or economy?

4. *Problem Area:* Growing number of lawsuits for accidents in high-risk recreation programs.

Possible Research Question: Given the possibility of being sued for negligence, does it make sense to sponsor high-risk, adventure recreation programs?

Each of these questions represents a potentially useful subject for research in the leisure-service field. However, they tend to be much too general, and need to be more precisely stated, if they are to serve as the basis for planning a research study. The following kinds of questions must be raised:

CLARITY OF QUESTION

Are the terms that are used in the question entirely clear, and will it be possible to operationalize them, in order to carry out measurements that yield useful data?

To illustrate, a phrase like "what are the typical effects" lacks precision. What does the word "typical" mean? Similarly, a phrase like, "Does it make sense?" may be heard in informal conversation, but does not represent a precise or clear question that can be meaningfully answered.

BALANCE BETWEEN BREADTH AND SPECIFICITY

Does the research question strike a proper balance between breadth and specificity? Often, beginning problem statements are far too broad and must be narrowed down to be researchable. However, it might also be a mistake to have a problem statement that is overly limited and that would therefore lack significance or generalizability.

To illustrate, the term, "the effects of fees and charges," might be rephrased to refer to three specific elements: (*a*) the effects on attendance and participation; (*b*) the effects on the income of an agency;

and (c) the effects on the public's perception of the agency. At the same time, to deal only with the effects of fees and charges applied to a single event or type of program might be too narrow for a worthwhile study.

Similarly, in the fourth question, it would be helpful to know more specifically what types of agencies are being considered. For example, it might make sense for commercial organizations to undertake high-risk programs, but not for nonprofit, voluntary organizations.

APPROPRIATE LEVEL OF INVESTIGATION

If the problem area is a relatively new one and has not been investigated before, the question might be a simple or exploratory one. On the other hand, if considerable research has already been done on a subject, any new research question dealing with it should build on what has already been done, and should examine a more specialized or in-depth aspect of the problem.

DEVELOPING THE PROBLEM STATEMENT

Identifying an appropriate research question is followed by the need to develop a statement of the research problem. This statement serves two important functions. First, it compels the researcher to begin to come to grips with exactly what he or she wants to accomplish in the study. The problem statement should make quite explicit whether the research is intended to gather descriptive information, develop a classification system of phenomena, compare two or more agencies or systems, identify and test possible relationships among variables, or test a formally stated hypothesis.

Second, the problem statement usually serves as a key section in a research proposal. It may actually take two forms: (1) the introduction, a brief, carefully worded statement that presents the overall area of concern, arouses the reader's interest, and provides some general background information or indication of the problem area's significance and (2) a more explicit statement of the overall purpose and subpurposes of the study, or of the hypotheses to be investigated, along with a concise summary of the variables to be examined, including the nature of the population and settings that will be involved in the research.

The basic purpose of the problem statement is to make absolutely clear, in succinct terms, what is to be investigated and why it is to be investigated. Mason and Bramble suggest that problem statements must meet three important criteria: (*a*) A problem should raise a question about a relationship between or among variables; (*b*) the relationship must be stated clearly and precisely; and (*c*) the problem statement should suggest a method of researching the question or determining the exact nature of the relationship.[3] While some studies may not necessarily explore possible relationships—such as a descriptive study that seeks primarily to gather a broad sweep of knowledge and to organize findings into logical categories or classification systems—these criteria are applicable to most recreation, park, and leisure-studies research problems.

Following development of the problem statement, the researcher begins to develop a study plan that makes key decisions with respect to defining key variables, selecting instruments or data-gathering procedures, choosing subjects for the study, and other important research tasks. Thus, what may have begun in the investigator's mind as a rather casual or offhand question, stemming from curiosity or informal observation, begins to take form in the development of a proposal that will provide the formal plan for carrying out a research study. Chapter 6 describes the process of preparing such a proposal.

SUMMARY

There are eight major steps involved in carrying out research: (1) identifying the broad problem area; (2) defining the research question and/or its hypotheses, and identifying important study variables; (3) selecting a study design and key procedures; (4) operationalizing the research methodology; (5) obtaining approval for the study; (6) actually carrying out the data-gathering process; (7) analyzing and interpreting the data; and (8) preparing a final report.

Before initiating a study, the researcher should examine his/her personal motivations or purposes for doing research, since they are likely to influence the choice of a research topic. It is also possible to undertake research under several different kinds of auspices, which may provide special kinds of support or assistance. Identifying a problem area is a key step in research; it may begin with a simple, casual question or point of curiosity, but must be transformed into a more detailed, analytical, and precise question that lends itself to systematic investigation. The researcher should ask a number of specific questions about the potential research topic, in terms of its significance and researchability, as well as his or her own interest

in it and suitability for investigating the area. With fuller exploration and reworking, the research question is transformed into a
detailed statement of the problem, and ultimately a convincing
study proposal.

ENDNOTES

1. Clifford J. Drew, *Introduction to Designing and Conducting Research* (St.
   Louis: C. V. Mosby Co., 1980): 73.
2. F. S. C. Northrop, cited in Claire Selltiz, Lawrence S. Wrightsman, and
   Stuart W. Cook, *Research Methods in Social Relations* (New York: Holt,
   Rinehart and Winston, 1976): 11.
3. Emanuel J. Mason and William J. Bramble, *Understanding and Conducting Research* (New York: McGraw-Hill Book Co., 1977): 59.

QUESTIONS FOR CLASS REVIEW
AND DISCUSSION

14. What are the key factors to be considered in selecting a problem area for
    investigation?

15. This chapter points out that one's motivations for doing research may
    vary greatly. Which of these do you think are the most important and
    valid, and which are least significant?

16. Probably the key step in developing a research study is developing a
    specific, concrete research question from a broad problem area. What
    are the desired characteristics of a meaningful research question?

WORKSHOP ACTIVITY TO BE CARRIED OUT
IN CLASS

17. Divide the overall class into two teams, and each team into several
    subgroups. Each subgroup then identifies and briefly describes a possi-
    ble problem area in recreation, parks, and leisure studies. They then
    exchange written summaries of these problem areas with a subgroup in
    the other team. Each subgroup must develop a specific research ques-
    tion based on the problem area it has been given. Subgroups then report
    their results to the overall class for discussion.

18. Similar subgroups select research reports in professional journals.
    Reviewing these reports, paired subgroups attempt to identify three
    elements in them: (a) the overall problem area; (b) the statement of the
    specific issue or area of concern; and (c) the research question that the
    research seeks to answer. They then compare their findings with the
    group with which they have been paired.

6

DEVELOPING THE RESEARCH PROPOSAL

The importance of the student's first formal proposal is measured by the fact that in most instances the decision to permit the student to embark on a thesis or dissertation is made solely on the basis of that document. The quality of the writing in the proposal is likely to be used by advisors as a basis for judging the clarity of thought that has preceded the study, the degree of facility with which it will be implemented if approved, and the skill of presentation the student will bring to reporting the results. In sum, the proposal is a document in which the student will reveal whether there is a reasonable hope that he can conduct any research project at all.[1]

INTRODUCTION

A key step in the research process is to develop a research proposal. This represents a carefully designed and written plan for doing the research, including a clear statement of the problem and the purposes or hypotheses of the investigation, a review of the related literature, and a step-by-step outline of the methodology to be followed. Usually the proposal is submitted for review and approval by a faculty committee or other group before the researcher is authorized to conduct the study.

This chapter describes the process of preparing a research proposal, describing the key elements that they normally contain and offering a number of illustrations of how different sections may be phrased. It is intended as a general guideline, rather than as a precise model to be followed, and is primarily concerned with academic research proposals, although it also applies to the preparation of other types of proposals.

ROLE OF THE PROPOSAL

David Krathwohl describes the way in which many students tend to regard the research process. The typical novice in this field, he writes:

> . . . envisions the researcher as one who dreams up creative ideas, the needed resources miraculously appear, and the hero, in a state of eager anticipation, begins his investigation.[2]

The reality of course is that developing a proposal is a complex task, which may involve careful preparation and possibly a drawn-out series of presentations and revisions before the plan is finally approved. Locke and Spirduso point out that the completed research proposal in a college or university graduate program serves three functions: (1) it communicates the student's research plans to those who may give consultation and advice; (2) it serves as a detailed plan of action; and (3) it constitutes a bond of agreement, or contract, between the student and his or her advisors.[3] Similarly, in a proposal that is placed before a foundation or other funding agency for support, or that is submitted in a bid to carry out an advertised study, the proposal provides the basis for reviewing the researcher's intentions and providing a basis for judging the intended study.

As described in Chapter 5, a research proposal normally begins with the identification of a problem area, which in turn is refined or distilled into a specific research question. Following a thorough review of the literature, major decisions are made regarding the specific purposes or hypotheses of the research, and the design that it will follow. Variables are identified, and the data-gathering procedures selected. All of these elements must be fitted into a proposal which presents a full and accurate picture of the researcher's intentions.

FORMAT OF THE PROPOSAL

The authors of this text have done graduate study or served on the graduate faculties of six well-known universities. In no two of them were the required formats of thesis or dissertation proposals exactly alike. However, they all tended to require that certain common elements appear in research proposals. While the names of these elements may vary from institution to institution, their essential functions are the same.

KEY ELEMENTS IN THE PROPOSAL

Typically, most academic research proposals contain three sections, or chapters, as they are often called. These chapters consist of the *Introduction,* the *Literature Review,* and the *Methodology.* They include the following subelements:

Chapter One: Introduction
1. Introduction
2. Statement of the Problem
3. Purposes and/or Hypotheses
4. Definitions of Terms
5. Limitations and Delimitations

Chapter Two: Review of the Literature
1. Summary and Discussion of Related Research
2. Implications of Literature Review for Proposed Study

Chapter Three: Methodology
1. Study Design
2. Study Variables: Subjects and Settings
3. Data-Gathering Instruments and Procedures
4. Data-Analysis Plan
5. Study Timetable
6. Permissions and Human Subjects Approval

MANNER OF PRESENTATION

The writing style of the proposal should be simple, matter-of-fact, and very clear and precise. Slang or overly light or humorous usages are to be avoided, as are excessively technical phrases or unnecessarily elaborate language. What is particularly important is that all statements are understandable and can be documented or supported, and that they flow in a logical sequence, in terms of conveying to the reader the purpose and methodology of the proposed research. The author of the proposal must be able to defend his or her plan before an examining committee—both in terms of the need for the study, its conceptual framework, and the actual research process that is advanced.

It is essential that the physical appearance of the proposal be highly professional and attractive. Usually, it should be double-spaced and should either be neatly typed or computer-generated (different graduate faculties may specify the exact nature of the typing that may be required, and other details such as weight of paper, width of margins, nature of headings, and similar details). References and other format elements should follow specified style guidelines, which often are based on an approved publications style manual. The proposal should be carefully proof-read and free of all errors or hand-written corrections. Since it is a reflection of the researcher's scholarly capability and degree of motivation and effort, it should convey a very positive impresson to the reviewer!

DETAILED DESCRIPTION OF PROPOSAL ELEMENTS

The following section of this chapter provides a detailed description of the three chapters that normally constitute academic research proposals, beginning with guidelines for the study title.

TITLE

The title should be fairly brief, but should contain a very clear indication of the major thrust of the proposed study or the key elements that are contained in the study. Normally, a study title would not be presented as a question or as a declarative statement. Instead, it usually takes the form of a descriptive caption, sometimes with a semicolon followed by an explanatory phrase or qualifying phrase. Examples of several titles which illustrate typical kinds of study headings follow:

Sex-Role Stereotypes and Evaluations of Administrative Performance by Municipal Recreation and Park Administrators

Imaginal Rehearsal Training: A Technique for Improving Simulation Training for Park Law Enforcement Officers

Data-Based Research in Therapeutic Recreation: State of the Art

Park and Recreation Directors' Perceptions of Organizational Goals

Social Interaction, Affect, and Leisure

The Effects of Direct and Indirect Competition on Children's State Anxiety

Systematic Observation of Use Levels, Campsite Selection, and Visitor Characteristics at a High Mountain Lake

The Publications Manual of the American Psychological Association presents guidelines for writing titles of published articles, which apply also to proposal titles:

... avoid words that serve no useful purpose; they increase length and can mislead indexers. For example, the words *method* and *results* do not normally appear in a title, nor should such redundancies as "A Study of" or "An Experimental Investigation of" begin a title. Do not use abbreviations in a title. .... The recommended length for a title is 12 to 15 words.[4]

CHAPTER ONE

The first major section of the proposal, Chapter One, is intended to provide a clear picture of the problem area, the specific research question or questions that the research is designed to investigate, and its actual purposes and/or hypotheses. In addition, it may clarify the terms used in the study by providing definitions, and should indicate the ways in which the investigation is to be limited, either through the researcher's intention or for other reasons. It contains the following subsections:

Introduction

This is an opening statement of the problem and describes it briefly. It is almost like an abstract, which is the summary page (usually about 300 or 400 words) that appears in the beginning of many thesis or dissertation reports or articles in research journals. However, an abstract is usually presented in the past tense, since it describes work that *has* been done. Instead, the Introduction normally describes the problem situation in the present tense, and the proposed study plan in the future tense.

Within two or three pages, the proposal should give a concise picture of the area of investigation, the specific problem or research question under study, and the intended research strategy. After reading the Introduction, one should have a clear idea of the problem and the basic thrust of the research. An abridged example of an Introduction intended to achieve these purposes follows:

Example of Introduction

This study is concerned with the impact of selected off-road recreational vehicles on the natural environment in selected state parks in the midwest region of the United States. It seeks to measure the extent of damage caused by different types of vehicles, and to learn both the factors related to more serious negative environmental impact, and the effectiveness of different types of control procedures in limiting such negative impact.

The rapidly growing use of off-road vehicles such as snowmobiles or four-wheel drive jeeps or dune buggies has been shown to have a serious environmental impact on different outdoor recreation environments. State and federal park officials have sought to develop policies and regulations to protect vegetation and wildlife from such incursions, while at the same time making it possible for those recreationists who enjoy the use of off-road vehicles to do so in appropriate settings.

This study will identify a sample of five park areas in each of the state park systems of four Midwestern states. The park areas must include examples of the types of areas described in the proposed classification system developed in the Report of the Outdoor Recreation Resources Review Commission, including: wilderness, primitive, natural, historic, and intensive-use areas.

Over a four-season period (fall, winter, spring, summer), the investigation will examine each of the selected parks through direct monitoring of park areas, measurement of physical forms of environmental damage, measurement of types and volume of off-vehicle use, determination of park policies and restrictions regarding the use of vehicles, and the effectiveness of such policies and regulations.

STATEMENT OF THE PROBLEM

This section provides a more detailed discussion of the problem area, showing its dimensions or background more fully, summarizing its implications in terms of professional significance or theory development, and giving the reader a fuller understanding of what has been learned thus far by other researchers. Statistics may be cited and the literature may be discussed briefly; there may also be a historical review, if appropriate. If earlier works are summarized, it is best to avoid nonessential details and instead emphasize pertinent findings and methodological issues. The reader should be referred to general reviews of the topic if they are available. In developing the background, it is best to:

> ... demonstrate the logical continuity between previous and present work. Develop the problem with enough breadth and clarity to make it generally understood by as wide a professional audience as possible. Do not let the goal of brevity mislead you into writing a statement intelligible only to the specialist.[5]

In discussing controversial issues, it is essential to avoid animosity or overly impassioned opinion statements. Instead, a simple statement that certain studies support one position and other studies support others is preferable to an extensive but inconclusive essay or a one-sided presentation of a partisan argument. When this section of the proposal emphasizes the theoretical background of the proposed study, it may be referred to as the Conceptual Framework. It is important that this section not simply repeat the points covered in the Introduction. Instead, it provides a fuller discussion and overview of the background of the problem, and concludes with a concise statement of the research question or questions. For example, a problem statement based on the Introduction just presented would stress: *(a)* the need to gain a comprehensive and systematic picture of the impact of off-road recreational vehicles on the environment and *(b)* the need to identify the measures that have been used to control such vehicles and to learn their degree of success.

PURPOSES AND/OR HYPOTHESES

This section of the proposal presents a specific, detailed statement of the thrust of the intended research. At this stage, an important decision must be made with respect to the study: whether it is to test one or more hypotheses through statistical analysis. It is sometimes assumed that the *only* kind of worthwhile study is based on hypothesis testing. However, it has been shown that 94 percent of all studies reported in a recognized recreation research journal over a recent five-year period involved surveys, rather than other research designs.[6] Typically, relatively few surveys involve hypotheses; instead their purpose is to gather descriptive information about a subject. This may involve comparing two or more subjects or systems, categorizing or classifying groups of phenomena, developing and testing models, *or* measuring relationships among different variables.

Therefore, the proposal may simply contain a statement of purposes of the research. For example, in a study designed to determine the effect of increased fees and charges on certain population groups in public recreation and park programs within a designated region of the country, the following major purposes and related subpurposes might be advanced:

Purpose No. 1

To examine the impact of new and increased fees and charges on participation by selected special population groups in public recreation and park programs in the Delaware Valley region.

Subpurposes

a. To measure the impact of new and increased fees and charges on recreation participation in selected settings by the following population groups: (1) the economically disadvantaged; (2) the physically and mentally disabled; and (3) the aging.

b. To determine the specific program areas or facilities (i.e., sports and games, arts and crafts, trip programs, adult classes, etc., *or* use of community centers, swimming pools, skating rinks, etc.) which have had the sharpest increase in fees and charges, and then to measure the specific rates of increased or decreased participation in each of these types of programs or facilities.

Purpose No. 2

To analyze management techniques employed in determining the level of fees and charges and the methods used in presenting them to the public, including possible "waiver" or "scholarship" arrangements with special populations.

Subpurposes

a. To identify any special measures which may have been taken to ensure that individuals are not excluded from participation, such as the use of special rates for handicapped groups or families on welfare, fee waivers for the handicapped or aging, free sessions or days, or scholarships or work-exchange practices; and also to measure the degree of success of such practices.

b. To identify techniques that have been used effectively to increase revenues through fees and charges without negative public feedback or decline in participation, and to develop a set of guidelines based on these practices. Linked to this subpurpose, to determine whether the public's perception and support of public recreation and park programs has been influenced by such fiscal practices, and whether governmental support of leisure-service agencies has been affected by them as well.

Examples of Hypotheses

If this study had hypotheses, they might be formulated to test such assumptions as the following:

Working Hypotheses

a. Selected administrative policies or procedures may be useful in modifying the effect of excluding special populations from program participation because of increased fees and charges.

b. Fees and charges may be successfully applied in certain types of communities, such as wealthy suburban townships or smaller communities, but may not be feasible in others, such as high-density central city areas.

Statistical Hypotheses

a. Participation by certain population groups will be significantly decreased by the imposition of new or higher fees, in contrast with other population groups.

b. The imposition of fees and charges will result in a significant increase in participation by some population groups

In framing statistical hypotheses, the following guidelines are helpful. Normally, hypotheses have five key characteristics: (1) They should be stated in declarative form; (2) they should identify and describe a relationship between two or more variables; (3) they should be testable through empirical measurement that lends itself to statistical confirmation; (4) they should be so clearly stated that there is no ambiguity in the variables or the relationship that is being tested; and (5) they should lend themselves (particularly in the case of applied research) to developing a solution or outcome to a problem recognized as a key area of difficulty in the field.

In addition to stating the purposes and/or hypotheses of the proposed study, this section may include a brief discussion of the rationale underlying these elements. Based on the preceding background section, it should be possible to make clear the logic behind each of the hypotheses, or the way in which the purposes, when carried out, will contribute to fuller understanding of the problem area.

DEFINITIONS OF TERMS

This is a brief section, consisting of a series of definitions of the key terms or concepts found in the study proposal. Since words like recreation or leisure may have various meanings, it is important to clarify the way they are being used in the proposal. Other words, which may be less familiar to the reader, may also require more precise definitions. The term "environmental quality," for example, may require a definition drawn from a governmental handbook, specifying exactly what it means and possibly even indicating levels of quality. Other terms like "professionalization," "mental retardation," "senility," or professional processes like "zero-based budgeting" or "orientation" may also require a clear definition.

Each definition should be as brief as possible, rather than a rambling discussion or essaylike presentation. The following distinction can be made between "operational" and "attribute" definitions:

> *Operational* definitions are to be distinguished from *property* or *attribute* definitions, in which something is defined by saying what it *consists of.* For example, a crude attribute definition of a college might be "An organization containing faculty and students, teaching a variety of subjects beyond the high-school level." An operational definition of university might be "An organization found in *The World Almanac's* listing of 'Colleges and Universities.' "[7]

Operational definitions differ sharply from dictionary definitions, which tend to rely on comparisons or synonyms, to give the meaning of a term or to help translate a word not known into words already known. In contrast, the operational definition provides a complete, independent understanding of the term. Usually it is best to draw definitions from widely accepted, authoritative sources. However, it is always possible to present your own definition of a term as it is being used in the proposal, with a logical justification or explanation as necessary.

The following example of a definition of special populations, which might be used in a study of the impact of increased fees and charges on such populations, contains both operational and attribute elements.

Special Populations

As a general definition, refers to any subgroup within the community which, either because of disability or impairment of a physical or mental nature, or because of economic or other social factors, is limited in recreational participation, and therefore requires special programming or adapted activities and facilities. In the proposed study, the preliminary plan will be to identify three special populations: *(a)* the mentally or physically disabled (including the blind, deaf, orthopedically or neurologically impaired, the mentally ill or mentally retarded); *(b)* the economically disadvantaged, based on Federal poverty guidelines; and *(c)* senior citizens.

LIMITATIONS AND DELIMITATIONS OF PROPOSED STUDY

These refer to areas of possible weakness in the methodology of the study plan, or to exclusions that are deliberately planned. Isaac and Michael comment that an important step in planning research is to ask:

> What are the limitations surrounding your study and within which conclusions must be confined? What limitations exist in your methods or approach—sampling restrictions, uncontrolled variables, faulty instrumentation, and other compromises to internal and external validity?[8]

LIMITATIONS: These are certain conditions of the study methodology which you cannot overcome or strengthen, and about which you are warning the reader. For example, it may be a limitation that you are drawing information only from program leaders rather than participants, or that you are exploring events that occurred several years ago, with the likelihood that participants' memories are somewhat faulty.

Another limitation may be that you have not been granted access to a particular facility or source of information, or that you will be unable to check the reliability of a given test procedure. If these are too serious, it may be that members of a study advisory committee might feel that the study design is inadequate or unacceptable, and that a new plan must be submitted. Normally, however, statements of limitations are accepted as an honest presentation of possible weaknesses of the study, made in advance, rather than in the form of an apologetic rationalization, at a later point. In some cases, when there are serious limitations in the proposal plan, the researcher may choose to describe it as an "exploratory study," which suggests that he or she is opening up the subject for research with admittedly crude methods, and with the expectation that future researchers will apply more rigorous methods.

DELIMITATIONS: These represent decisions made by the researcher, in which the study plan *deliberately* excludes certain areas of information, or limits the scope or depth of the investigation. For example, setting limits to the population to be examined, the time period to be covered, or the region to be studied would all be types of delimitations.

Realistically, many research studies have too broad a scope or complex a problem, and try to do too much with inadequate resources. Therefore, it may be desirable to reduce the scope of the study, and to carry it out in greater depth and with more rigorous procedures. To illustrate, a study of therapeutic recreation service in mental health centers might deal with the entire nation, a region, a state, or a single community. With limited resources, it might be desirable to delimit it to a narrow geographical focus.

CHAPTER TWO: REVIEW OF THE LITERATURE

Although earlier sections of the proposal may include references to the literature, it is at this point that a full-scale review is normally provided. The Literature Review's purpose is to give the proposed study a scholarly background, by discussing it conceptually and by showing the kinds of research that have already been done on the subject, along with their findings. It also has the purpose within an academic setting of assuring the faculty committee guiding the study that the graduate student planning to carry out the research is highly knowledgeable within his or her area of special interest.

While the primary source of citations would normally be research reports found in scholarly journals or other professional publications, it may also be appropriate to cite references from textbooks, general articles in popular publications, conference proceedings and symposium reports, and similar sources. Isaac and Michael point out that the scope of the research topic should be clearly defined and illustrated in the literature review:

> Searching too broad an area often leads to the student's becoming discouraged or doing a slipshod job. Searching too narrow an area causes him to overlook many articles that are peripheral to his research topic but contain information that would help him design a better study.[9]

The literature review normally takes the form of an essay which moves from the general question or topic to the more specific area or question you are researching. It should be carefully organized, so that it is not simply a collection of random citations or earlier research findings. Instead, each major topic or subtopic should be blocked out in a logical sequence, with appropriate transitions, from area to area. It should conclude with a statement that, ideally, confirms the need for the research you are planning to carry out as a continuation of what has already been done.

If you cannot find relevant research on the exact issue that you are planning to investigate, you may cite related studies that provide helpful information, parallel findings, or useful research designs and methods. Rather than indicate that yours is a poor proposal, this might support the need for your research, in that it is directed at a significant *gap* in the available research literature.

Literature Retrieval Process

In exploring sources for research references, it is helpful to use the following techniques: *(a)* direct review of the publications likely to contain relevant articles, usually extending back in time for several years; *(b)* follow-up of research references found in the bibliographies or footnotes of these articles; *(c)* examination of textbooks in areas related to the research subject; *(d)* use of subject indices identifying articles on a wide range of topics in areas such as sociology, psychology, education, urban planning, or environmental education, drawn from many publications and published on an annual or semiannual basis; *(e)* use of general subject indices, such as the Reader's Guide to Periodical Literature; *(f)* use of annual collections of abstracts of studies reported at research symposia of professional societies; or *(g)* other special bibliographies or reports of research within specialized subject areas in recreation and leisure studies.

Increasingly, computer searches are used to locate relevant articles conveniently, although this method may have the disadvantage of producing numerous articles only vaguely related to the topic or in difficult-to-locate publications. The use of "keywords," which identify the major themes found in a research report, is essential in exploring such sources. The literature retrieval process may also be facilitated by the use of interlibrary loans of theses or dissertations in microfilm or microfiche form.

CHAPTER THREE: METHODOLOGY

Customarily, the third major section of the proposal includes a detailed description of the methods that will be used to conduct the research.

Study Design

This section should specify the nature of the study design (survey, case study, experimental, etc.), and give a brief description of the nature of the investigation. For example, it might state that the study will consist of an experiment carried on with preschool-age children in a playground setting, in which their use of several different kinds of play equipment will be observed and analyzed.

Study Variables: Subjects and Settings

The variables, both dependent and independent, that will be the focus of the investigation, will be identified. The methodology section should show how they are to be operationalized; i.e., how they will be described in terms that can be measured.

In research studies where variables will be introduced or controlled by the investigator, as in experimental studies, it may be necessary to describe the different levels at which a given variable may be applied. For example, the responses of players on a team to different coaching techniques may be categorized at different levels, and the coaching methods themselves may be graded in intensity, frequency, or in other ways.

The methodology section should give specific information regarding the subjects who will be involved in the study, including who they are, how they are to be selected, and other relevant information about them.

It should also indicate the locations where the study will be carried out, or the agencies that may be involved. In some cases, subjects and settings may be combined, as in a study that compares the performance of several teams within a women's softball league, or that gathers information from a number of nursing homes.

Data-Gathering Instruments and Procedures

The actual methods that will be used to gather data should be described here, including how the observations, interviews, or surveys will be carried out, or how groups will be organized and tested. The instruments that will be used to gather the data should also be described.

In some cases, the study may require the proposal to include the actual instrument in refined form. In others, it may be acceptable to indicate the nature of the instruments and its subsections, or the method that may be used to develop and test it. If the study is to be a historical one, this section might include a description of the sources that will be examined, including an assessment of their availability. If the researcher plans to develop an entirely new instrument, he/she should indicate how it is to be formulated and tested, with emphasis on determining its validity.

Data-Analysis Plan

The techniques that will be used to analyze the data are presented in this section. If the study is to be primarily quantitative in nature, the statistical tests that will be applied should be presented. In the case of a historical study, a preliminary plan for organizing the findings according to a sequence of chronological periods might be presented. In a case study, a system for analyzing the data might be suggested—if appropriate, within a theoretical framework described earlier in the proposal.

It is critical that this section be carefully reviewed in terms of the stated purposes or hypotheses of the study proposal. The data analysis *must* be planned to ensure that the study's findings are directly relevant to the major thrust of the research. Otherwise, no matter how interesting the investigation, it will not be a success.

Timetable for the Investigation

The methodology section may include a listing of the various steps that are to be taken in carrying out the study, in the appropriate sequence, and with a calendar or "flow chart" of the time frame in which they will be accomplished. While graduate students or other professional researchers are not normally held rigidly to such a precise schedule, when a funded research study is carried out under contract with a sponsoring organization, normally it has a set of deadlines for carrying out each step of the investigation and completing the study. Often these steps may be keyed to payment for the work done, as separate sections of the study are carried out satisfactorily.

Permissions and Human Subjects' Approval

The permissions, authorization, or approval statement that will be needed to carry out the study should be identified here. For example, if the investigator plans to carry out an observational study of patients in a mental hospital, or do an evaluation of the recreation program within a penitentiary, it will obviously be necessary to obtain permission from the director of the institution to be studied— and possibly even from the director of the state mental health department, or the department of corrections. Similarly, if the researcher intends to carry out the study in cooperation with a professional organization or government agency, or with their approval and under their letterhead, it will be necessary to have this arrangement formally approved. Increasingly, it has also become necessary to have any piece of formal research that involves subjects in any way reviewed and cleared by a committee responsible for providing such clearance.

Normally, when study proposals are first reviewed by a study committee, such permissions and authorizations need not be in hand. However, before final approval is granted and the research study is authorized to get under way, it is customary to require them.

OPTIONAL ELEMENTS IN THE PROPOSAL

In some situations, the proposal may also be required to include a preliminary breakdown of the chapters that will appear in the final report, or the sections that it will include. In masters' theses and doctoral dissertations, a set format may be required by the graduate school or graduate research council. In funded research, the contracting organization may indicate the sections that the report must include, and it is therefore not necessary for the proposal to include this information. Proposals for funded research studies may also require a detailed preliminary budget, outlining the various costs to be incurred for personnel, printing, and similar expenses. Customarily, they also require a description of the individuals on the study team, with a detailed resumé of their qualifications and research experience, or a summary of other studies that the study team has carried out. Since proposals to do funding research are often submitted on a competitive basis, such information helps the sponsoring or granting organization determine the qualifications of the research groups that are applying for a study grant.

Finally, the research proposal normally includes an Appendix, which may contain other background information, preliminary drafts of study instruments, maps, listings of agencies to be examined, or similar elements.

REVIEWING THE RESEARCH PROPOSAL

As indicated earlier, developing a sound research proposal is a major task. Often, when it has been carried out and approved, half the battle has been won. Therefore, the researcher should ask himself or herself the following kinds of questions before submitting it for consideration, or meeting with a faculty committee for final approval.

INTRODUCTION

Does this opening section provide a brief but helpful explanation of the problem area and the essential thrust of the study? Is it easily understood? Is unnecessary or irrelevant information presented?

STATEMENT OF THE PROBLEM

Is the problem area convincingly presented, and does it appear to be a significant one? Is it placed within a logical context, and is it related to other research efforts and to a meaningful conceptual background? Does it end with a presentation of the key questions that the study will attempt to explore?

PURPOSES AND/OR HYPOTHESES

Do these tell us exactly what we need to know—or what the study intends to discover or test? Are the purposes or hypotheses directly in line with the Statement of the Problem, or do they go off in some new directions? Are they sharply focused, in that they tell us in precise, specific terms what we are going to investigate? Is any significant purpose left out, or are there any purposes which are not necessary and make the study too broad?

DEFINITIONS, LIMITATIONS, AND DELIMITATIONS

Do these effectively clarify any ambiguous terms or concepts in the proposal, and do they show possible limitations in the methodology and the reasons why these exist? Are the delimitations supported by a logical rationale?

REVIEW OF THE LITERATURE

Has a comprehensive search been carried out, to uncover all important references on the subject? Has any important source, or type of source, been ignored? While chief emphasis should be given to research reports, have other types of documentation—such as quotations from books, professional articles, newspapers, planning studies, etc.—been used? Are all references correctly footnoted? Does the treatment move logically forward in a chronological way, or from a broad analysis of the subject to a sharper focus on the actual key issues of the proposed study? If adequate references dealing with the exact subject of the study could not be found, were other related research findings cited? Does the Literature Review provide support for carrying out the study?

METHODOLOGY

Have all of the necessary elements been described, either in a preliminary or finished form—including the design of the proposed research, the nature of the subjects and settings, the instrumentation and method of data analysis, the needed permissions or authorizations, and other relevant information? Most important: Will the study, as presented, gather the kinds of data that will relate directly to the purposes and hypotheses of the investigation? Does it meet high professional standards, in terms of being a carefully planned, systematic, and rigorous search for knowledge? Will it contribute meaningfully either to effective professional practice or to theory in the field, or to both?

Finally, will the study be feasible? Will it be possible to carry it out, in terms of its scope and complexity, or will it be too difficult or expensive, given the resources of the investigator or study team? Should it be reduced in scope or redesigned to make it more feasible?

SUMMARY

The proposal represents a key step in the conceptualization and design of any research study. Chapter 6 describes the role and format of proposals of various types, and discusses in detail the sections that are typically found in most academic or scholarly research proposals. In each case, illustrations are given of how a given section might be approached, using case materials drawn from recreation, parks, or leisure-studies research themes.

The chapter concludes with a set of questions that should be asked before submitting a study proposal for approval.

ENDNOTES

1. Lawrence F. Locke and Waneen W. Spirduso, *Proposals That Work: A Guide for Planning Research* (New York: Teachers College Press, 1976): x.
2. David Krathwohl, *How to Prepare a Research Proposal* (Syracuse, N.Y.: Syracuse University Bookstore, 1966): 3.
3. Locke and Spirduso, op. cit., 1–2.
4. *Publication Manual of the American Psychological Association* (Washington, D.C.: American Psychological Association, 1983): 22–23.
5. Ibid., 25.
6. Carol Cutler Riddick, Meg DeSchriver and Ellen Weissinger, "A Methodological Review of Research in the Journal of Leisure Research From 1978 to 1982," *Journal of Leisure Research,* Vol. 16, No. 4 (1984): 314.
7. Julian L. Simon, *Basic Research Methods in Social Sciences: The Art of Empirical Investigation* (New York: Random House 1978): 14–15.
8. Stephen Isaac and William B. Michael, *Handbook in Research and Evaluation* (San Diego, Cal.: EdITS Publishers, 1971, 1980): 4.
9. Ibid., 6.

INDIVIDUAL ASSIGNMENTS TO BE PREPARED AND PRESENTED TO CLASS

19. Select and review several proposals for research (thesis or dissertation proposals) by graduate students in the recreation, parks, and leisure-

studies department. Critically analyze them for their strengths and possible weaknesses.

20. Individual students select problem statements or research questions that were developed by others in question No. 4 in Chapter 5. They then develop specific statements of purpose or research hypotheses, based on these questions. The class reviews and critically analyzes them.

21. Individuals or small groups of students select a research problem and develop brief outlines of the opening section of a proposal for it, including: *(a)* title; *(b)* introduction; *(c)* background of the study; and *(d)* purposes, hypotheses, and rationale. These outlines are presented to the class for discussion.

22. Students prepare literature reviews on an assigned topic. It is usually helpful to give specifications for this preliminary task, such as: The review should be approximately three to five pages in length, and must include a minimum number of references, such as eight or ten.

7

IMPLEMENTING THE STUDY: THE DATA-GATHERING PROCESS

In most cases, the research idea must be distilled into a very specific question, which tends to take the form of a hypothesis or several hypotheses. Once this has been accomplished, the study must be designed in a manner that will avoid potential difficulties and pemit the researcher to answer the question. The research design part of the overall process is critically important and essentially involves a rigorous and meticulous planning procedure (including) the operational details of actually conducting the study. You are now ready to begin.[1]

INTRODUCTION

When the proposal to carry out a research study has been approved, it is time to put the plan into effect. This chapter examines several key tasks involved in carrying out a research study. In so doing, it reviews the sampling process that is used to select appropriate subjects and/or settings to be studied. It then presents guidelines for developing and applying research instruments as part of three data-gathering methods: surveys, interviews, and observation.

The concluding section of the chapter describes some of the common pitfalls that researchers encounter in the effort to achieve high levels of validity and reliability, particularly in experimental research. It offers a number of constructive techniques through which these hazards may be overcome.

THE NEED FOR ORDER

One of the most important characteristics of effective research is that the researcher must have a sharply defined purpose in mind. He or she is not just throwing out a net to gather a collection of facts at random, or to see what "turns up." Then, once the research question has been selected, the study must be designed so that every step that is taken is well thought out, and based on scientific principles that will ensure valid findings.

To illustrate, Backstrom and Hursh suggest a checklist of steps in survey research which clearly outlines each stage of the process:

1. Hypothesizing—deciding what it is you want to study.
2. Designing—establishing the procedures and methods to use.
3. Planning and Financing—figuring materials and personnel needed, and arranging support for the survey.
4. Sampling—choosing which people are to be interviewed.
5. Drafting—planning the format of the questionnaire and framing its questions.
6. Pre-Testing—determining whether the questions elicit the data desired and revising as necessary.
7. Training—training interviewers in correct use of the questionnaire.
8. Controlling—seeing that the interviewing is carried out correctly, and verifying the collected data.
9. Coding and Processing—preparing the data for analysis, and carrying it out mechanically or electronically.
10. Analyzing—reviewing and interpreting the study data.
11. Reporting—sharing the new knowledge.[2]

Within this sequence of tasks, steps 4 through 8 represent the actual data-gathering process found in every type of empirical study. Obviously, not all research will involve framing questionnaires or carrying out interviews. However, the essential tasks are quite similar, with the specific objectives of the research determining the kinds of methods that are most useful.

NEED TO SELECT SUBJECTS

At an early point, the investigator must decide exactly what subjects will be studied, and on what basis they are to be chosen. Typically, subjects are people—either individuals to be surveyed or interviewed in a descriptive study, or members of experimental and control groups in experimental research studies. However, subjects might conceivably consist of other types of units, such as agencies that will be examined, communities, companies, or other social organizations.

SAMPLING PRINCIPLES AND METHODS

Since for practical reasons of cost and time it is usually not possible to measure an entire population, it is customary to pick a sample of subjects to work with, who will be more manageable than the entire group would be, in terms of sheer numbers and accessibility. Best defines a sample as:

> . . . a small proportion of a population selected for observation and analysis. By observing the characteristics of the sample, one can make certain inferences about the characteristics of the population from which it is drawn.[3]

On all levels of survey research, heavy reliance is placed on the use of samples. For example, the Gallup Poll typically surveys approximately 1,500 adults across the nation to gain a picture of changing social attitudes, and the Nielsen survey organization monitors television sets in 2,400 homes to draw inferences about all of the television watching in the country.

TYPES OF SAMPLES

There are two general types of samples: convenience samples and probability samples. A *convenience sample* is what its name suggests—a selection of subjects that makes use of subjects who are readily available, without a systematic method of choosing them that would help to ensure their being representative of the overall population. An example of a convenience sample might involve interviewing people casually on the street without any concern about the location, the time, or the makeup of respondents.

In contrast, a *probability sample* is more scientifically chosen, and is therefore statistically more likely to be representative of the entire population. However, it must take into account the realistic factor of time and cost. Backstrom and Hursh write:

> A good . . . probability sample, by practical definition, is one that yields the desired information within expected but tolerable limits of sampling error, for the lowest cost.[4]

STEPS IN THE SAMPLING PROCESS

Determine Unit of Analysis

The first step in the sampling process is to establish the group of persons or things to be investigated. These objects of study are referred to as the unit of analysis. Usually this consists of a number of individual subjects. However, it may also be composed of families, clubs, or other social groups; companies; public or private agencies; or other types of subjects. The sum total of units of analysis represents the population or universe; each entity in the population is called a sampling element.

Defining the Study Population

The next step in the process is to determine the exact nature of the population the sample is to be drawn from. If one plans to survey voters, would it be *all* voters, those in a certain district, or of members of one party? Depending on the purpose of the survey and its available resources, different choices might be made. It therefore becomes necessary to define the population exactly, in terms of its personal or demographic characteristics, its geographical or location limits, and similar elements. It also becomes important to recognize that it may simply not be possible to reach *all* individuals within a given population. If one wanted to use all adults living within a city as the overall population from which to draw a city, it would be necessary to recognize that some people have no telephones or permanent residences, or may be temporarily away from the metropolis, or in institutions or prisons, or other inaccessible settings.

If one seeks to draw a random sample that is representative of all the members of a given population, but if some members of that population cannot possibly be reached, then they are excluded automatically from the possibility of being chosen—and the random sampling process has been faulty. Therefore, the choice of a population to begin with may depend on knowing its accessibility, and may represent one of the delimitations of a study. One might define as a study population all the registered voters within a city, knowing that they constituted only 85 percent of the actual adults in the city, but that at least all of them have recent addresses and are presumably available to be interviewed.

Establishing the Sampling Frame

The sampling frame is a complete list of sampling units from which the sample will be drawn. As stated above, it is virtually impossible to list every element in a population. The sampling frame is the most comprehensive list one can obtain. Common sources for the sampling frame are: voter registration lists, telephone books, city directories, club memberships, utility hook-up lists, school directories, or publication subscriber lists. The sampling frame may use a combination of these sources, with duplicate entries eliminated.

RANDOM SAMPLE

The most common type of probability sample is the random sample. In this method, subjects are chosen according to a selection process that ensures that all possible subjects have an equal opportunity to be picked. If a random means of selecting subjects is used, the likelihood is that they will be characteristic of the entire population or universe. The characteristics found in the sample can then be projected to describe the overall population, usually stated with an estimate of the percentage of possible or probable error. For example, in a political poll, a survey may conclude that a given candidate is favored by 60 percent of the voters, with a three-percent margin, plus or minus, of possible error.

Random sampling may be accomplished by simply placing the complete list of sampling elements in a hat and drawing them out one by one until the desired sample size is reached. Other random sampling methods include the use of a table of random numbers or other computer-based selection methods which ensure that the choice of subjects is absolutely arbitrary, without any bias that might exclude some subjects or favor others.

Location and Time Factors

Certain factors may distort the accuracy of a random sampling approach. The location in which subjects are questioned and the time at which the interviews are held might influence their representativeness. For example, people found at a major street intersection in many large cities today at 11 o'clock at night would be very different from those who would be there at 11 o'clock in the morning. In a small, readily accessible and homogeneous population, simple random sampling in a limited number of locations and at a few times might be adequate. In a more diversified population, it might be necessary to take a considerable number of locations and times to draw a representative population. To make an analogy from nature, if a chemical pollutant had found its way into a lake, and you wanted to measure the degree of its concentration in the water, a small sample taken at one location might be adequate.

However, if the chemical pollutant did not diffuse easily or if the lake was stagnant, with little water movement, different conditions would probably prevail in different parts of the lake. Therefore, it would be necessary to take several tests in different locations.

Systematic Sample

Systematic sampling is used when it is not reasonable or possible to randomly select subjects from the population. Probably the simplest way of drawing a systematic random sample is to determine the number of subjects or respondents that would represent an adequate sample and then to divide this number into the overall population. If, for example, a state recreation and park society had 1,500 members and it was decided that 300 would constitute an acceptable sample, every fifth name on an alphabetical membership list would provide the sample. The first element is selected randomly.

Specific characteristics of the population must be carefully examined to prevent possible bias. For example, if the plan was to select every tenth house on a given street, it might be found that there were ten houses on each block and therefore the sample consisted only of corner houses, which tend to be larger and more expensive than others. The sample would therefore be faulty. One must be careful to avoid any such inherent bias in the sampling frame when using systematic sampling.

Stratified Sample

Another variation of the random sampling method involves stratification—that is, dividing the overall population into several different subgroups which are homogeneous within themselves, based on such criteria as ethnic identity, age groupings, sex, socioeconomic status, or similar factors. These groups would be given allocations in the sample, with subjects selected from each of them randomly. Ideally, this should be done proportionately, so that each stratum or special group in the sample is represented in numbers keyed to its size in the total population. If all important demographic variables can be blended into a mix in this way, a cross section of subjects will be achieved that guarantees a high degree of representativeness.

In general, stratified random samples require fewer cases than simple random samples. However, they may be difficult to obtain, particularly when the effort is made to match several demographic factors within individual subjects. Therefore, although stratified samples are often used in marketing or political polls, they may prove too complex for most research studies in recreation.

CLUSTER OR AREA SAMPLE

This method is most useful when the overall population is very widespread, difficult to identify, or not readily accessible. For example, to do a survey of recreation therapists drawn from all of the psychiatric hospitals in the country might be difficult as a sampling problem. Instead, it might be feasible to select a random sample of 10 states from the existing 50 states, and then to list all counties in these 10 states and draw a random sample of 100 counties. Within these areas, all existing psychiatric treatment centers would be identified, and a random sample of forty such institutions would be chosen. This method would ensure that the final set of subjects would be chosen in a relatively efficient and inexpensive way.

OTHER TYPES OF SAMPLES

Two other types of samples involve double samples and partial samples. A *double sample* is a follow-up survey or retest of a random sample of nonrespondents to a survey, to attempt to determine whether those individuals who did not reply to the initial investigation were, in any major respect, significantly unlike those who did reply. This is a way to check on the reliability of a survey that had a disappointing response rate. The question may always be raised, "Are those who did not reply significantly different from those who did reply? If this is the case, how much credibility can we give to the findings we have gathered, as representative of the *entire* population?"

A *partial sample* is similar to cluster sampling, in that the researcher deliberately narrows the overall population by region, age, or other characteristics, and then studies the limited sample intensively.[5]

TIME-SAMPLING STRATEGIES

As indicated earlier, the *time* when a survey or other descriptive study is carried out may influence or distort its findings. Efforts must be made to avoid this, if a study is to be valid. From a time perspective, data may be gathered in several different ways:

1. All at once in a single procedure, such as a mailed question-naire that goes out to all subjects simultaneously.
2. In a period of continuous observation or analysis over a period of time, such as a community planning study over a three-month or one-year period.
3. In a time series, through a set number of observations or data-gathering steps at predetermined intervals (hourly, daily, weekly, etc.) intended to give an accurate picture of subjects under different circumstances.

In any cross-sectional or comparative research, all observations must be done at exactly comparable times, to ensure that the time factor does not distort results. Time-series data gathering is especially useful in showing change; for example, political polling at one-week intervals is commonly done to show shifts in public interest or preference.

SIZE OF SAMPLE

A critical question that researchers must resolve is the size of the sample they will use. There is no absolute guideline on this; typically, it becomes a compromise between the ideal of having a very large number of cases (or a number that represents a high percentage of the cases in the overall population) and the fact that more cases lead to greater expense. Backstrom and Hursh point out:

> The length of time and amount of money you have to collect information in the field, hire assistants, hire interviewers, process data, as well as the number of interviewers and office personnel available are restrictions on sample size.[6]

One factor to be considered is the homogeneity of the population being studied; as indicated earlier, the more alike subjects are in major demographic respects, the smaller the sample size can be. Other factors include the nature of the sampling method: (a) Usually, stratified sampling requires the smallest number of cases; (b) simple random sampling a somewhat larger number; and (c) cluster sampling a large number, to obtain the same degree of precision.[7] Other factors have to do with the method of analysis that will be used with the study data. For example in some types of statistical analysis, there must be a minimum of at least thirty cases for procedures to be applied—depending on whether parametric or nonparametric tests are used.

Percentage of Response

A related point is the percentage of the sample that must respond in a survey or poll for the findings to be considered valid. For example, one would normally have confidence in a survey with a 98 percent response rate; however, a survey with a 2 percent return would obviously lack credibility. At what point between these extremes can one say, "This is an acceptable rate of return?"

There are no hard rules as to the minimum percentage rate of return that a survey should have, to be considered acceptable. Usually, surveys with a return rate of over 50 percent are considered acceptable, and lesser rates of return are frequently reported. Kerlinger writes:

> Responses to mail questionnaires are generally poor. Returns of less than 40 to 50 percent are common. High percentages are rare. At best the researcher must content himself with returns as low as 50 or 60 percent.[8]

Often, the rate of the return is influenced by the nature of the study and the population it is directed to. In those surveys where respondents are readily accessible to the researcher, are members of an organization that is cooperating in the study, or have a strong personal or professional interest in the subject of the study, a high rate of return may be expected. However, in surveys of the public at large, including many individuals who have little interest in the study, much lower rates are likely to occur. Factors influencing the rate of return include making sure that the survey is as brief as possible; that it is highly professional in makeup and appearance, with precise, clear directions; and that its purpose and significance are explained to the respondent in a covering letter or introduction.

Among strategies that may be used to increase the response rate to a desirable 70 to 90 percent range are the following: (a) using follow-up mailings or reminder cards or telephone calls to encourage response, even if late; (b) providing letters of support from community leaders or public officials, to encourage response; (c) gaining support for the study from relevant organizations, including their sponsorship or direct support, when appropriate; and (d) offering respondents a summary of the findings as an inducement to participate.

SAMPLING ERROR

Even if a sample has been carefully drawn, using one of the methods just described, it is likely to deviate to some degree from the actual characteristics of the overall population. Best points out that if a considerable number of researchers each selected samples of 100 teachers from the population of all teachers in California, the mean weight of the samples would not be identical. A few would be relatively high and others relatively low, while most would tend to cluster around the population mean. He writes:

> This variation of sample means is due to what is known as sampling error. This term does not suggest any fault or mistake in the *sampling process;* it merely describes the chance variations that are inevitable when a number of randomly selected sample means are computed.[9]

Estimating or inferring a population characteristic (parameter) based on data drawn from a random sample (statistic) is not an exact process. Since each set of sample means will differ from the others to some degree, it is also logical to assume that any one of them will also differ from the mean of the overall population. Recognizing this, statisticians have developed ways of estimating the degree of variation of sample means on a probability basis. To minimize sampling error, the following suggestions are useful: (a) Recognize that the larger a sample is, the smaller the sampling error is likely to be; (b) in general, surveys should have larger samples than experimental studies; and (c) when sample groups are to be subdivided into smaller groups, the original sample should be large enough so that the subgroups can be large enough for appropriate analysis. Beyond this, every effort must be made to prevent nonsampling errors, which may stem from mistakes of recording responses, misunderstanding the meaning of questions, or other mechanical or clerical errors which result in inaccurate data. Sophisticated procedures can be used to estimate the degree of sampling error that will occur, based on the kind of question that is being explored, and the size of the sample in relation to the overall population. Usually this is expressed as an estimate of a "degree of confidence" at a 95 or 99 percent level of accuracy. Backstrom and Hursh write:

> ... confidence is expressed as assurance that in 95 (or 99) out of 100 samples like ours the true value is within the estimated range of tolerated error. So, in a survey where we permit 6 percent error and set 95 percent confidence limits, we are sure that 95 cases out of 100 would contain the population value in an interval within 6 percent in either direction of the estimate.[10]

INSTRUMENT DEVELOPMENT

A second important phase of the research process consists of developing effective data-gathering instruments. If research is to be systematic and acccurate, it must make use of carefully developed and consistently applied instruments and procedures. They provide a framework for gathering, classifying, and recording data, and making sure that all surveys, observations, interviews, or other data-gathering activities are carried out in a comprehensive, uniform way.

To illustrate, if several investigators were asked to examine a group of county parks and to report on their condition, the resulting reports would be likely to vary greatly—*unless* there was agreement in advance as to the kinds of data that should be gathered, and the standards that would be applied. Such issues are usually determined by the choice or development of a data-gathering instrument which specifies exactly how an investigation is to be carried out and provides the framework for questioning, observation, or otherwise recording data.

TYPES OF INSTRUMENTS

Data-gathering instruments are of many types. Among the most commonly used in social research and the types of applied studies that are carried out in recreation, parks, and leisure studies are: (a) questionnaires; (b) rating scales; (c) checklists; (d) observational recording forms; (e) psychological tests; (f) tests of physical attributes or performance; (g) sociometric tests; and (h) other specialized instruments for environmental, economic, or other special research studies.

Questionnaires

These are the most common form of survey research instrument, and usually consist of a series of questions or statements to which subjects are asked to respond, as in marketing surveys or political polls. They may deal with items of fact or personal knowledge, with reported behaviors, with attitudes and beliefs, or with professional practices. Customarily, they may be distributed to members of a sample either directly or by mail and filled out, usually on an individual basis, although a test may be administered to a group of individuals simultaneously by an investigator. Questionnaires may also be used in telephone or face-to-face interviews. If a person receives a questionnaire by mail, he or she must fill it out and return it. In the case of a telephone survey, the interviewer asks the questions and records the responses. Often, in face-to-face interviews, responses may be tape-recorded.

Rating Scales

These are quite similar to questionnaires, except that they tend to be narrower in their format and scope, and usually to involve judgments or ratings on a scale of possible responses. Rating scales are commonly used to measure or evaluate behavior, the quality of performance, the level of participation, the effectiveness of maintenance or administrative procedures, or such elements. For example, respondents may be asked to rate their own attitudes or leisure behaviors, usually selecting the most appropriate or correct choice of ratings from a ranked continuum of possible responses (see pg. 125).

Checklists

These are similar to both questionnaires and rating scales, except that they tend to have lists of items which can be replied to by "yes" or "no" responses or by other concrete pieces of information, rather than opinions or judgments. They are particularly useful in measuring professional practices, facilities, or other types of evaluation studies. For example, in camp accreditation procedures, a number of items regarding camp practices in areas such as food services, safety and health, programming, or facilities might simply require that the director indicate whether or not a particular procedure is carried out. Obviously, in such procedures, the investigator might also require evidence substantiating the director's response and might rely on observation, interviews, or other means of obtaining documentation that supports the use of the checklist.

Observational Recording Forms

These are instruments or forms that are based on direct observation of practices, facilities, behaviors, or other variables. They may be very much like checklists with respect to carrying out routine observations of facilities, as an example, or may require more subtle judgment. Examples:

a. Direct observation of behavior; they might involve observation of employees at work, participation of children in a play setting, group interaction in a planning group, or similar activities. The form itself might list a number of typical behaviors, and the observer might note when these occur, who demonstrated them, and with what frequency or duration.

b. Mechanical recording processes, such as the use of film or video tape recording, or the use of electronic feedback through computer cards which provide information about those entering facilities, or measure the physiological responses of subjects to stimuli.

Psychological Tests

These may involve tests of beliefs, attitudes, personality traits, self-concept, and similar variables. In some cases, they are taken directly, as paper-and-pencil tests, by subjects. In others, they may be filled out by observer/researchers. They may also include projective tests which involve the subject's interpretation of pictures, associations with words or phrases, or other tests of perception, memory, or emotional response to stimuli.

Measurement of Physical Attributes or Performance

In some research areas involving motor performance or fitness programs; factors such as size, height, weight, strength, speed, performance of skills tests; or ability to solve puzzles or perform tests of coordination or agility, standardized instruments and recording forms may be used. They may be used to test individual or group performance in both cooperative and competitive social frameworks.

Sociometric Tests

This is a special form of observation of group behavior, in which the researcher notes the relationships and cliques within the group, the leadership/followership roles held by individuals, and similar behaviors or structures. It can also be done through a self-reporting process, in which group members report their feelings toward others, those they would choose to work or associate with, and similar information.

Other Types of Instruments

Numerous other specialized types of instruments may be developed to carry out other data-gathering tasks. Typically, within each basic discipline, such as sociology, psychology, economics, marketing, political science, business management, or environmental studies, certain kinds of instruments tend to be used to meet special needs within the field.

SOURCES OF INSTRUMENTS

In many cases, instruments used in scientific research have been published or otherwise made available for general use. However, as in the case of a number of psychological inventories (tests of personality, intelligence, or self-concept), they may be standardized and protected by copyright. In such cases, they may be used only by permission with a designated commercial fee for use. In other cases, instruments which have been developed for a particular study and which have been carefully validated (tested to determine their scientific accuracy), may be used again by other researchers in new studies, with the permission of the original researchers but without charge. A number of instruments measuring leisure attitudes or behaviors have been used again and again in published research studies, following their initial presentation to the field.[11]

For other studies, there may be no appropriate instruments available and so the research team or individual investigator must devise their own instruments. This typically involves a process of examining similar instruments in order to identify potentially useful models; selecting the elements or variables that should be in the new form; possibly getting advice or approval from a jury of experts; pilot-testing or field-testing the instrument; and assigning values to given questions or groups of questions. Particularly if a research study is to be used for scholarly or academic purposes, any new instrument that has been developed for it should be tested for validity and reliability (see page 130). Often, when a professional organization conducts a specialized study of trends in the field, a team of practitioners and educators is formed to develop appropriate survey tools.

GUIDELINES FOR QUESTIONNAIRE CONSTRUCTION

The most commonly used instrument in survey research is the questionnaire, used either through mailings or distribution to a sample of respondents, or in administered, face-to-face situations. While questionnaires may vary greatly in length and complexity, the following guidelines apply generally to questionnaire construction.

1. Determine the major areas that are to be covered, based on your proposal. Consult with others and examine the literature carefully, both to ensure that you have identified the key topics and to gather ideas for questions and the overall format of the questionnaire. Make sure that the areas fulfill the stated purposes of your study, or relate directly to the hypotheses.

2. Develop a preliminary set of questions for each of these areas. Questions or items (as they are sometimes called) may deal with: (*a*) information about the respondent: (*b*) matters of fact or knowledge; (*c*) personal attitudes, values, or opinions; (*d*) judgments or ratings of others, or of programs, policies, or procedures; (*e*) rating of priorities; (*f*) statements of needs and interests; or other types of information.

3. Determine whether the questions should be *closed-end* (with limited, predesignated choice of possible responses), or *open-end* (with unstructured opportunity for response). Closed-end questions in effect restrict the respondent to forced choices or categories of replies; they are very clear and unambiguous, and are simple to tally and analyze. Open-end questions provide a fuller range of possible responses, but may be much more difficult to tally.

4. In composing individual questions or items (a question asks for a response and is phrased with terms like "How would you . . .?" or "Are there any . . .?" while an item might state "Please rate the following procedures . . ." or "Indicate the frequency with which . . ."), the following guidelines are helpful:

a. It is usually best to start with short, easy, or familiar questions that are nonthreatening and encouraging to the respondent, to get him/her started comfortably, rather than more complicated or challenging questions.

b. If necessary, define the terms used in individual questions. For example, a question like "How many children live on the average farm in Jones County?" has at least three terms that might be misinterpreted, and that should be defined: "children," "live on," and "average farm."

c. Avoid vague terms. A question like "Do you play sports often?" is ambiguous, because what is "often" for one person might be "infrequent" for another. Such words are best translated into specific categories, like "daily," "weekly," "monthly," etc., or into specific numbers. Similarly, even the word "sports" might have different meanings for different people, and possibly should be explained with a phrase like

". . . such as tennis, golf, or racquetball." Also avoid words with which the respondent may not be familiar.

d. Avoid questions that might give incomplete information, like "Are you married?" A negative response will not give you the detailed information you need. Instead, asking respondents to indicate their marital status and giving them all possible or appropriate responses (married, separated, divorced, widowed, single, etc.) will provide an exact answer.

e. In asking for judgments or attitudes, questions should be specific, rather than general. The question, "What do you think of the cafeteria?" will not yield as precise information as one which asks them to rate the cafeteria for cleanliness, service, quality of food, pricing policy, and similar items, and then to provide a general rating. The actual response may be handled several ways: by having respondents check the appropriate point on a numbered scale (from Poor to Excellent), select the correct descriptive adjective, or assign an identified value to the subject.

f. Avoid multiple questions like "Do you go to the movies, theater, or circus?" Each such choice should be presented separately, preferably on a scale which might indicate specific attendance over the past year.

g. Avoid questions that might show any bias or leanings on your part. Respondents will be quick to detect such items and to resent what they may perceive as manipulation or brainwashing, even if you have not consciously framed questions in this way. Questions must be perceived as neutral, and should avoid characterizing any element of choice in an unfavorable way.

h. Avoid any questions that might be embarrassing or self-incriminating, or that may deal with sensitive information, such as the respondent's income, religion, or political affiliation. Consider assuring anonymity to the respondent, although even this may not persuade individuals to reply to such questions. Note: This does not mean that sensitive or personal questions can never be explored in surveys; numerous studies of sexual behavior and attitudes show that this is not so. However, it *does* mean that such questions or issues must be treated very carefully in routine surveys.

5. General guidelines that are useful in composing the overall questionnaire and in ensuring a maximum rate of accurate response include the following:

a. Give complete directions as to how a question should be answered, or how questions that provide for several possible responses should be handled (i.e., "Mark the correct response with an X in the appropriate box, etc."). If possible, provide a rating system that does allow for different choices, such as a Likert-type range of responses, unless you deliberately wish to have a "forced choice" format that compels a "yes" or "no," or other sharp "either/or" decisions. Typically, in Likert-type questions, the subject might be asked to respond to a statement by indicating one of five possible opinions: *Agree Strongly; Agree Moderately; Neutral* or *Undecided: Disagree Moderately; Disagree Strongly.*

b. Whenever possible, all questions should be precoded (assigned code numbers or letters, to permit easy transfer to computer cards or tapes for analysis). Some survey questionnaires have attached answer sheets, where the replies should be marked, and in some cases may make use of answer strips attached with perforations to the questionnaire, so they may be electronically tabulated, without the need for a keypunching or other transfer process.

c. Keep the questionnaire as short and simple as possible, to encourage respondents' completing and returning it, particularly if it is going to the general public. More lengthy or difficult forms may be sent to people who have a direct interest in the research or are members of professional groups or organizations related to it, and who therefore are likely to be more highly motivated to respond.

d. Make sure the survey form is attractive, readable, and professional in its appearance, while at the same time being careful not to have it too elaborate, ornate, or obviously expensive (set in fancy type, on embossed paper, with several colors, etc.). People who resent surveys or feel that they are a waste of time and money sometimes criticize them because of their cost, or argue that the money could be better spent. The form should not look crowded or confusing; it is important to use white space effectively as a design element. Pastel colors may also be used if there is sufficient contrast between the paper and the print for legibility.

e. Usually, although not always, it is desirable to get specific information about each respondent, in order to be able to break down responses by age, sex, income level, or similar categories. Therefore, questions about such identification factors, or other demographic variables should be included, with the assurance that the respondent's name will be kept confidential. While most questionnaires ask for such information in the opening section, some place these questions in the back, feeling that if they appear in the beginning the subject may decide not to answer the survey.

f. Also, make sure to group questions by content areas; for example, place all questions regarding recreation participation together, rather than space them throughout the instrument. When feasible, also group similar question formats together; i.e., all Likert-type questions together, and all open-end questions together. People respond more readily when they do not have to jump back and forth, in terms of either content or format.

6. When the first draft of the questionnaire has been completed, it should be pilot-tested with appropriate subjects, to make sure that it is workable in terms of its clarity, the appropriateness of questions, the simplicity of its language, the length of time it takes to complete it, and similar concerns. It should be carefully reviewed, with a checklist that includes such questions as:

Are you satisfied that the questionnaire is the best method available to obtain the needed information?

Has a workable method for distributing and collecting the questionnaire been devised?

Is the title of the survey accurate and concise? Are the instructions for taking it or applying it also easily understood?

Is the personal information that is requested necessary, and does it run the risk of offending or "turning off" possible respondents?

Are questions arranged in an appropriate sequence, both in terms of grouping subjects and moving generally from simple to more difficult items?

Are there any questions which might "lead" the respondent or might show bias?

Is there sufficient space for responding to open-end questions?

Are questions arranged so that answers can be easily tabulated?

Following the pilot-testing procedure and application of such a checklist, the instrument should be revised as necessary. If it is to be used in a scholarly project, or if it is expected to meet standards of academic rigor, it may also be necessary to determine its validity and reliability as a research instrument (see page 130).

7. If it is a mailed questionnaire, encourage response by providing a self-addressed, stamped envelope for its return. A carefully written cover letter should appeal to the respondent's sense of responsibility or citizenship, professionalism, or other motivations, to encourage response. This letter should establish the credibility of the survey and the researcher by explaining who is conducting the survey and with what purpose; naming individuals or organizations who are supporting it; telling respondents how they were chosen and why the study may be of value to them; assuring confidentiality of responses; providing additional directions for filling out the form; and thanking the respondent in advance for his/her assistance.

In addition, it may well require additional postcard or telephone reminders or follow-up mailings to achieve an acceptable percentage of response. Studies have shown distinct differences between respondents and nonrespondents (both in terms of their characteristics and their opinions) and therefore it is highly desirable that as high a percentage as possible of the original sample respond, to avoid an inaccurate or biased set of findings.

PROBLEMS IN THE USE OF QUESTIONNAIRES

There are a number of inherent problems in the use of questionnaires that researchers must guard against—both in designing an instrument and in its application. These include the following:

1. Respondents' lack of knowledge about a subject. People may often answer surveys with information that is hazy or insecure, in order to "play along," or to appear cooperative. A special problem has to do with the fallibility of memory; elderly people in particular may not remember the past accurately, and should be advised not to answer questions if they are not sure of their replies. In some cases, it may be helpful to consult records or other sources to support or enrich one's answers.

2. Respondents' failure to understand questions or to mark responses in the correct columns or spaces may result in invalid responses that must be rejected, or in some cases incorrect data being tabulated. Careful directions and pretesting of the survey help to prevent such faulty responses. In some cases, the best procedure is to have the survey administered in person, rather than by mail.

3. Cover-up, embarrassment, self-defensiveness, and similar factors may influence respondents to give inaccurate replies—either

to make themselves appear in a positive light, or because they are influenced by the identity of the interviewer (in the case of an administered questionnaire). Studies have shown, for example, that people will respond differently to a survey depending on the gender or ethnic identity of the person interviewing them.

INTERVIEWING METHODS

A second important method of data gathering consists of personal interviews. These are of two types: (*a*) brief interviews which are usually tightly structured, with a questionnaire schedule or form, which may be administered either in person or over the telephone, usually as part of a survey or (*b*) lengthier and more loosely structured interviews, which tend to use open-end questions for a more flexible discussion of a topic or problem area, and which may be part of a survey or case study approach.

In either case, it is important that the interviewer make use of an interview schedule or outline, to ensure that the same topics are covered with all subjects. If specific questions are included, as in a formal questionnaire, they may be followed by open-end questions to get fuller detail or more subtle nuances of response. When a research study is concerned not only with facts and details, but also with the dynamics of a situation, or with the perceptions of the respondent, such questions are essential.

GUIDELINES FOR INTERVIEWING

1. The interviewer's appearance should be normal and appropriate to the setting. Interviewers should avoid provocative or unusual clothing and should not wear dark glasses unless it is absolutely essential, since they do not permit subjects to look into their eyes, and may create a sense of suspicion.

2. If possible, interviews should be arranged and scheduled in advance, to ensure that subjects will be available and willing to take part. If not, and if an interviewer is hoping to question a group of randomly selected respondents in a recreation setting, it would be advisable to get the approval of the center director, and have him or her assist in setting up interviews.

3. In asking questions, make sure they are thoroughly understood. If necessary, restate them, or ask the subject if he or she is absolutely clear on their meaning. If responses are still uncertain, press to make sure that you are getting an accurate response, and one that the subject really intends to deliver.

4. Record responses immediately, using a precoded tally sheet or answer form for closed-end questions (see p. 161). This may be reinforced by using a tape recorder with the subject's permission. Take additional written notes as necessary.

5. Do not indicate with any personal expression (humor, disapproval, surprise, disgust, etc.) that you disagree with or disapprove of any of the subject's responses. Never argue with or discuss a point with him or her, other than through follow-up questions. Subjects should be treated in a respectful, friendly, but impersonal way and no attempt should be made to influence them in any way.

6. If the interview is a long one, encourage respondents with comments like, "We're doing very well," or "We are halfway through now," if they are getting restless or seem to want to stop.

7. When the interview is completed, thank respondents for their cooperation. Keep detailed notes on when and where the interview was conducted, and transcribe your written notes as soon as possible, to ensure accuracy and make sure they are not misplaced.

Although most interviews are conducted on a formal, structured basis, with subjects knowing that they are taking part in an actual research study, Moeller and associates argue that formal interviews frequently result in biased or misleading responses. Instead, they suggest that informal interviews, in which the subject is not aware of being purposefully examined but in which responses are still solicited to specific questions, may provide a useful alternative. This approach, they argue, serves as a useful cross check on the validity of data gathered by other methods and avoids some of the sources of bias associated with formal interviews and questionnaires. They write:

> In addition, the relaxed atmosphere of the informal interview may elicit responses that more closely approximate people's private feelings, as opposed to "public" sentiments that they might report on a questionnaire.[12]

OBSERVATIONAL STUDY METHODS

A third data-gathering technique which may be used in both natural, field settings and in experimental or laboratory settings involves behavior recording by observers who are part of the study team. Again, this may be carried on in a highly structured way, with the observers using checklists or other forms recording behavior frequencies, or may be much freer, with the researcher participating inconspicuously in a group situation and simply recording whatever occurs. In either case, it is desirable to develop a clear understanding of the kinds of behavior or communication that are to be identified and recorded, as well as the varieties of group relationships, roles played by participants, and other aspects of group involvement. While it might appear desirable to have an organized method of categorizing or coding behavioral occurrences from the outset, often it is necessary to observe a group situation over a period of time in order to develop such a method.

VALIDITY AND RELIABILITY OF RESEARCH PROCESSES

It is essential that all research instruments and data-gathering procedures be as valid, reliable, and objective as possible.

VALIDITY

The validity of an instrument or research procedure refers to its accuracy in measuring what it seeks or claims to measure. Selltiz and associates point out that, to be useful, data-collection techniques must produce information that is not only relevant but also correct:

> Two crucial aspects of correctness are reliability (that is, the extent to which measures give consistent results) and validity (that is, the extent to which they correspond to the "true" position of the person or object on the characteristic being measured).[13]

A test may be a very good test, quite accurate and consistent in its findings, but may simply not measure what it is intended to measure. For example, a supposed test of *intelligence* may accurately measure a subject's reading skill, memory, or fund of information, but may *not* be a valid test of intelligence. Or a test may be correctly focused on a particular element or quality, but may be an incomplete or inconsistent measure of that element. There are two main ways of judging the validity of a test or instrument:

Content Validity

This refers to the degree to which an instrument or test examines the total content of the element or area being measured. For example, in developing a test of fitness, researchers should include all those elements which authorities generally agree are essential parts of physical fitness, such as speed, strength, coordination, endurance, balance, and flexibility. The identification of such elements and the weight they are given in the test may be drawn from the literature or established with the help of a jury of experts. Since content validity is not based on the actual performance of subjects or the results of other tests but rather on its content as rationally analyzed, it may also be called *rational* or *logical* validity.

Closely related to content validity is so-called *face* validity, which refers to the relevance of the measuring instrument to what one is trying to measure, based "on the face of it"—or through simple common sense or judgment.

Criterion-Related Validity

This is determined by whether the results of a test or other data-gathering instrument are in agreement with the findings of other criterion measures. It takes two forms: (1) *concurrent* validity, the degree to which the new instrument agrees with scores of other measurements taken at the same time and under similar conditions, or (2) *predictive* validity, in which the instrument is shown to be accurate with respect to predicting future outcomes, based on the actual performance of the subjects. For example, the validity of a test of sportsmanship or sportswomanship might be determined by comparing its findings to those of another test or the ratings of a group of experts who judge participants' behavior in later game situations. Criterion-related validity may also be called *empirical* or *statistical* validity, since it is supported not only by logical analysis, but also by concrete, empirical evidence that supports its findings.

Construct Validity

Construct validity is concerned with the underlying construct or theoretical basis for developing a research instrument. It seeks to examine the degree to which given explanatory concepts or constructs may account for the performance of subjects. Determination of construct validity requires both logical or rational analysis and the use of empirical evidence; thus it may be considered to have elements of both content and criterion validity. To draw an illustration from the field of psychology, construct validity may be employed in examining a test of personality types, to determine how well the theoretical implications of the different typologies account for the actual results obtained in using the test.

Two other applications of the term "validity" are *internal* and *external* validity and were discussed in Chapter 4. Although related, they should not be confused with the concept of validity that is discussed here.

Many tests that are used in research and that may be found in the professional literature have had their validity determined in statistical terms as a prerequisite to publication or scholarly acceptance. Tests may be analyzed internally, so that different groups of items are given weights according to their importance within the overall instrument. In some cases, a lengthy test may be given in a "short" form, which uses the most powerful or predictive items (items that correlate most highly with the overall test score, or with other criterion scores) as a valid form of the test.

RELIABILITY

Reliability is another important quality of research instruments or testing procedures. It refers to the stability and consistency of the instrument or measure itself. Very simply, it is a question of whether one obtains the same results on repeated administrations of an instrument, given that test conditions remain the same. The repeated measures (test results) would be correlated to obtain a reliability estimate, referred to as a coefficient of stability. A second type of reliability refers to the consistency of various forms of an instrument. The responses to two different forms of the instrument would be correlated to yield a measure referred to as the coefficient of equivalence. Beyond such factors, the reliability of any measurement depends not only on the test itself but on how and when it is applied. Several examples of problems related to making sure that testing procedures or observations are reliable follow:

Environmental Conditions

Measuring speed in a dash might be affected by the type of surface (dirt, grass, cinder, blacktop, or rubber composition), by the weather (wind, rain, or other atmospheric conditions), or by other physical factors affecting the measurement.

Time of Application

If a given test is applied to patients in a hospital or nursing home, they may respond very differently, depending on whether they have just received medication or have had other forms of therapy just before the test. If subjects are shown a test of agility or coordination and are asked to do it one person at a time, the last ones to perform may have a better idea of how it is done (because they have observed it repeatedly). They may therefore perform at a higher level than the first subjects to be tested.

Objectivity of the Investigator

Investigators must be absolutely objective and unbiased as they carry out interviews, rate subjects, observe behaviors, or interpret data, if their results are to be trustworthy. This means that they must be consistent in their recording of data and application of standards; often, they mut be carefully trained to ensure objectivity and accuracy. Drew writes:

> . . . observation studies often (and should always) include certain precautions that attempt to determine observer reliability. This is typically accomplished by using two or more observers (either continually or on a periodic, spot-check basis) and calculating the degree to which they agree. Such procedures are known as determining interobserver reliability.[14]

It is often helpful to have observers carry out practice sessions, comparing and discussing their ratings, until they can consistently arrive at very similar results.

OTHER ISSUES OF EXPERIMENTAL VALIDITY

Particularly in experimental research, a number of special techniques are used to control extraneous variables or other threats to validity. For example, the so-called "Hawthorne effect," in which subjects in an experiment tend to feel better or perform more effectively simply because they know that they are receiving special attention, can distort the findings of an experimental study. In medical research, when a control group is being given a "placebo," or inert medication, it is common practice to conceal this information from subjects. This is referred to as a "blind" experiment. When both the subjects and the raters are kept ignorant regarding the real treatment, it is known as a "double blind." In social research, it is necessary to maintain similar controls in experimental studies, in order to avoid possible contamination of the findings.

It is difficult to conduct effective experimental research in recreation, parks, and leisure services for two reasons: (a) If the experiment is structured in an artificial, laboratorylike environment, it is difficult to make it realistic for the subjects and to create a truly recreational kind of climate for participation, and (b) if it is carried on in a natural, field setting, it is difficult to maintain effective controls over subjects that would shield them from extraneous variables that might distort the study findings. A number of specific threats to experimental validity were described in Chapter 4. In addition, two other areas of difficulty include:

1. Investigator bias, either in terms of the experimenter not being totally objective or consistent in his or her group direction or assessment of study effects, or in terms of subjects' response to different types of investigators.

2. Difficulty in maintaining the ceteris paribus principle—the Latin phrase which describes the need to keep all factors other than the experimental and control variables constant, so that if significantly different outcomes are noted, it can be concluded that the experimental factors had to be responsible for them.

A number of interesting experimental studies have been carried out in therapeutic recreation settings, particularly in residential situations where it is possible to maintain careful controls and to keep groups intact over a period of time. However, relatively few such research studies have been carried out in the overall field of recreation, parks, and leisure services. Instead, studies which seek to measure program outcomes or causal relationships are more likely to be designed as quasi-experimental studies (see pg. 66), or as forms of action research or demonstration projects. While such research is less acceptable to academic scholars, it tends to be useful to the profession at large in assessing the effects of programs through empirical documentation, rather than through opinion or unsubstantiated claims.

SUMMARY

Implementing descriptive and experimental research studies requires careful planning and use of appropriate sampling techniques to ensure representative study populations. This chapter describes convenience and probability sampling, and outlines approaches to developing random, stratified, and cluster samples. It also discusses the appropriate size of samples and needed percentages of response in survey research, in connection with sampling error.

It then describes seven types of data-gathering instruments, with emphasis on the development of questionnaires, rating scales, checklists, and observational rating methods. Problems in the use of questionnaires are discussed, along with methods of conducting formal and informal interviews. The chapter concludes with a discussion of types of validity (content, criterion-related, internal, and external) and reliability, and threats to experimental validity.

ENDNOTES

1. Clifford J. Drew, *Introduction to Designing and Conducting Research* (St. Louis, Mo.: C. V. Mosby Co., 1980): 10.
2. Charles H. Backstrom and Gerald D. Hursh, *Survey Research* (Evanston, Ill.: Northwestern University Press, 1963): 19.
3. John W. Best, *Research in Education* (Englewood Cliffs, N.J.: Prentice-Hall, 1981): 8–9.
4. Backstrom and Hursh, op. cit., 24.
5. For a fuller discussion of sampling, see Drew, op. cit., Chapter 8.
6. Backstrom and Hursh, op. cit., 27.
7. Ibid., 26.
8. Fred N. Kerlinger, *Foundations of Behavioral Research* (New York: Holt, Rinehart and Winston, 1973): 414.
9. Best, op. cit., 265.
10. Backstrom and Hursh, op. cit., 31-32.
11. See for example M. Ragheb and J. Beard, "Measuring Leisure Attitudes," *Journal of Leisure Research* (2nd Quarter 1982): 155–167.
12. George H. Moeller, Michael A. Mescher, Thomas A. More and Elwood L. Shafer, "The Informal Interview as a Technique for Recreation Research," *Journal of Leisure Research* (2nd Quarter 1980): 180.
13. Claire Selltiz, Lawrence S. Wrightsman, and Stuart W. Cook, *Research Methods in Social Relations* (New York: Holt, Rinehart and Winston, 1976): 161.
14. Drew, op. cit., 133.

WORKSHOP ACTIVITIES
TO BE CARRIED OUT IN CLASS

23. *Sampling.* Select one of the problems identified during the activities for Chapters 5 and 6. Then carry out the following steps:
  a. Determine the exact population you will investigate, and the means of identifying the full list of potential subjects or respondents; i.e., the sources that will be used to identify the entire population.
  b. Identify alternative approaches to drawing a sample from this population, including both convenience and probability methods.

    c. Indicate the approximate size of the sample you would seek to obtain, and the percentage of response or completed investigations that you would set as a minimum acceptable figure.

24. *Instruments.* Select several different research problems and, using a small-group approach, develop appropriate instruments for them of the following types, to be presented and reviewed in class:

    a. Questionnaire.

    b. Rating scale or checklist.

    c. Observational form.

    If possible design these instruments so that different types of studies (surveys, experiments, case studies, etc.) are represented.

25. *Interviews.* Prepare an interview schedule for a specific research investigation, and carry out several mock interviews in class, using a role-playing approach. Have the class review each performance in turn, and develop additional guidelines for effective interviewing.

8

DATA ANALYSIS I: DESCRIPTIVE STATISTICS

The general study of statistics is usually divided into two topical areas: descriptive and inductive statistics. *Descriptive* statistics or, more accurately, the *descriptive statistical* method is any treatment of numerical data that does not involve making generalizations from a sample to a population. That is, when we are interested in describing a group of elements (people, test scores, etc.), we use descriptive statistics. When we make generalizations, predictions, estimations, or otherwise arrive at decisions in the face of uncertainty, we are using *inductive statistics* by a process called *statistical inference.*[1]

INTRODUCTION

When all the data in a research study have been collected, they must be organized, analyzed, and interpreted. It is desirable to use quantification as a means of organizing and reporting data whenever possible. *Quantification* has been defined as a numerical method of describing or presenting the events or elements that are part of a study. It provides a valid, precise, and readily understandable means of measuring a sample, and a useful basis for statistical analysis. Since so many aspects of our lives involve numbers—our ages, our salaries, the distances we must travel each day—it is natural that research depends heavily on being able to present findings in terms of numbers. This chapter introduces the use of statistics in recreation and leisure research and evaluation.

STATISTICS AS AN ESSENTIAL PROCESS

Statistics is the basic process of organizing and interpreting numbers in order to arrive at their meaning. Throughout the business world, in science, the military, education, psychology, and sociology, statistics are relied upon to clarify trends in our lives, patterns of behavior, the effectiveness of different products, or similar concerns.

Too often, the claims or conclusions of statistics are poorly understood by the average person—particularly when they are being used to sum up marketing research studies or support advertising claims. One popular saying has been, "There are three types of liars: plain liars, damn liars, and statisticians." Another saying is that "Researchers too often use statistics the way a drunk uses a lamppost—more as a means of support than for illumination."

Nonetheless, statistics represent an essential means of dealing with research data today, particularly with the help of computers, which make possible extremely rapid and complicated analysis of great bulks of data. Essentially, it is divided into two basic types: descriptive and inferential.

DESCRIPTIVE AND INFERENTIAL STATISTICS

These two forms of statistics have the following characteristics.

DESCRIPTIVE

This is the branch of statistics that is primarily concerned with the organization, display, and interpretation of data describing all members of the group under investigation. Typical descriptive measures include the mean, mode, median, and measures of dispersion. It limits its conclusions to the particular group of individuals observed or tested; no conclusions are extended beyond this group, and any similarity to others outside the group cannot be assumed. The term *descriptive statistics* may also be used to describe a collection of observations, whether of the total population or a sample from the population.

INFERENTIAL

This is the branch of statistics that uses data from a sample of individuals to infer one or more characteristics of the entire population. The summary value of each such characteristic is called a *statistic*. A statistic is simply a measure (number, figure, etc.) based on observations of the study sample. For example, samples of consumers are studied with respect to their preferences of products; the characteristics found in these samples are assumed, within the limits of probable error, to be those of the entire consumer population. The small group is known as the sample; the larger group is the population.

STEPS OF STATISTICAL ANALYSIS

Any of the following steps may be used in the analysis of research data. In more basic studies, the first two or three steps may be sufficient, while in more scholarly or academic reports, the more advanced methods are usually employed.

ORGANIZING DATA FOR ANALYSIS

At the outset, it is necessary to determine which variables or elements are to be measured, and to organize them by grouping them into several major categories or sections for tabulation and analysis. At this point, the researcher must decide exactly which comparisons, relationships, time sequences, or other kinds of characteristics of the data he or she wishes to explore. The data analysis relates directly to the original research questions and/or the hypotheses established by the investigation.

SIMPLE DESCRIPTIVE MEASURES

This represents the most common type of analysis, and involves carrying out procedures that are used to describe only the subjects that have been analyzed. This includes measures of central tendency (mean, median, mode), percentage breakdowns, standard scores, spreading of scores away from the center, correlations, and similar types of analysis.

PRESENTATION OF DESCRIPTIVE FINDINGS

The findings of such analyses may then be summarized, with interpretations and possible recommendations for action or further research. This should be directly keyed to the stated purposes or hypotheses of the study in precise, definitive statements. In the case of an evaluation study, it may also involve developing a profile of the agency and its programs, and comparing it to established norms or standards, as well as identifying areas of strength, weakness, and needed improvement. Frequently, tables, graphs, or charts may be used to visually summarize and present data so the findings may be readily understood in a simplified, fairly dramatic form.

INFERENTIAL ANALYSIS

If appropriate to the study's purposes and the kinds of data that have been gathered, inferential statistical techniques may be used to explore characteristics of the larger population from which a study sample has been drawn. These methods are used to determine if significant relationships exist among variables, including both correlation and causal (cause-and-effect) relationships, and generally to determine whether the study's hypotheses have been accepted or rejected.

LEVELS OF MEASUREMENT

The process of assigning a value or score to any observed phenomenon or variable is known as measurement. Measurement is done on several different levels, commonly identified as *nominal, ordinal, interval,* and *ratio.* Knowledge of these levels is essential for statistical analysis, because each statistical technique is designed for data measured only at certain levels.

NOMINAL

Nominal-level scales represent the lowest or least sophisticated level of measurement, and apply to data which are classified only by *name* (the word itself drawn from the Latin word *nomen,* meaning name). Examples of subjects of nominal measurement include: *animals* (horses, cows, goats); *trees* (oak, birch, maple, cherry); or *professions* (doctor, lawyer, architect). The categories and the examples within each category have no numerical value and no assigned order of value or precedence, although one could assign numbers to them purely for identification purposes, by listing them as: (1) class; (2) workshop; (3) league; etc. But this would only be for convenience in grouping and referring to them; the numbers would have no other purpose. Any statistical procedure that assumes a meaningful order or distance between the categories should not be used.

ORDINAL

This is the next lowest level of measurement. It indicates not only that things differ from each other by belonging in different groups, but that they are recognizedly different in amount or degree, and fit into a given *order.*

Ordinal scales are the result of ranking procedures and show the relative positions of individuals within a group, usually based on information about the relative amount of some trait possessed by subjects, such as intelligence, or performing skill. For example, tennis players might be ranked in the following sequence: (1) beginner; (2) novice; (3) intermediate; (4) advanced; (5) tournament level. These show the relative level of ability for each rank or category, although they do not provide an exact measurement of the amount of skill, or the difference between different ranks or groups. While these categories may be based on quantitative measures of performance, in themselves they have no absolute values or scoring weights, and the differences between adjacent ranks may not be equal. The characteristic of *ordering* (placing in a rank order) is the sole mathematical property of this level.

INTERVAL SCALES

This level of measurement implies that the distances between the categories or intervals of measurement are defined in fixed and equal terms. For example, an examination with fifty questions, each worth two points, would provide an interval scale. Each question answered correctly would raise you two points on the scale; each incorrect answer would lower you by two points. The difference between an 88 and a 90 is the same as between a 62 and a 64. Similarly, a thermometer records temperatures in terms of degrees, and a single degree refers to the same amount of heat, whether the temperature is in the 20s or the 40s.

However, an interval scale does not have a true zero point, at which there is nothing of the element being measured. For example, the zero point on a thermometer does not imply a total absence of heat. Thus, interval-level measurement lets us measure the difference between things but not their proportionate size in terms of ratio. It is not possible to say that an I.Q. score of 120 means that an individual is twice as smart as one with an I.Q. of 60. In social research it is often difficult to find true interval-level measures; many statistics assume no more than an ordinal level of measurement.

RATIO-LEVEL MEASUREMENT

Ratio scales have all the properties of interval scales, with one added feature—they do have a true zero point, at which it is assumed that there is a complete absence of the element being measured. Physical distance provides a useful example; it can be measured in exactly equal units of distance, such as inches, feet, or yards. Yet, it can have a true zero point; for example, if two objects are exactly side-by-side, with no distance between them, or if a car travels *no* distance. Weight too might constitute ratio-level measurement, with the possibility of absolute weightlessness. Ratio-level measurements have all the properties of actual numbers and may be added, divided, or multiplied, or expressed in ratio relationships.

IMPLICATIONS OF LEVELS OF MEASUREMENT

An important rule of statistical analysis is that statistics which are useful at one level of measurement can always be used with higher-level variables, but not with variables measured at lower levels. In other words, if a type of data is interval in nature, statistics that are useful for it can also be used with ratio-level data. However, they could not be used with ordinal or nominal data. This has important implications for the use of parametric and nonparametric tests:

> Selection of the appropriate type of statistical analysis depends on a number of factors including the nature of the data being gathered, the size of the sample, and certain assumptions about the population . . . . For example. a given parametric statistic may require that the scores be normally distributed in the population. For that particular statistic to be appropriate, this assumption must be valid or the results of computation may not be accurate. The population values (e.g., mean, distribution, and standard deviation) are known as parameters, and since this category of statistics requires assumptions about these values, they are called "parametric" statistics . . . . Nonparametric statistics do not, in general, require as many or as rigorous assumptions.[2]

OTHER BASIC CONCEPTS

In addition to levels of measurement, two basic concepts underlying the statistical analysis of data involve the distribution of data and the normal curve, and probability. To illustrate, commonly encountered kinds of data found in educational and behavioral research often are interval or ratio data, involving surveys, tests of

self-concepts, leisure interests or attitude scales, reports of attendance, or measures of other personal characteristics. Typically, such
findings fall into so-called normal distributions.

NORMAL DISTRIBUTION AND PROBABILITY

A key to understanding statistical analysis is the normal probability distribution. Early mathematicians found that the
distribution of measurements of many phenomena approximated
what we now call the normal curve. If one were to plot quantifiable
scores of some phenomena on a graph, the frequency distribution of
these measurements fit a bell-shaped curve with the most frequent
occurrences at or near the center of the distribution. This finding is
now commonly used to describe a set of data and make predictions
about future investigations. For example, in a graph showing the
number of basketball shots that individuals in a youth sports program are able to make within a two-minute period, one might
expect to find a pattern like the following (see Fig. 8.1). The most
commonly occurring scores are 8, 9, and 10, while higher and lower
scores occur less frequently. The further one moves from the center
of the distribution (the mean), the less scores are likely to occur.

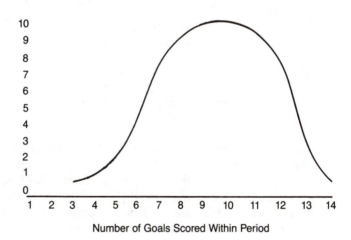

Number of Individuals Scoring at Each Level

Number of Goals Scored Within Period

FIGURE 8.1.
Example of the normal curve.

Normal Curve

The definition of the normal curve says that it is symmetrical
around its vertical axis, with the scores clustering around the

mean. If it is fully symmetrical, all measures which mark the center of the scores (mode, median, mean) would be in exactly the same location. However, in real life, this would rarely occur, particularly when a relatively few cases are involved.

Theoretically, the curve has no boundaries in either direction, and never touches the baseline at its ends. In real distributions, however, scores obviously do occur very infrequently at either end. The curve is most likely to be symmetrical if the subjects measured are homogeneous in major respects. If they are not, the curve may be distorted. For example, in a population where half the group is active in exercise programs and half the group is not, a test of physical fitness might show a *bimodal* distribution, with two peaks or high points of central tendency, and a valley between (see Fig. 8.2).

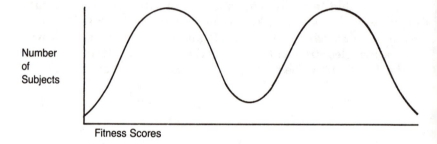

FIGURE 8.2
Example of bimodal distribution.

If many participants were active in fitness programs but a small number were inactive or had special problems such as illness or malnutrition, there would be a *skewed* curve, with a concentration of scores at one end of the distribution. Figure 8.3 shows a negatively skewed distribution with a preponderance of scores at the upper end of the distribution. A positively skewed distribution would have a preponderance of scores at the lower end of the distribution.

Standard Deviation and Standard Scores

Other concepts related to the distribution of scores on an interval or ratio scale involve *standard deviation* and *standard scores*. Standard deviation is a way of showing how scores scatter away from the

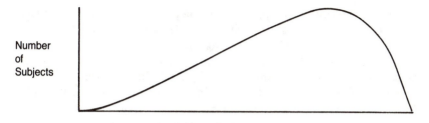

FIGURE 8.3
Example of skewed distribution.

mean of the distribution. If the standard deviation of scores is small, most scores will cluster tightly about the mean and the distribution will be very peaked. If the standard deviation is large, the scores are widely distributed above and below the mean and the distribution will be quite flat.

The standard deviation measure permits us to calculate the percentage of scores which fall at various intervals under the normal curve. This is done through the use of standard scores, a means of translating a score into a standard unit of measurement indicating its percentile location within a distribution. Given this information, we can determine the probability of a new score's occurring within the existing normal distribution curve (for fuller explanation, see pg. 156).

PROBABILITY: Probability has to do with the likelihood—or probability—that given events will occur. As a concept, it is illustrated in many ways in everyday life. Sports betting provides an example, when odds are given on a game, or when a player's performance is expressed in terms of percentages.

To illustrate, if a player has a batting average of .300, this means that he has hit safely three out of ten times at bat, and the probability is that he will do so his next time at the plate—i.e., the odds are three out of ten that he will get a hit. Obviously, other factors may affect the outcome, such as the opposing pitcher's skills or his own confidence or physical health. Thus, the odds may not stand up on a single day, or even a week or two. However, during a season, the likelihood is that the player's performance at the plate will be very close to his past record; a .300 batter will probably be close to that, and a .225 batter will be close to his own customary performance.

In terms of weather, when the forecaster predicts that there is a 30 percent chance of rain, this means that when the conditions presently existing have appeared in the past, it rained 30 percent of the time. Therefore, the prediction is that there is a 30 percent probability that it will happen again. Chance always influences isolated events. In tossing a coin, there is a 50 percent probability that it will come up heads. In a series of a few tosses, the 50/50 heads/tails percentage will probably not prevail; instead, it might be eight heads and two tails, or seven and three. However, in the long run, with hundreds of tosses, the percentage should move toward an even distribution, 50/50, unless the coin is "fixed."

Probability and the normal distribution are directly related to one another. By knowing the mean and standard deviation of a distribution, we can establish the probability of any particular score occurring in the distribution, as well as determine if a specific score is actually a part of the distribution with which we are working.

DESCRIPTIVE PROCEDURES

We will begin our discussion of descriptive statistics by examining a set of raw scores which might represent any of hundreds of possibilities in recreation and leisure: (1) figures of attendance at programs or facilities; (2) physical fitness scores of a group of participants; (3) per capita spending of communities on recreation and park budgets; (4) agency employees' salaries; or (5) scores on a test of leisure attitudes. If one were to look at such scores in a totally unorganized way, it would be difficult to make sense of them. Therefore, it is necessary to organize them so they can be conveniently tabulated and analyzed. Customarily this is done by means of frequency distributions.

USE OF FREQUENCY DISTRIBUTIONS

These represent a means of counting the frequency with which each score has been recorded, and placing them within a framework that permits easy statistical calculations. There are two types of frequency distributions: *simple* and *grouped*.

Simple Frequency Distribution

Starting with an unorganized set of scores which appear just as they were recorded, all scores would be listed in order of their size or value. A hypothetical set of scores would then appear as:

59	56	52	50	50	47	46	44	44	43	42	42	40
39	38	38	38	37	37	37	36	36	36	36	35	35
34	34	33	32	32	31	31	31	31	30	30	29	29
28	27	27	27	25	24	22	22	21	21	20	19	17

Each score would then be listed in order, with the number of times it occurs in the distribution, as follows:

59-1	58-0	57-0	56-1	55-0	54-0	53-0	52-1
51-0	50-2	49-0	48-0	47-1	46-1	45-0	44-2
43-1	42-2	41-0	40-1	39-1	38-3	37-3	36-4
35-2	34-2	33-1	32-2	31-3	30-2	29-2	28-1
27-3	26-0	25-1	24-1	23-0	22-2	21-2	20-1
19-1	18-0	17-1					

Simple frequency distributions are useful in getting a quick picture of the scores. For example, the *range* of the scores just shown (meaning the distance between the highest and lowest scores) is from 17 to 59, or 43, when one includes both the top and bottom scores. Simple frequency distributions also make it possible to identify the most common scores. In this case, the *mode* (the most common score) is quickly indentified as 36, with a frequency of four. Beyond this, it is necessary to group the scores to carry out other calculations.

Grouped Frequency Distribution

This consists of a method of grouping data within a series of equal intervals, extending from the highest to the lowest scores. Within each interval, the number of scores occurring within the interval is recorded.

INTERVAL DEFINED: An interval is one of the equal divisions or units of the overall grouped frequency distribution. It is a mutually exclusive subset within the larger set of scores. The upper and lower limits of the interval control the scores that might be tallied within the interval. To design a grouped frequency distribution correctly, it is necessary to understand that individual pieces of data, or scores, may be of two types: discrete and continuous.

Discrete pieces of data are those which record single, whole events or units. For example, one can shoot a basket 10 times or 11 times, but not 10½ times. There may be six people in a room or seven, but not six and a half.

On the other hand, *continuous* data involve scores with finer measures, as in weight, time, or distance. A person rarely weighs exactly 136 or 163 pounds, instead it is likely to be 136.7 or 163.2 pounds—or, with highly sensitive scales, it might be extended to several decimal places.

If all scores were single whole numbers, like 5, 8, or 10, there would be no need to define the limits of the intervals into which they are to be placed, other than 4 to 6, 7 to 9, or 10 to 15, as examples. However, when a whole score is accompanied by a fraction or decimal place indicating an additional amount, how is it to be placed in a frequency distribution? If the intervals in a grouped frequency distribution are 8 to 10, and then 11 to 13, where would one record a score of 10.6?

UPPER AND LOWER REAL LIMITS: The answer is that intervals are considered to have upper and lower *real limits,* to accommodate continuous data. The real limit is at the midpoint of the bottom integer of an interval and the top integer of the one below. For example, the midpoint between the interval of 8 to 10 and the interval of 11 to 13 would be 10.5. To avoid the possibility of getting a score of 10.5 and not knowing where to place it, we will call the upper real limit of the interval of 8 to 10, 10.49, and the lower real limit of the interval 11 to 13, 10.5.

This makes it possible to locate any score that falls within the space between the two intervals. For example, a score of 10.3 would belong to the interval of 8 to 10, because it is below 10.49. A score of 10.6 would belong to the 11 to 13 interval, because it is above 10.5.

CONSTRUCTING A GROUPED FREQUENCY DISTRIBUTION: To construct a grouped frequency distribution, it is necessary to decide on an appropriate width or size of each interval. For example, in the table below (Table 8.1), the width of the interval is 3, and can be determined by counting up from the beginning of one step to the beginning of the next (i.e., from 16 to 19). It is usually advisable to have between 10 and 20 steps in a grouped frequency distribution. One selects the interval by determining the range, and then fitting possible intervals into it.

To illustrate in Table 8.1, the actual range of 43 (59 − 17 + 1) is extended by adding one number at both the top and bottom, to give a total range of 45 without affecting the distribution. An interval width of 3 can be divided into this 15 times, which is perfect, yielding the table below.

TABLE 8.1

Example of Grouped Frequency Distribution

Interval	Tallies	Frequency	CF*
58-60	1	1	52
55-57	1	1	51
52-54	1	1	50
49-51	11	2	49
46-48	11	2	47
43-45	111	3	45
40-42	111	3	42
37-39	~~HHT~~ 11	7	39
34-36	~~HHT~~ 111	8	32
31-33	~~HHT~~ 11	7	24
28-30	~~HHT~~	5	17
25-27	~~HHT~~	4	12
22-24	111	3	8
19-21	111	3	5
16-18	11	2	2

N (Number) = 52

*Cumulative frequency, added from lowest interval up

By grouping a large number of individual scores into a frequency distribution with a lesser number of intervals, the data have been made much more compact and easy to work with. The overall shape of the distribution and the most common scores are easily recognized. A limitation of grouped distributions is that one loses sight of individual scores, once they have been placed within an interval. In fact, for the statistician, they no longer exist as actual scores and instead are assumed to be spread out evenly along the interval in which they appear.

MEASURING CENTRAL TENDENCY: MODE, MEDIAN, MEAN

In descriptive statistics, a common beginning procedure is to measure central tendency—i.e., to see where the center of the scores seems to lie, or to identify the most common or typical scores. This makes it possible to interpret the overall group performance and to compare it to other groups, or to see how any single score or performance falls within the group itself. The word "average" (meaning the sum of all the scores divided by the number of scores) is often used to imply central tendency, but is often applied incorrectly. Actually, the three best-known measures of central tendency are: *mode, median,* and *mean.*

MODE

This is the single score (either the actual individual score in a simple frequency distribution, or the midpoint of the interval that has the highest frequency) that occurs most frequently in a set of scores. In a frequency polygon (see Fig 8.8, it is the value along the horizontal axis at which the height of the curve is the highest.

The mode provides a quick but crude measure of central tendency, and cannot be used for any complex analysis. It is highly unstable, and may occur at points which are not actually near the real center of the scores. In the grouped frequency distribution we have been using (Table 8.1), it is found in the interval of 34 to 36; the mode itself would be 35.

MEDIAN

This is the middle measure, or score, in a series in which all scores have been arranged in their order or size or value. Stated differently, it is the point above which and below which half the scores lie; thus, it divides the top half of the scores from the bottom half. Simply calculated, it would be identified as the middle case (for example, in a series of 31 scores, it would be the 16th score, with 15 scores above it, and 15 scores below). Calculated statistically, it would be the 50th percentile.

The median is a useful measure, although it does not reflect the actual weight of the scores on either side of it. In other words, in a distorted or skewed distribution, the median would not give a true picture of central tendency. On the other hand, a strength of the median is that it honestly shows the midpoint of the scores, and is not influenced by a few scores that might otherwise radically affect its position.

Procedure for Calculating the Median

The following method is used to calculate the median statistically. It is illustrated based on the grouped frequency distribution shown in Table 8.1.

1. Identify the number of cases that would represent 50 percent of the total group. Since there are 52 scores, it would be one-half of 52, or 26. This actually refers to the point that is at the very top of 26, so

there are 26 cases above it, and 26 cases below it. If it were an odd number, such as 53 cases, the point would be 26.5.

2. Starting with the lowest interval, count up the scores through each interval using the Cumulative Frequency (CF) column, until you reach the interval just *below* the one that will have the required number of cases. In this case, it would be the interval of 31–33; there are 24 cases in or below this interval. The 26th case will be found in the next interval, 34–36.

3. You need to find the distance that you will have to travel in the 34–36 interval, in order to reach the 26th case. This makes use of the following formula:

$$\frac{\text{No. of cases needed}}{\text{No. of cases in next interval}} \quad \times \quad \text{Width of the interval}$$

or

$$\frac{2}{8} \times 3 = \frac{6}{8} \text{ or } 0.75$$

4. This must be added to the lower real limit of the interval in which the median (26th case) will be found, which is 33.5. Thus, the median will be 33.5 + 0.75, or 34.25. Fifty percent of the scores lie below this, and 50 percent lie above it.

The key to understanding step 3 is to realize that you already have 24 cases below the 34–36 interval, and therefore you must travel a distance of 2 cases into the interval to locate the 26th case. Since there are 8 cases in the interval, spaced evenly throughout it, it is necessary to go 2/8 of the way through the interval (which is 3, the interval's width) to locate the median.

Remember, the median is the 50th percentile. The same procedure can be used to locate the 25th percentile or the 75th percentile, in order to identify the bottom quarter of the scores, or the top quarter. Similarly, each decile, or 10 percent point may also be readily identified.

MEAN

This is the actual arithmetic average, which can simply be determined by adding up all the scores, and then dividing this sum by the number of scores. To illustrate, the mean weight of all of the students in a class could be calculated by adding all their individual weights, and dividing by the number of students. A useful statistical method of calculating this makes use of the grouped frequency distribution. The mean is an effective way of showing central tendency, although in a skewed distribution a few scores at the extremes can radically affect it out of proportion to their number.

Procedure for Calculating the Mean

As indicated earlier, the mean is the arithmetic average of all the scores in the distribution. Each score exerts an influence on it but the further away a score is, the more influence it will have. To illustrate, if two new houses are to be built in a neighborhood of predominantly $50,000 homes, a new home costing $300,000 will have far more influence on the mean value of the homes there than a house costing $55,000.

Using the same frequency distribution as before, we create a new column, the Deviation (d) column. This indicates the distance that a given interval is from the interval, containing the assumed mean. The further away it is, the greater the deviation and the greater its effect on the mean. This principle is basic in the statistical procedure for calculating the mean of a set of scores. Using the same figures found in the earlier procedures, the steps are as follows.

1. Select an interval close to the center of the distribution as an arbitrary starting place or estimated location of the mean. This may be called the "arbitrary origin," or "assumed mean." This interval is given a weight or value of zero (0). Give the next higher interval a deviation (d) weight of +1, the next +2, the next +3, and so on, to reflect the added influence each interval has on the mean, by virtue of its greater distance from it. Do the same for the deviations below the mean, but make them −1, −2, −3, and so on.

2. For each interval, multiply the number of cases in it by the weight or value of the interval (d) next to it, to combine the plus or minus effect of the interval with the number of cases in it. Those above the assumed mean are positive and "pull" the mean up. Those below it are negative and "pull" it down. This gives you a column of frequency times deviation (fd) scores, showing the total amount of the deviation of the cases in each interval, from the assumed mean. (see Table 8.2).

3. Sum (Σ) the values in the fd column, taking account of the plus and minus signs. Sum the frequencies in the column headed Frequency (f) to get the total of cases, or N, as a check.

4. Divide the sum of fd values by N, to get the average of the deviations from the assumed mean. Then multiply by the width of the interval (3), to express the deviation in score units. Add the result to the midpoint of the assumed mean, and the result is the mean.

The formula may be summarized as follows:

$$\text{Mean} = \frac{\Sigma fd}{N} \times \text{Interval} + \text{Assumed Mean (midpoint)}$$

$$\text{Mean} = \frac{-7}{52} \times 3 + 35 = 34.6$$

The result, 34.6, is quite close to the median, which was calculated as 34.25. If the distribution was uneven or markedly skewed, they probably would be quite different.

TABLE 8.2

Procedure for Calculating the Mean

Score Interval	Frequency f	Deviation d	fd
58–60	1	8	8
55–57	1	7	7
52–54	1	6	6
49–51	2	5	10
46–48	2	4	8
43–45	3	3	9
40–42	3	2	6
37–39	7	1	7
34–36	8	0	0
31–33	7	−1	−7
28–30	5	−2	−10
25–27	4	−3	−12
22–24	3	−4	−12
19–21	3	−5	−15
16–18	2	−6	−12
$N = 52$	$\Sigma f = 52$		$\Sigma fd = -7$

MEASURES OF DISPERSION
(SCATTERING OF SCORES)

In descriptive statistics, it is important to be able to measure the dispersion, or scattering of scores away from the mean, to get a true picture of a distribution. For example, one might select a vacation destination on the basis of what appears to be mild or moderate temperature. Yet, two locations that appear to have exactly the same average temperature, 72° Fahrenheit, might have radically different climates. In one vacation site, a South Seas island, the temperature over a 24-hour period might vary only from the low 60s to the 80s. In another site, a camping area in the Grand Canyon, the temperature might shift from freezing at night to over 100° during the day. Yet both would have the same average temperature. Thus, it is important to know not only the central tendency of scores, but how they are dispersed away from the mean.

The simplest way to measure the spread of scores in any distribution is to examine the range, which is the highest score minus the lowest score, plus 1 ($X_{max} - X_{min} + 1$ = range). This is a quick, rough measure which is useful only to indicate the extreme scores. While easy to calculate, it is not reliable and gives no information about how scores may vary within the distribution. Instead, standard deviation provides a better measure of the variability of scores.

STANDARD DEVIATION

One method of looking at the variation in scores is to determine how much individual scores (x_i) deviate on the average from the mean of the distribution ($\bar{x}$). This calculation would theoretically result in zero since the positive scores above the mean would be equivalent to the negative scores below the mean. Therefore, one uses the absolute values of the deviations, without noting the pluses or minuses, to establish the *average absolute deviation*. The following calculation shows how the average absolute deviation is determined:

Raw Scores x_i	$N=6$	*Absolute Deviations* $\|x_i - \bar{x}\|$
2		2
3	$\bar{x} = \dfrac{\Sigma \mathrm{x}}{u} = \dfrac{24}{6} = 4.0$	1
7		3
4	(mean of the	0
2	distribution)	2
6		2
$\Sigma x = 24$		$\Sigma\|x_i - \bar{x}\| = 11$

$$\text{Average absolute deviation (AD)} = \frac{\Sigma|x_i - \bar{x}|}{N} = \frac{11}{6} = 1.83$$

On the average, these six scores deviate 1.83 points from the arithmetic mean of this distribution. Although this measure is easily calculated and interpreted, another measure known as standard deviation is preferred because of its utility in other statistical analysis.

The standard deviation is the square root of the variance (s^2) where the variance is the average of the squared deviation of scores from the mean. The formula for the standard deviation(s) is:

$$s = \sqrt{\frac{\Sigma(x_i - \bar{x})^2}{N}}^{*}$$

*This formula yields a slight underestimation of the population standard deviation. The underestimate can be corrected by using N-1 in the denominator of the formula. In most cases the sample size is sufficiently large so that the effect of this correction is negligible.

Using the data from the previous discussion, the calculations of the standard deviation are as follows:

	Raw Scores x_i	Differences $(x_i - \bar{x})$	Squared Differences $(x_i - \bar{x})^2$
	2	−2	4
N=6	3	−1	1
	7	+3	9
$\bar{x}$=4.0	4	0	0
	2	−2	4
	6	+2	4
	$\Sigma x_i = 24$	0	$\Sigma(x_i - \bar{x})^2 = 22$

$$s = \sqrt{\frac{22}{6}} = \sqrt{3.67} \quad s = 1.91$$

The standard deviation of this distribution is calculated at 1.91, which is slightly different from the average absolute deviation of 1.83. The value of 1.91 is also referred to as one standard deviation unit; 3.82 is considered two standard deviation units, and so on.

Interpretation of Standard Deviation

Within the normal, bell-shaped curve, about ⅔ (68.2 percent) of the scores will fall within one standard deviation unit (S.D.) of either side of the mean (plus or minus 1 S.D.). About 95 percent of all scores will fall within 2 S.D.s, and almost all scores within 3 S.D.s (See Fig. 8.4).

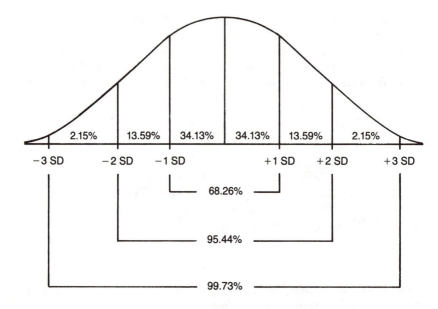

FIGURE 8.4
Interpretation of standard deviation.

Applied to the distribution shown in Table 8.2, the standard deviation of this set of scores is 9.6. This means that about two-thirds of the scores are between 25.0 and 44.2 (9.6 above and below the mean of 34.6). The larger the standard deviation in relation to the range, the wider the spread or dispersion of scores. When different sets of scores are compared, the standard deviation provides useful information. It may also be used to interpret the meaning of any single score. For example, an individual who is one standard deviation above the mean is higher than about 84 percent of the entire group (50 percent below and 34 percent above the mean).

STANDARD SCORES (z Scores)

Comparisons among individual scores within a single distribution or across distributions can be facilitated through the use of standard scores. They provide a method of expressing a score in a distribution in terms of its distance from the mean, in standard deviation units. For example, in a distribution with a mean of 27 and a standard deviation of 3.5, an individual score of 30.5 would have a standard score of 1. This can be found by using the following formula:

$$z = \frac{(x_i - \bar{x})}{s}$$

$$z = \frac{30.5 - 27}{3.5} = \frac{3.5}{3.5}$$

$$z = 1$$

A score of 1 indicates that the individual score is 1 standard deviation unit above the mean and reveals that 84 percent of the individuals had scores less than or equal to 30.5 (see previous discussion of area under the normal curve). As a second example, an individual with a score of 34 would have a z score of 2, and would lie at approximately the 98th percentile, with only 2 percent of the scores being higher than 34.

MEASURES OF ASSOCIATION BETWEEN SCORES

Another important task in descriptive statistics is to measure the degree of association among scores. This involves what are commonly called "proportionate reduction in error" measures, or PRE measures. The PRE measures state the proportion by which one can reduce errors in predicting one's score or value on one variable by using information from a second variable.

Very simply, there are two ways of predicting one's score on a variable. The first involves predicting individual scores by using the modal or average response of the overall study population as a guide. For example, if you know that 200 students played summer softball and 300 did not play, you would arbitrarily predict that each student in the population did not play, since you would have a higher probability of being correct making this prediction. You would be correct 300 times, and incorrect 200 times.

	Softball Participants	
	Yes	No
Students	200	300

However, in the second situation you now have information regarding the distribution of softball participation by sex. It is as follows:

	Softball Participants		
Students	Yes	No	
Male	150	75	225
Female	50	225	275

Knowing the sex of students, one could successfully predict softball participation 375 times. If the student were a male, you would predict "yes," and if a female, "no." You would be incorrect only 125 times, using the second method. The PRE measure describes the reduction in errors in predicting participation in the first situation, based on using the second set of information.

PRE Measures for Nominal Variables

Lambda and Goodman and Kruskal's tau-*y* are two PRE measures suitable for use when both variables are interpreted to be nominal variables. Both measures are asymmetric; that is, a distinction is made between independent and dependent variables. Normally, two different asymmetric coefficients are computed; the value of predicting *y* from knowledge of variable *x*, and the value of predicting *x* from knowledge of variable *y*. It is up to the discretion of the researcher as to which value to present. Also, both measures vary from 0.0, indicating no reduction in error to +1.0 for perfect reduction. However, the measures do differ on one dimension. Lambda is concerned with prediction of the optimal value of the dependent variable, i.e., the mode, while Goodman and Kruskal's tau-*y* is used to predict the distribution of the dependent variable.

PRE Measures for Ordinal Variables

Kendall's tau-*a*, Kendall's tau-*b*, gamma (G), and Somer's *D* are four common PRE measures for ordinal data (rank order data). The first three measures are symmetrical, meaning that there is no distinction between a dependent and independent variable while Somer's *D* is an asymmetric measure. All four measures have a range of −1.0 to +1.0. A negative PRE value is associated with a negative or inverse relationship, i.e., as one ranking increases, the other ranking decreases, while a positive PRE value involves a direct or positive relationship between the rankings under investigation. Tau-*a* can be utilized when there are no ties in the rankings on either variable while tau-*b* takes into account ties in the rankings on one or the other variable. Gamma, on the other hand, eliminates ties from its calculation; however, it has been criticized on this point because several pairs of observations could potentially be discarded and the measure could actually be based on limited pairs of observations. As stated previously, Somer's *D* is the only asymmetric measure; two values would be computed, testing both variables as the dependent and independent variable.

PRE Measures for Interval Variables

The most common measure of association found in recreation research is the product-moment correlation coefficient (PMCC). The PMCC, r, can be used with two variables measured on interval or ratio levels. We include this coefficient as a PRE measure because r^2 indicates the proportionate reduction in errors, given the use of a prediction equation, rather than merely using the overall mean of the dependent variable. Further explanation of the prediction equation is presented in Chapter 9. For now, let us focus our attention on the nature of the correlation coefficient.

The correlation coefficient provides a quantitative expression of the degree of relationship between two interval variables. In a rating process or test which gives scores on different attributes or performance measures for each subject, it seeks to determine whether these scores are related. If this relationship were assumed to be positive (as in the case of study habits and grades on examinations), one would expect that a high score on one variable would mean that the individual would *tend* to have a high score on the other. This does not mean that every individual would have such a clear positive relationship between the two variables, but rather that it would be a general pattern for the overall group.

If two sets of scores are simply plotted on a chart, a positive correlation will be indicated if the scores tend to fall in a diagonal line from the lower left to the upper right. The higher the degree of positive correlation, the tighter the line in the sense that all scores will tend to be closer to it. If there is little or no correlation, the scores will tend to be randomly scattered. If the correlation is negative (meaning that the higher one is on a given attribute, the more likely one is to be lower on the other), the line will fall in the other direction (from upper left to lower right). The correlation coefficient, r, ranges from $+1$ (perfect positive correlation) to -1 (perfect negative correlation). An r of zero means that there is no relationship at all. Figure 8.5 shows four examples of correlations between variables, with the rs that have been recorded for each of them.

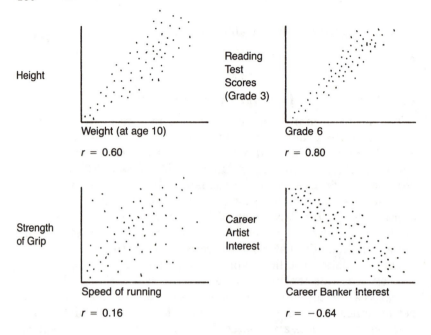

FIGURE 8.5
Different degrees of correlation.

METHODS OF TABULATING AND ANALYZING DATA

The preceding section of this chapter has presented a number of the key principles and procedures found in descriptive statistics. The concluding section presents guidelines for organizing, tabulating, and analyzing data, particularly the kinds of data which may be derived from surveys or other descriptive research studies.

It would be a mistake to think of the data-analysis process as something that happens *after* you have gathered your study data. Instead, this should have been carefully planned at an early stage in developing the study proposal. In identifying the study purposes and selecting an appropriate research design, the selection of the variables you intend to identify and measure should have been thought out carefully in advance. Similarly, in designing study instruments, it is desirable to precode all test items and responses, so that each potential response is identified by a number and/or letter, with additional space left for other possible replies.

PLANNING THE ANALYSIS

As you prepare to tabulate and analyze data, it is helpful to identify in outline form the tables or charts you expect to develop, based on the information you have gathered. Printing the specific variables across the tops and down the sides of tables and charts forces you to state the variables explicitly and to decide exactly what totals, percentages, or trends over time you will report, or what relationships you may wish to explore.

For example, in a survey which reports recreational participation by a diverse sample of community residents in programs sponsored by a public recreation and parks agency, you might decide to develop findings on any of the following:

1. Ranked order of the most popular activities, with the percentage of the overall population that engages in them, or with reported frequencies of participation for each activity, by the week, month, or year.

2. A breakdown of the most popular groups of activities (such as active sports or creative arts), with respect to participation by different age groups.

3. Identification of the major districts of the city, showing patterns of popularity of individual activities, or groups of activities, within each geographical area.

4. Tables showing seasonal participation (for fall, winter, spring, and summer) for overall listing of activities, or selected groups.

5. Tables showing estimated spending on recreation for different age groups, or for areas of the city or types of activities.

6. Tables contrasting participation by age, by sex, by race, by socioeconomic status, or other demographic variables.

To develop such analyses, it is necessary to transfer scores from the data-gathering instruments, such as survey questionnaires or survey rating forms, to a form in which they can be systematically analyzed. This can be done in two ways: (1) through simple hand-tabulating procedures, in which the data are first tabulated and then analyzed and (2) through computer analysis, in which the scores are transferred onto the computer and then all tabulation and analysis is done automatically, using a specific program to treat the data.

HAND-TABULATING PROCEDURES

In simple research or evaluation projects, hand-tabulating procedures are convenient and inexpensive, particularly if few subjects are involved, and if the information sought is of a basic nature. Customarily, a tabulation sheet is prepared, on which all responses can be recorded. Usually, this is designed based on the questionnaire or rating sheet itself, with all questions and response items listed in turn, with all possible responses following them, and with space for tabulation of scores. Closed-end questions normally have very simple kinds of response choices, such as:

Yes	_____	or	Married	_____
No	_____		Divorced/Separated	_____
No Opinion	_____		Widowed	_____
No Reply	_____		Single	_____

In some cases, questions may call for respondents to fill in the appropriate items in a listing of possible activities or other types of information, such as:

Tennis	_____	or	$10,000–$19,999	_____
Golf	_____		$20,000–$29,999	_____
Basketball	_____		$30,000–$39,999	_____
Softball	_____		$40,000 and over	_____

Thus, a tabulation sheet simply represents an expanded form of the questionnaire, which provides space for tallying the responses. To save time and ensure greater accuracy, it is recommended that one person read the data, while another person records them on the tabulation sheet.

Presorting of Responses

At this stage, it is desirable to presort all response sheets first into categories or subgroups, to avoid unnecessary steps later. For example, if all the sheets reporting a survey of community residents were tabulated directly when they were turned in to the survey office, without sorting, an accurate tabulation of the entire study population could be done. However, if it were later decided that it would be helpful to compare the findings from each district in a city, it would be necessary to sort the replies and tabulate them again. If it had been thought of in advance, the responses could have been put into separate stacks and compiled according to these groups. The separate totals could then be combined, to provide an aggregate total for the entire study population.

Findings for separate groups may be combined in tables which show in assembled form how they have responded to specific questions. For example, Table 8.3 shows how the responses of four age groups to a question regarding program priorities could be presented.

Table 8.3.

Levels of Priorities Assigned to Activity, by Age Groups

	High Priority	Middle Priority	Low Priority
Children			
Youth			
Adults			
Elderly			

Tallying Open-End Questions

If a survey form or observation sheet consists entirely or partially of open-end questions, the tallying process is somewhat more complicated. A question like, "What is your opinion of the center's cultural arts program?" may yield dozens of different kinds of responses. However, they must be tallied, and it is usually not feasible simply to list all the different responses to the question. The procedure in such cases is usually to examine a good range of responses, in order to identify the most common responses that should be included on the tabulation sheet. All important or frequent responses should be included—and those doing the scoring should review them to ensure that they are interpreting responses correctly and assigning them to response categories in a consistent way. Other scattered or infrequent replies may be included under the heading of "other" or "miscellaneous" replies. The entire effort should be designed to be as simple, accurate, and economical as possible, in terms of the time and effort required to do the job.

COMPUTER ANALYSIS OF DATA

Increasingly, electronic data processing has taken the place of hand-tabulation and analysis procedures. Certainly, in more extensive investigations where complex analysis is called for, computers provide the most efficient means of tabulating and analzying data. This is particularly true where large numbers of responses are involved. A tremendous advantage of computer data-analysis capability is that, once the original findings are placed on cards or tapes, it is possible to examine them at any level of complexity—from simple totals or percentages to more sophisticated questions involving the relationship of different subgroups or variables in the study population. The investigator may return to the data again and again to test hypotheses or explore other study findings.

Several statistical packages have been developed which have greatly simplified use of the computer for statistical analysis. Three of the most common computer statistical packages are Statistical Package for the Social Sciences (SPSS), Bio Medical Programs (BMDP), and Statistical Analysis System (SAS). Each one possesses both descriptive and inferential statistical procedures ranging from simple frequency distributions for descriptive purposes to highly complex multivariate analysis, such as cluster analysis and canonical correlation. The beauty of these statistical packages is their flexibility. Operation of these packages has been developed so virtually any data set can be analyzed. Each statistical procedure can be adapted to the number of subjects, number of variables, and even, in some cases, the level of measurement. One can run the same statistical procedure for one research question or literally over 100 research questions simultaneously. The packages accommodate the transformation of variables, the creation of new variables through arithmetic operations of existing variables, the redefining of variables, and the selection of specific levels of a variable.

Although each package provides an explanation of the various statistical procedures it contains, the document is not a complete textbook on statistical application. One must possess a basic understanding of statistical analysis to utilize these packages effectively. Further, because of the flexibility of the packages, their use becomes quite involved since one must set up the statistical procedure to address the research hypothesis and/or research question and fit the nature of the data set.

To illustrate the use of a statistical package, we will utilize information gathered in a large leisure-services marketing study conducted by the authors of this text. We will illustrate a very basic cross-tabulation program from the Statistical Package for the Social Sciences (SPSS)[3,4].

To use a statistical package, a set of control statements and procedure statements must be prepared according to rigidly specified procedures. These statements are organized into a program file contained in the computer where they can be called upon when the researcher desires to conduct a specific statistical analysis. The program file must conform to the data. In addition to the program file, the data must also be entered into the computer so they can be read and analyzed through use of the program file. Sometimes the data are actually contained within the program file, but more often they are organized in a separate file simply called the data file.

CODE BOOK

Normally, when we collect data through any of a variety of mechanisms, we develop a code book. This code book specifies how the data should be entered into the data file and also how the program file must be developed to utilize these data. A code book is a very simple but essential aspect of the research process. Earlier we talked about hand-tabulating our data. Even with this manual procedure, aspects of the code book are needed for ease of tabulation. If we asked people to list their favorite leisure activities, with 1,000 subjects we might easily have hundreds of different activities mentioned. Rather than writing out the activity each time it is mentioned, we assign it a code. For example, jogging could be the code "0001," swimming the code "0002," etc. Now a number represents an activity. This same principle can be applied to all data we collect; we code the data using numeric symbols. We say numeric symbols because they may not possess any mathematical properties. For example, a "1" may be the code for male and a "2" the code for female. These are only symbols for categorical (numeral) data and have no numerical value. However, a 135 may represent the weight of an individual and in this case the data do have numerical value with arithmetic properties.

When using the computer for analysis, the code book not only specifies the code for each piece of datum, it indicates the name of each piece of datum to be used for the program file and the placement of the data in the data file. Figure 8.6 presents one page of a code book used for the leisure-services marketing study previously mentioned. The code book has four essential items of information. The first item, in this case, is the survey question. This indicates the piece of information which is to be coded; i.e., township zone, age of adult No. 1, etc. The second item of information is the column in which the data will be placed within the data file. For example, the identification number (I.D. No.) is the first piece of datum to be placed in the data file. Therefore, it goes in the first four columns

Survey Question	Column	Code	Computer Name
I.D. No.	1-4	0001-1000	VAR001
Township zone	5	1-5 9 = missing value	VAR002
Individual Information			
Length of residence	6-7	01-98 99 = Missing value	VAR003
Marital status	8	1 = Single 2 = Married 3 = Divorced 4 = Other 9 = Missing value	VAR004
Adult No. 1 age	9-10	01-98 Years 99 = Missing value	VAR005
Adult No. 1 sex	11	1 = Male 2 = Female 9 = Missing value	VAR006
Adult No. 1 race	12	1 = Black 2 = White 3 = Hispanic 4 = Oriental 5 = Other 9 = Missing value	VAR007
Facility Maintenance			
Large community center	13	1 = Very good 2 = Good 3 = Fair 4 = Poor 9 = Missing value	VAR008
Neighborhood park	14	Same	VAR009
Tennis courts	15	Same	VAR010
Soft/baseball fields	16	Same	VAR011

FIGURE 8.6.
Leisure-services code book.

(1-4) of the file. (Traditionally, data files have been set up with 80 columns of information; however, this need not be the case.) Since the identification number can be four digits in length, it will utilize four columns. The third item of information in the code book is the actual numeric symbol to be used in the data file. In the case of the I.D. No., the codes will range from 0001 to 1000. This is because there were potentially 1,000 respondents in the study. Notice that, for marital status, the codes are 1 through 4 with a "9" indicating a missing value. The missing value simply tells the computer that the individual didn't respond to this question. The last item of information in the code book is the name of the variable which will be used in the computer program file. Each statistical package has very specific requirements for the "computer names." In this case, we have simply named our variables VAR001 to VAR011. This code book was set up for an SPSS program file using sequentially named variables and involves a saving of time in writing the program file.

PROGRAM FILE

As stated previously, the program file consists of control statements and procedure statements. Control statements provide information about the variables to be analyzed and general information about the nature of the file itself. The procedure statements address the specific types of statistical analysis the researcher would like to run. Figure 8.7 illustrates the SPSS program file used to conduct the cross-tabulation analysis in Table 8.4.

The SPSS program file must be developed using only 80 columns regardless of whether the researcher is entering the program through computer cards or a terminal device. The name of each control and procedure statement begins in column 1 and the description of the statements always begins in column 16.

The RUN NAME statement in Fig. 8.7 provides a title for the particular analysis the researcher will be performing. The name of the control statement begins in column 1 and the title begins in column 16 and may continue to column 80.

The DATA LIST statement is the most important statement in the program file. It names the variables to be studied and indicates the columns in which the data can be found within the data file. The DATA LIST statement may be continued on several lines with the description always starting in column 16. The term FIXED means the data are placed in the data file in exactly the same way for all respondents. The number in parentheses indicates the number of lines of data for each respondent. In this case, we could have omitted the number "1" since the default in SPSS is one line per respondent. The number following the slash indicates the data line to be read by the computer. Again, since we have only one line of data, we use a "1." However, if there were several data lines per respondent and we desired to only use data from line three, for example, we would have placed a "3" in this position. Following a blank space, the names of the variables and the columns in which each variable is located in the data file are defined. For example, VAR001 is the first variable in

PROGRAM
PROGRAMMER
DATE
PUNCHING INSTRUCTIONS
GRAPHIC
PUNCH
PAGE   OF
CARD ELECTRO NUMBER*
STATEMENT NUMBER

	FORTRAN STATEMENT
RUN NAME	LEISURE SERVICES MARKETING STUDY
DATA LIST	FIXED(1)/1 VAR001 1-4, VAR002 5, VAR003 6-7, VAR004 8, VAR005
	9-10, VAR006 TO VAR011 11-16
MISSING VALUES	VAR002,VAR004,VAR006 TO VAR018(9)/VAR003,VAR005(99)
VAR LABELS	VAR001 RESPONDENT ID NO/VAR002 TOWNSHIP ZONE/
	VAR003 LENGTH OF RESIDENCE/VAR004 MARITAL STATUS/
	VAR005 AGE ADULT 1/VAR006 SEX ADULT 1/VAR007 RACE ADULT 1
	VAR008 MAINT COMM PARK/VAR009 MAINT NEIGH PARK/
	VAR010 MAINT TENNIS CT/VAR011 MAINT SOFT-BASEBALL FLD
VALUE LABELS	VAR002(1)ZONE 1 (2)ZONE 2 (3)ZONE 3(4)ZONE 4(5)ZONE 5
	VAR004(1)SINGLE(2)MARRIED(3)DIVORCED(4)OTHER/
	VAR006(1)MALE(2)FEMALE/VAR007(1)BLACK(2)WHITE(3)HISPANIC
	(4)ORIENTAL(5)OTHER/VAR008 TO VAR011(1)VERY GOOD(2)GOOD
	(3)FAIR(4)POOR
CROSSTABS	VARIABLES=VAR007(1,5)VAR008(1,4)/TABLES=VAR008 BY VAR007

FIGURE 8.7
SPSS program file.

the data file and its value is contained in columns 1 through 4. This process is continued for each variable. Notice that VAR007 through VAR10 are not explicitly defined in the statement. Since SPSS allows implicit definitions using the "TO" convention, these variables are defined by the term VAR006 TO VAR011. The variables VAR007 through VAR10 are implicit within this term. The term "11-16" indicates the columns in which the values of those variables are located. There are six variables and six columns available; therefore, the SPSS program recognizes that each variable is a single digit, each using one column. The variable name can be up to eight alphabetic or numeric characters but the first character must be alphabetic. Also, notice that each variable definition is separated by a comma.

The MISSING VALUES statement provides a means of defining when a respondent does not provide a piece of information. For this case, the digit "9" is used to indicate a missing value of all single-digit variables and a "99" is used for two-digit variables. Not all variables need a MISSING VALUE definition, only those which are critical to the researcher's analysis. Note the use of the "TO" convention again in this statement.

The VAR LABELS statement provides a description for each variable. The description may be up to 40 characters. First, the variable name is listed and, following a blank space, the description is provided. Each description is completed with a slash, indicating that another variable name is to follow. For example, VAR001 refers to the respondent's identification number, RESPONDENT I.D. NO.

The VALUE LABELS statement describes the meaning of each value given to a variable. For example, VAR004 is the marital status of the respondent; a value of "1" indicates that the respondent is single, a value of "2" indicates the respondent is married, and so on. A VALUE LABEL is necessary only for those variables in which the numeric symbols do not have a specific numerical value but rather have some non-numeric meaning. Note that the numeric symbol is placed in parentheses immediately following the variable name and then the value for each symbol is described. The description for each variable symbol (value) can be up to 20 characters but may not include / or). A slash is used to separate the value label descriptions between variables.

Up to this point, we have discussed control statements only. A program file also must contain procedure statements. In our example, we only have one procedure statement; the CROSSTABS statement allows a very simple analysis of the relationship between two or more variables. In its simplest form, it is a joint-frequency distribution of two categorical variables. Various types of statistical analyses can be conducted with this procedure statement; however, our purpose is only to illustrate the use of a computer package (SPSS in this example) and not to explain various statistical procedures at this time.

In our example, the CROSSTABS statement is developed for integer data. In the description section of the statement, the name of all the variables to be analyzed and their limiting values must be stated. The limiting values refer to the numeric symbols used to designate the various categories for each variable; i.e., a "1" for VAR007 refers to a black respondent. First, all variables are listed using VARIABLES = followed by the name of each variable and their limiting values in parentheses. All variables to be presented in a table must be listed in this section; then in the TABLES section, the specific tables to be produced are defined. In this example, we are only producing one table, VAR008 by VAR007. The first variable is always the row variable. Several tables may be defined using multiple tables statements; however, we have presented just one table for illustrative purposes.

Table 8.4 presents the resulting computer PRINTOUT from the CROSSTABS procedure defined in our program file. Respondents were asked to rate the quality of maintenance of a large community center they were attending. This table presents the cross tabulation of their responses, grouped by race of the respondent. Tables of this type are very common in recreation and park research studies.

The clue to understanding the printout is in the upper left corner in which the four items (COUNT, ROW PCT, COL PCT, and TOT PCT) explain the meaning of the four numbers in each cell of the table.

The first key, COUNT, refers to the first (highest) number in each box. For example, 75 Blacks rated maintenance as Very Good; 167 Whites rated maintenance as Good; and so on.

The second key, ROW PCT, means Row Percentage, and refers to the second number in each cell. Since it says "Row," it means that the numbers are to be read horizontally, across the rows of cells. It tells each group's percentage of the total number that gave that rating. For example, of the total of 384 respondents who rated maintenance as good, 52.1 percent were Black, 43.5 percent were White, 3.6 percent were Hispanic, none were Oriental, and 0.8 percent were "Other."

The third key, COL PCT, means Column Percentage. It refers to the third number in each cell, and indicates the percentage of the

TABLE 8.4.

How Respondent Rates Maintenance Of Facility: By Race

VAR008	Count Row Pct Col Pct Tot Pct	Black 1.	White 2.	Hispanic 3.	Oriental 4.	Other 5.	Row Total
Very good	1.	75 36.2 15.1 7.6	131 63.3 28.9 13.3	0 0 0 0	1 .5 100.0 .1	0 0 0 0	207 21.1
Good	2.	200 52.1 40.3 20.3	167 43.5 36.8 17.0	14 3.6 58.3 1.4	0 0 0 0	3 .8 37.5 .3	384 39.1
Fair	3.	147 58.1 29.6 15.0	95 37.5 20.9 9.7	8 3.2 33.3 .8	0 0 0 0	3 1.2 37.5 .3	253 25.7
Poor	4.	74 53.2 14.9 7.5	61 43.9 13.4 6.2	2 1.4 8.3 .2	0 0 0 0	2 1.4 25.0 .2	139 14.1
	Column total	496 50.5	454 46.2	24 2.4	1 .1	8 .8	983 100.0

total in the column that a particular number represents. For example, of the 496 Blacks who took part in the survey, 15.1 percent rated maintenance as Very Good, 40.3 percent as Good, 29.6 as Fair, and 14.9 percent as Poor. In each such case, the row or column percentages must add up to 100.

The fourth key, TOTAL PCT, means Total Percentage. It indicates the percentage that any cell represents, of the total group of respondents. For example, 8 Hispanics of the total of 983 respondents (0.8 percent) rated maintenance as Fair. In another column, 200 Blacks out of the total number of 983 respondents, or 20.3 percent, rated maintenance as Good.

The other values to be interpreted are: (1) the column on the far right, which shows the absolute number and the percentage for each rating (Very Good, 21.1 percent; Good, 39.1 percent, and so on and (2) the row on the bottom, which shows the absolute number and percentage of each ethnic group responding to the survey (50.5 percent Blacks, 46.2 percent Whites, and so on).

VISUAL PRESENTATION OF SCORES:
CHARTS AND GRAPHS

In addition to using tables, it is often helpful to present findings in visual form through the use of charts and graphs. Figure 8.8 gives two examples, drawn from the data presented earlier in this chapter (pg. 149).

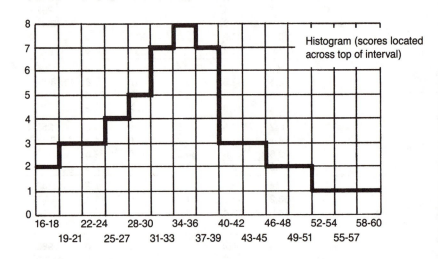

Histogram (scores located across top of interval)

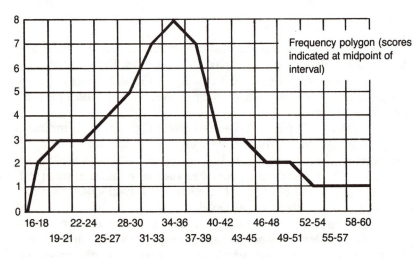

Frequency polygon (scores indicated at midpoint of interval)

FIGURE 8.8
Examples of graphs: histogram and frequency polygon.

Other types of visual materials include:

Pie Charts

These show the composition of any subject, such as a budget or program content, by depicting its elements with proportionately sized wedges within a circular, or "pie-shaped," chart.

Charts of Changes Over Time

These may show how a particular process or index may rise and fall over a period of time; examples might include participation totals, vandalism occurrences, or revenues.

Charts Showing Comparisons

These include bar graphs or charts showing change over time, with two or more different elements being represented by different textures, or different types of lines on a graph (solid line, punctuated line, line of dots, etc.)

Examination of business reports, annual reports of agencies, and similar sources will reveal several other examples of visual materials designed to present statistical findings concisely.

LEVELS OF ANALYSIS: PREPARING RESEARCH REPORTS

In concluding this chapter, it should be stressed that the level of statistical analysis tends to be strongly influenced by the nature of the research itself, and by the audience for which it is intended. For example, reports of applied research studies are read primarily by practitioners or the public at large; this audience is largely unfamiliar with statistical concepts and techniques. In addition, it is likely that the research questions that form the focus of the study will call for fairly basic kinds of analysis. Therefore, the methods used and the reporting of the data should be very simple and clear— relying heavily on totals and percentages that are descriptive in nature, and on simple tables, charts, or graphs that serve to illustrate the study findings.

In contrast, any research study that is intended to develop or test theory, and that is "pure" or abstract in nature, is likely to use more sophisticated and difficult methods of statistical analysis. This is often true in academic research and in the research studies that are reported at research symposia and in the scholarly journals in the field. A number of the concepts and methods found in inferential statistics, which are of this nature, are summarized and discussed in Chapter 9.

SUMMARY

This chapter introduces the use of statistics as an essential function in analyzing quantitative research data, and describes two major forms of statistics: descriptive and inferential. It defines four levels of measurement: (a) nominal, (b) ordinal, (c) interval, and (d) ratio data, and discusses the normal distribution curve and principles of probability. It then outlines a number of important concepts of descriptive statistics, including the use of grouped frequency distributions to measure central tendency. The mode, median, and mean are described, along with measures of dispersion. Standard deviation and standard scores are explained.

Measures of association between scores are presented, with illustrations of the coefficient of correlation. The remaining section of the chapter suggests approaches to planning data-analysis techniques in designing study instruments, as well as methods of tabulating and organizing study findings. Tallying closed- and open-end questions and interpreting computer printouts conclude the chapter, along with a brief presentation of the use of charts and graphs to summarize study findings.

ENDNOTES

1. Sidney M. Stahl and James D. Hennes, *Reading and Understanding Applied Statistics* (St. Louis, Mo.: C. V. Mosby Co., 1980), 2.
2. Clifford J. Drew, *Introduction to Designing and Conducting Research* (St. Louis, Mo.: C. V. Mosby Co., 1980), 268-269.
3. S. H. Nie, C. H. Hull, J. Jenkins, K. Steinbrenner, and D. H. Bent, *Statistical Package for the Social Sciences,* 2nd ed. (New York: McGraw-Hill, 1975).
4. Mark L. Berenson, David M. Levine, and Matthew Goldstein, *Intermediate Statistical Methods and Applications: A Computer Package Approach* (Englewood Cliffs, N.J.: Prentice-Hall, Inc., 1983).

WORKSHOP ACTIVITIES TO BE CARRIED OUT IN CLASS

26. Have all students, individually or in small groups, prepare a frequency distribution of a set of scores. Ask them to determine the central ten-

dency (mean, median, and mode) and to chart the distribution, using a frequency polygon or a histogram. Compare the results.

27. As an extension of No. 26, have students determine the standard deviation of the scores. Assign several hypothetical scores to them, and have them determine the standard scores of these scores.

28. Have students actually apply a research instrument (a simple survey would be most convenient) to a selected population. Then have them estimate the degree of relationship between any two variables, using the simple plotting method to show correlation graphically.

29. Present the students with a set of computer printouts, like the one shown in Table 8.4. Have them respond to specific questions to test their ability to read and interpret the printout.

9

OVERVIEW OF INFERENTIAL STATISTICS

A mere quantitative superiority of the experimental group mean score over the control group mean score is not conclusive proof of its superiority. Since we know that the means of two groups randomly drawn from the same population were not necessarily identical, any difference . . . could possibly be attributed to sampling error or chance. To be statistically significant, the difference must be greater than that which can reasonably be attributed to sampling error.[1]

INTRODUCTION

This chapter presents a concise summary of information dealing with a number of the key principles and procedures in inferential statistics. It begins with a discussion of hypothesis development and testing and the difference between parametric and non-parametric analysis. It continues with the use of t-tests and one-way analysis of variance (ANOVA), then discusses factorial designs, repeated measures designs, and analysis of covariance.

The second section of the chapter deals with measures of association (including the chi-square test), Spearman rank-order correlation, the product-moment coefficient of correlation, and bivariate regression and multiple regression. The concluding section deals with multivariate procedures, including factor analysis, cluster analysis, discriminant analysis, and canonical correlation. *The reader should be warned:* much of this material is too advanced to be useful in an introductory or basic course on research and evaluation, and probably should not even be attempted in such a course. However, it provides a valuable explanation of inferential statistics principles and procedures for those in more advanced courses or seminars, particularly when students are having or will have additional courses in statistics. Therefore, course instructors must determine how much or how little of it should be covered in such courses.

USE OF INFERENTIAL STATISTICS

Descriptive statistics involves data from an entire population, while inferential statistics involves data from a sample of the larger population. Because it is virtually impossible to measure every element in a population, sample data are used to make inferences about the population based upon estimates of population parameters.

While there is always the potential for error in this approach, statisticians have developed mathematical models and established techniques in which the sample mean, x, is an unbiased estimator of the population mean, u. The theory underlying these techniques is based upon the central limit theorem as it applies to a sampling distribution.

SAMPLING DISTRIBUTION AND
THE CENTRAL LIMIT THEOREM

A sampling distribution merely involves calculation of the means from a large number of samples, all of the same size. Using this approach, one establishes a sampling distribution of sample means with the mean of this distribution (mean of sample means) being the same as the population mean, and the sample means being normally distributed around the mean of the distribution, with a standard deviation which approximates the population standard deviation. These qualities are the foundation of the *central limit theorem,* which states that "if random samples of a fixed N are drawn from *any* population (regardless of the form of the population distribution), as N becomes larger, the distribution of sample means approaches normality."[2] This suggests that, if we base our estimate of the population mean on a *single* sample drawn from the population, it is likely to be closer to the actual parameter as we increase the size of the sample.

It is difficult to identify the exact size of a sample required to approximate the population from which it is drawn, because the needed sample size depends on the shape of the population distribution. Some statisticians have specified thirty as the minimum sample size, while others suggest larger samples. Commonly, one establishes a sample which is within the economic and time constraints of the investigator. Specific sample sizes have been established for various size populations which allow for different degrees of precision as relating to the representativeness of the sample.

Chapter 8 pointed out that about 68 percent of all scores fall between $+1$ and -1 standard deviation units from the mean, and approximately 95 percent of all scores fall between $+2$ and -2 standard deviation units. This provides the basis for the estimation of population parameters from sample statistics—the core element in inferential statistics. Thus, 95 percent of all sample means, theoretically, will fall within two standard deviation units from the population mean. Essentially, this is what we do when we assess recreation behavior in a community or an institution; we draw conclusions regarding the larger population from data obtained from a sample of residents. The application of inferential statistics may be illustrated in the process of hypothesis testing.

STEPS OF HYPOTHESIS TESTING[3]

Generally, hypothesis testing involves five basic steps, as follows:

ESTABLISHING THE HYPOTHESIS TO BE INVESTIGATED

In Chapter 3, the nature of a hypothesis was explained. It is a proposition that is stated in testable form and predicts a particular relationship between two or more variables. In the actual research effort, the *null* hypothesis is always stated. This specifies that no relationship exists between the populations being compared. A statistical test is conducted to determine the probability that the null hypothesis is false and thus rejected. If the null hypothesis is rejected, the alternative hypothesis, which states that there is a relationship between the variables under investigation, is accepted.

ESTABLISHING CRITERIA FOR REJECTING THE NULL HYPOTHESIS

Since inferential statistics involves sample data, there is always the possibility of error. For example, the fact that two sample means are different from each other may be due to sampling error rather than a true difference in the two populations. The question becomes: At what point are the sample differences observed truly due to differences between the populations under investigation? To assist in answering this question, the researcher must select a level of significance. A significance level is based on the degree of probability that these differences are due to sampling error. If the probability is small enough, we reject the null hypothesis and conclude that true differences exist among our results. The significance level is usually set at 0.05 (5 percent of the time), or 0.01 (1 percent of the time). At the first level of significance, we conclude that the differences observed are due to sampling error 5 percent of the time or less, or conversely that they are due to real differences 95 percent of the time or more; thus, we reject the null hypothesis.

Although these levels are arbitrarily set, researchers normally feel the chances of differences being due to sampling error are too great to reject the null hypothesis beyond the 0.01 or 0.05 level. It should be pointed out that level of significance is sometimes referred to as the *alpha* level or level of probability, in the literature.

CALCULATING THE OBSERVED VALUE

Each inferential statistical test involves calculation of an observed value based upon the data collected. Various formulas have been established for calculating the observed value for appropriate inferential tests. As will be explained later, they may include: *t*-value, *F*-value, or *r*-value. These values are then compared to a critical value.

CALCULATING THE CRITICAL VALUE

Each statistical test has an accompanying critical value associated with it, based upon the size of the sample(s) and the level of significance chosen by the researcher. The critical value is the criterion which the observed value must meet or exceed for the null hypothesis to be rejected. As a more stringent level of significance is chosen, the critical value will necessarily increase. These criterion values have been established by statisticians and are available in tables in many statistics textbooks.

ACCEPTING OR REJECTING THE NULL HYPOTHESIS

This final step involves comparison of the observed value and the critical value for the appropriate statistical procedure. If the observed value is lower than the critical value, the researcher accepts the null hypothesis and normally indicates that there is *no* significant difference or relationship between the groups or variables under investigation. On the other hand, if the observed value is higher than the critical value, the researcher rejects the null hypothesis and accepts the alternative hypothesis, indicating that there *is* a significant difference or relationship.

In the literature, the researcher usually reports the probability level at which the null hypothesis was rejected. This is done in symbolic form where, for example, $p \leq 0.05$ indicates that the probability of the differences being due to sampling error was less than or equal to 5 times out of 100.

ERRORS IN HYPOTHESIS TESTING: TYPE I AND TYPE II ERRORS

The decision to accept or reject the null hypothesis always has the possibility of being incorrect because of the use of sample statistics to estimate population parameters. The conjectured differences or lack of differences may be due to sampling errors rather than the true nature of the populations under investigation. Because of this situation, we have the possibility of rejecting the null hypothesis when it is true (type I error) or accepting the null hypothesis when it is actually false (type II error).

The chance of making a type I error is equal to the level of significance established by the researcher. For example, at a significance level of 0.05, there are 5 chances out of 100 that the sample statistic is large enough to reject the null hypothesis when it is true. The researcher may wish to keep the likelihood of type I error as small as possible and may therefore use more stringent levels of significance, such as 0.01 or 0.001.

Unfortunately, there is no simple rule for the probability of making a type II error. However, type I and type II errors are inversely related; as the probability of making a type I error increases, the probability of making a type II error decreases. Whether the researcher should be more concerned about a type I or type II error depends on the nature of the investigation. If one is more concerned about making a type I error, the level of significance should be made more stringent, as indicated earlier. If, on the other hand, the researcher is more concerned about a type II error, the level of significance can be kept lower (for example, from 0.01 to 0.05). Table 9.1 presents a graphic display of the two types of errors.

TABLE 9.1

Errors in Decisions Based on Sample Statistics

	Reject H_o	Accept H_o
H_o is true in population	type I Error p	Correct
H_o is false in population	Correct	Type II Error

ONE-TAILED VERSUS TWO-TAILED TESTS

In many research situations, the null hypothesis is stated as: $u_1 = u_2$ where u_1 is the mean of population 1 and u_2 is the mean of population 2. Therefore, one has the possibility of rejecting the null if u_1 is significantly larger or smaller than u_2. In this case, the hypothesis testing is considered to be a two-tailed test since it is sensitive to significant differences in either direction. A study comparing males and females on their levels of leisure satisfaction would involve a two-tailed test because we would be looking for differences in either direction (i.e., are levels of males greater than or less than those of females?)

There are times, however, when the nature of the differences is hypothesized more specifically. Rather than look for significant differences in either direction, the researcher may be interested only in exploring differences in one direction. In such a case, the alternative hypothesis would be directional (for example $u_1 > u_2$) and the null hypothesis would state $u_1 \leq u_2$ (mean 1 is less than or equal to mean 2). When a test is concerned only with directional differences, it is called a one-tailed test.

For example, if we wish to examine the effects of a corporate recreation program on work productivity, we may decide to measure only the positive effects of the program. Thus, the null would be: u_1 (control group) $\geq u_2$ (treatment group), and the alternative hypothesis would be $u_1 < u_2$.

If the nature of the relationship is unknown, the researcher should use a two-tailed test. Only when the researcher is relatively certain of the direction of the relationship should a one-tailed test be used.

PARAMETRIC AND NONPARAMETRIC STATISTICS

The information presented thus far provides a basis of understanding for the broad area of statistical analysis called parametric statistics. Hypotheses that are tested using such procedures must meet certain assumptions. For example, one must assume that the variables being studied are normally distributed in the population from which the sample is drawn. Also, when two or more groups are being investigated, it is assumed that these groups have equal variances. Third, although researchers may not be as adamant regarding this criterion, it is normally required that parametric procedures be used only with interval-level data. As an exception, within the social and behavioral sciences many investigators use parametric procedures with certain types of ordinal data, including Likert-scaled questions.

Nonparametric statistics, on the other hand, are considered distribution-free procedures. Researchers would use such procedures when they feel the data deviate sharply from these assumptions. However, since many parametric procedures are robust with respect to assumptions regarding normal distribution and homogeneity of variances, nonparametric procedures are generally selected only when the sample size is quite small (for example, less than thirty subjects), or the data cannot be assumed to be at least at the interval level of measurement. In general, researchers prefer parametric procedures because they are more powerful than nonparametric ones.

STATISTICAL PROCEDURES

The following section discusses a number of frequently used inferential statistical procedures. Its purpose is to provide a conceptual understanding of these procedures, and not to present detailed mathematical formulas underlying them. The emphasis is on explaining the uses of these procedures, within the overall framework of inferential statistics.

TESTING HYPOTHESES OF POPULATION MEANS AND VARIANCES

One of the most common uses of hypothesis testing is to determine if a sample mean is significantly different from the population from which it was drawn, or to determine if two or more group means arise from different populations or the same population.

One Sample Case for Means

Assume that our purpose is to determine if a particular sample of adults ($N = 60$) participated in camping to the same extent as the general population within the state of Pennsylvania. From our sample of adults, we find that the average number of participation days per year is: $\bar{x} = 9.1$ days/year, with a standard deviation of $s = 2.4$. Also, we learn from the 1985 State Recreation Plan that the average number of participation days for all adults in the state is 11.2. To determine if our sample is significantly different from the population, we would use the t-test based on the t-distribution. The t-distribution is used in this type of analysis rather than the normal distribution, because the population's standard deviation is unknown. The t-distribution approximates the normal distribution with a slightly larger distribution of scores at each end of the curve. We can use the t-test because we meet the general assumption of parametric statistics and our data are interval scale of measurement. Since we will be using a two-tailed t-test (nondirectional), our null hypothesis will be: H_o: $u = 11.2$, and the alternative hypothesis will be: H_a:$u \neq 11.2$. The population mean, u, is used in the hypothesis, since we are using sample statistics to estimate population parameters. The formula for the t-test is:

$$t = \frac{\bar{x} - u}{s_{\bar{x}}}$$

where $\bar{x}$ is the sample mean, u is the population mean, and $s_{\bar{x}}$ is the estimated standard error of the mean. The standard error of the mean is an unbiased estimate of the population's standard deviation derived from the sample's standard deviation, using the following formula, $s_{\bar{x}} = s/\sqrt{n-1}$, where n is the sample size.

Therefore, $s_{\bar{x}} = 2.4/\sqrt{60-1} = 0.31$.

Then $t = \dfrac{(\bar{x} - u)}{s_{\bar{x}}} = \dfrac{(9.1 - 11.2)}{0.31} = \dfrac{-2.1}{.31} = 6.77$.

This value is referred to as a t-observed, or simply the t-value.

DEGREES OF FREEDOM. The concept of degrees of freedom is critical to the hypothesis-testing process. The term "degrees of freedom" refers to the number of independent observations minus the number of parameters being estimated in the procedure. In this case, there are sixty independent observations and we are estimating one population parameter, u. Thus, the degrees of freedom is $N-1$, or 59. Using the appropriate degrees of freedom and the selected level of significance, the researcher is able to determine the t-critical value.

From a table of t-critical values presented in most statistics books we would find the t-critical value for this example to be 2.00 when the df = 59 and the level of significance is 0.05. Our t-observed value is larger than the t-critical value; therefore, we reject the null hypothesis and accept the alternative hypothesis, which states that the annual number of camping days for our selected group of sixty adults was significantly different from the general adult population in Pennsylvania. In comparing the means, one would conclude the sample of adults participated significantly less than the general population.

Differences Between the Sample Means (Independent Samples)

In recreation research, we rarely compare sample data to population data. Instead, we tend to compare two different groups on selected variables. For example, if we were interested in knowing whether residents' attitudes toward leisure services varied significantly in two communities, we might randomly select two samples of adults from each community, with each sample consisting of 100 adults. Using a leisure attitude scale, we would determine scores for both groups. Our null hypothesis would be: H_o: u_1 = u_2. The alternative hypothesis would be: H_a: $u_1 \neq u_2$. Since we are looking for possible variations in either direction, this would be a two-tailed test. We can use a t-test since our investigation meets the basic requirements for parametric statistics and only two groups are involved (a t-test is not appropriate for more than two groups).

However, in this analysis we must use a different formula from the previous analysis, since we are comparing two independently drawn sample means rather than comparing a sample to the population. The appropriate formula is

$$t = \frac{\bar{x}_1 - \bar{x}_2}{\text{SD}_{\bar{x}}}$$

where $\bar{x}_1$ is the mean for town one, $\bar{x}_2$ is the mean for town 2, and $\text{SD}_{\bar{x}}$ is the standard error of the difference, which is a variability measure based upon the standard deviations from the two samples.

The formula for the $\text{SD}_{\bar{x}}$ is quite simple, although it looks rather involved:

$$SD_{\bar{x}} = \sqrt{\frac{N_1 s_1^2 + N_2 s_2^2}{N_1 + N_2 - 2} \left(\frac{1}{N_1} + \frac{1}{N_2}\right)}$$

In this formula, s_1 is the standard deviation for town 1, s_2 is the standard deviation for town 2, N_1 is the sample size for town 1, and N_2 is the sample size for town 2. The appropriate degrees of freedom is $N_1 + N_2 - 2$. Given $\bar{x}_1 = 8.2$, $\bar{x}_2 = 7.9$, $s_1 = 2.26$, and $s_2 = 2.10$, t-observed is 0.976 and t-critical is 1.96 for 198 degrees of freedom at the .05 level of significance. Therefore, we retain the null hypothesis and conclude that there is not a significant difference between the residents of the two towns regarding leisure attitudes and any differences we found were due to sampling error alone.

Difference Between Two Sample Means (Correlated Samples)

In many recreation studies, the t-test is used with correlated samples. For example, one may measure the level of leisure satisfaction of a group of individuals prior to their enrollment in a leisure education program, and following the completion of the class, to determine if there has been a significant change in their satisfaction. This is referred to as a "repeated measures" design.

In other situations, a researcher may match two groups of subjects on characteristics which are related to the specific variables under investigation. For example, if we wished to compare male and female institutionalized mentally retarded adults on their levels of leisure participation, using an observation procedure, we would match the groups of subjects with respect to length of institutionalization and I.Q., since these factors are likely to affect their level of participation. This approach is simply referred to as a "matched pairs" design; each pair of males and females in the study is matched, based on both factors.

The measurement in both of these studies is likely to be correlated. For example, if a subject scored the highest on the pretest for leisure satisfaction, she would also tend to score the highest on the posttest as well. We would therefore use a correlated t-test which takes this condition into account, such as the "direct difference" method. Applying this method, we use only the differences between the pairs of observations and not the means for the repeated measurement on the matched pairs. This would enable us to test the null hypothesis to determine whether there is a significant difference between subjects' pre- and posttest scores on leisure satisfaction, and thus make a statement regarding the effectiveness of the leisure education program. This judgment would be a limited one, in that we did not use a control group for comparison.

The formula for the correlated t-test is:

$$t = \frac{\bar{D}}{S_{\bar{x}_D}}$$

where $\bar{D}$ is the mean of differences between the pairs of observations and $S_{\bar{x}_D}$ is the standard error of the mean of the differences. The mean of the differences ($\bar{D}$) is found by summing the differences (ΣD) and dividing by the number of pairs, N. The standard error of the mean of the differences ($S_{\bar{x}_D}$) can be determined by dividing S_D, the standard deviation of the differences, by the square root of $N-1$ or $\sqrt{N-1}$. The formula for the standard deviation of the differences is:

$$S_D = \sqrt{\frac{\Sigma D^2}{N} - \bar{D}^2}$$

Finally, the degrees of freedom is equal to $N-1$. The t-critical value is again found using a table of t-values for varying degrees of freedom and significance levels.

Difference Between More than Two Sample Means: ANOVA

The t-test is an appropriate statistical test for comparing the means of two groups. However, when more than two groups are involved in the investigation, a different statistical test is required. The simplest test for comparing the means among two or more groups is the one-way analysis of variance (ANOVA), a parametric statistic.

A one-way ANOVA involves one independent variable (therefore one-way) and one dependent variable. The independent variable is normally either a nominal or ordinal scale of measurement involving two or more categories. ANOVA serves the same purpose as a t-test but can be extended for use with more than two groups. It should be pointed out that the term "groups" refers to the various categories of the independent variable. The hypothesis-testing process is similar to the process followed with the t-test, except that the null hypothesis may involve more than two groups. For example, we may investigate the number of times (dependent variable) randomly selected residents from four sections of town (independent variable with four categories) use the town's community park in one year. This type of investigation meets all the assumptions necessary for ANOVA: *(a)* the dependent variable is measured on the interval or ratio scale of measurement, *(b)* the residents are randomly selected, *(c)* the populations from which the residents are selected are normally distributed, and *(d)* the populations from which the sample is drawn have approximately the same variability (homogeneity of variance). The last two assumptions cannot be directly determined; however, we assume them to be true unless there is strong evidence to the contrary.

The results of a one-way ANOVA are commonly presented in a summary table. While various formats are used, certain items are normally included, as shown in Table 9.2, which is a summary table for the investigation just suggested.

TABLE 9-2

Example of ANOVA: Use of Park By Four Neighborhoods' Residents

Source	Degree of Freedom	SS	MS	F-Value
Between groups (section of town)	3	90	30	6
Within groups	196	980	5	
Total	199	1070		

The values in this table are fictitious and are used merely for illustrative purposes. The first column, labeled Source, describes the variation in scores among the residents in the study. Part of the variation in scores is attributed to the section of town in which residents live; this is presented in the Between Groups data. A second part of the variation is attributed to the different responses provided by residents within each group, and is referred to under Within Groups variation. The second column refers to the degrees of freedom for the three sources of variation. The Between Groups degree of freedom is calculated by subtracting 1 from the number of groups involved $(4 - 1 = 3)$. The Within Groups degree of freedom is the total number of subjects (4 groups, each with 50 subjects), minus 4 groups equals 196 degrees of freedom. The total degrees of freedom is merely the sum of the two previous degrees of freedom $(3 + 196 = 199)$.

The SS (sums of squares) is a measure of variability of scores. A relatively complicated procedure is used to calculate each SS, and it is beyond the scope of this textbook for presentation. The MS (mean square) column is a ratio of the SS divided by the degree of freedom for each Source. The F column contains only one value, and is found by dividing MS between groups by MS within groups. In this case, the resulting F-value would be 6. The F-value (also known as F-observed) is the most critical item of information in the table; it is compared to the critical F-value to determine if there are significant differences among the four groups (sections of town). If the comparison were to show that F-observed is larger than F-critical, we would reject the null hypothesis and conclude that there is a significant difference among the four sections of town. As with the t-critical value, F-critical is found using a table of F values for the associated Between and Within groups degrees of freedom and the selected level of significance.

It must be pointed out that the ANOVA procedure tells us only that there is a significant difference somewhere among the four sections of town, but does not tell us specifically where this is. In order to determine this, one would use any of several post hoc procedures to analyze each possible pair of means to determine which ones were significantly different from the others.

EXTENDED FORMS OF ANOVA: Analysis of variance is a very versatile procedure which can be used for a variety of research designs. In this section, we will describe three of the most common extensions of the basic ANOVA model: factorial design, repeated measures design, and analysis of covariance.

Factorial designs: A factorial design involves more than one independent variable (factor). If we were interested in the effects of gender and age on one's attitude toward leisure, we would use a two-way ANOVA procedure. The "two-way" refers to two independent factors: gender and age. Each factor has a specific number of categories, normally referred to as levels. Obviously, gender has two levels, male and female. However, age may have several categories; it is up to the discretion of the researcher to determine these. To illustrate, age might be categorized into three groups: young adults (20 to 35), middle adults (36 to 60), and older adults (60 plus). The two-way ANOVA would be a 2 x 3 ANOVA, with the 2 and the 3 indicating the levels of the factors (gender and age), respectively. The factorial design can be logically extended to more than two factors, but rarely do these designs go beyond three factors in the recreation literature.

A factorial design not only allows the researcher to examine the effect or influence of each factor; it also allows one to analyze the effect of two or more factors in combination with each other. This is referred to as the "interaction effect," while the effects of the individual factors are called the "main effects." To illustrate the interaction effect of age and gender on leisure attitudes, we have constructed a fictitious set of scores which show group means of scores on a leisure attitudes test (see Table 9.3).

TABLE 9-3

Factorial Design of Leisure Attitudes Interaction by Age and Gender

		Gender		
		Male	**Female**	
Age	Young adults	$\bar{x} = 38$	$\bar{x} = 27$	$\bar{x} = 33$
	Middle-aged adults	$\bar{x} = 32$	$\bar{x} = 32$	$\bar{x} = 33$
	Older adults	$\bar{x} = 27$	$\bar{x} = 38$	$\bar{x} = 33$
		$\bar{x} = 33$	$\bar{x} = 33$	

Examining the overall means (means outside the cells on right side and below) would suggest that males and females, as well as the three different age groups, all have the same leisure attitude. However, the individual cells show that in fact males and females are different at two of the age groups, and leisure attitudes are inversely related across age. This illustrates the importance of the interaction effect; it allows us to determine the effect of a factor at each level of the other factors. If we had conducted two one-way ANOVA analyses, this potential interaction effect would not have been detected. In research reports, it is frequently depicted in graphic format.

Repeated measures design: Often, studies are carried out in which subjects are tested or measured more than once. For example, we might test subjects during each of the four seasons to determine if their leisure satisfaction varies with respect to the time of year. In such a case, we would have four repeated measures on the same subject. Or, we might compare a group (treatment or experimental group) of subjects who went through a leisure education program with a group (control group) that received no special program. We would test both groups before the program and at its completion to determine any potential behavioral or attitude change.

The one-way or factorial ANOVAs previously discussed are not appropriate for either of these situations because they do not account for inherent relationships between the individual subject's repeated measures (i.e., the fact that one has already taken a given test might influence performance on a retest). The ANOVA for repeated measures is developed specifically to calculate such possible influence and its summary table is similar to the more basic ANOVA except that it includes a separate "error" term to estimate the effect of the test-retest procedure.

As shown earlier (see pg. 64), the pre-post testing procedure with a control group is one of the most common experimental research designs. The ANOVA for repeated measures is an appropriate analysis to use with this design, and is commonly referred to as a 2 x 2 ANOVA with repeated measures. In it, there are two factors, each with two levels. Factor one is a grouping factor, with the two levels being the treatment group and the control group. Factor two is the testing factor, with the two levels being the pretest and posttest. This analysis also involves an interaction effect, since it is a factorial design and is intended specifically to measure the influence of experimental variables. Theoretically, the researcher hopes to find no difference between the two groups in the pretest procedure, but a substantial difference in the posttest. The interaction effect permits the researcher to make this kind of determination.

Analysis of covariance (ANCOVA):   In many instances, two or more groups of subjects are compared on a dependent variable. In such studies, it is important that the groups be as similar as possible; for example, if we are examining the effect of a recreation program on mentally retarded participants in two groups, it is essential to have comparable ability levels in both groups at the outset. Since it is not always possible to hand-pick subjects in order to match them exactly, the analysis of covariance procedure is used. A comparison of group means on the dependent variable is conducted, after they are adjusted for the influence of the covariate variable.

When using the traditional pre- and posttest, treatment-and-control group experimental design, for example, the covariate may be the pretest score for the two groups. The posttest scores are adjusted on the basis of the covariate (pretest) scores and then compared to determine if there is a significant difference between the groups. The covariate need not always be the pretest score; it may be any characteristic which the researcher believes may be influencing the study results, and may in fact be more than one characteristic. Analysis of covariance may be used with one-way, factorial, or repeated measure designs. Summary tables are similar to other ANOVA tables, except that the results are adjusted for the covariate. This procedure is most useful when the covariate exerts a strong influence on the dependent variable.

TESTS OF ASSOCIATION

Chapter 8 points out that there are many situations in recreation research where the investigator wishes to learn whether two or more variables are related. By determining this, it is possible to achieve a fuller understanding of leisure behavior or other phenomena. The measures of association that are used in descriptive statistics may also be extended to inferential analysis. In this section, we will discuss several measures of association which may be used to make inferences about relationships among variables in recreation research.

CHI-SQUARE TEST

Since much of the data collected in recreation research is on the nominal or ordinal scale of measurement, one of the most common statistical tests applied is the chi-square test. It is referred to as a test of independence because the researcher seeks to learn whether the distribution of scores on the variables being investigated are independent of each other, or related in some way. Chi-square is considered a nonparametric test because it need not meet all the assumptions established for parametric statistics. It may be used with data sets which meet the assumptions for parametric statistics, except that they are not interval- or ratio-level data. However, simple random samples must be used to justify generalizing findings to the population under investigation.

Chi-square analysis is frequently used with analysis of demographic variables. Cheek, for example, conducted a study to determine the use of parks by individuals on different occupational levels.[4] Subjects were queried regarding their use of local parks, and were classified as "blue-collar" or "white-collar." Cheek's null hypothesis stated that the two variables (use of parks and occupational level) were independent of each other; i.e., that there was no association or relationship between them. The data fit a 2 x 2 table, in that there were two levels of each variable; occupation was blue-collar or white-collar and park attendance was either "yes" or "no." Cheek's finding was that the chi-square value (X^2) for the data was 0.151, which did not exceed the critical value of 3.841, which was identified through a chi-square table of critical values. At the 0.05 level of significance, this meant that the null hypothesis was retained and that park attendance was not related to occupational level.

Chi-square tests may be used with more than two variables, and with more than two levels as well. However, more than three variables are rarely investigated simultaneously, since interpretation becomes much more complex with greater numbers and/or levels of variables. It is suggested that the minimum number of subjects needed for chi-square analysis is the product of the variable levels multiplied by five. For example, if an investigation has three levels of one variable and two levels of a second variable, the number of subjects needed would be $3 \times 2 \times 5 = 30$ subjects.

The chi-square test for independence indicates whether or not there is a relationship between two or more variables, but does not measure the strength of the relationship. It is possible to obtain a significant X^2 when the strength of the relationship is quite weak; after rejecting the null hypothesis in a chi-square analysis, one would then use other measures such as Cramer's V to determine the actual strength of the relationship. In studies where variables are measured at the ordinal level, Gamma and Kendall's tau are useful procedures, since they are more appropriate for ordinal variables than is chi-square analysis. Both measures are nonparametric and can therefore be used with data which are not normally distributed in the population.

SPEARMAN RANK-ORDER CORRELATION COEFFICIENT

Spearman rank-order correlation coefficient (rho or r_s) is another correlational procedure appropriate for use with ordinal level data. It is a nonparametric procedure, although it has many similarities to the product-moment coefficient of correlation. Like the product-moment coefficient of correlation, Spearman rho has a range of $+1$ to -1, with a value of 0 indicating no relationship. Both of these procedures can be used as descriptive or inferential measures, and tests of significance can be conducted for both. The Spearman rho is used, however, when data represent subjects' rankings on variables under investigation.

PRODUCT-MOMENT COEFFICIENT OF CORRELATION(r)

This procedure was described as a descriptive statistic in Chapter 8. However, the product-moment coefficient of correlation can also be used for inferential tests. When this is done, a test of significance must be conducted to determine if the r-observed value is large enough to confirm a true relationship between the variables under investigation. A null hypothesis is established and tested at significance levels that are usually at the 0.05 or 0.01 levels. The r-observed value is compared to the r-critical value, which is identified using a table of critical values.

To use the product-moment coefficient of correlation, interval- or ratio-level data must be used. However, in some situations when ordinal data have been collected using Likert-type instruments, data have been assumed to meet the criteria of interval data and the product-moment method has been used. All other assumptions for parametric statistical procedures must be met. It is essential not to interpret a high correlation as a *causal* relationship between the variables under investigation. The coefficient of correlation merely states that there is a relationship between the variables, but *not* that one causes the other.

BIVARIATE REGRESSION

Beyond exploring the relationship between two variables, the researcher may also use one variable to predict the value of another. Bivariate regression is used in this process. To illustrate the use of bivariate regression analysis, you might apply it to the task of predicting the number of days adult members at a private swim club use the pool facilities during the season. Suspecting that there is a relationship between members' ages and their use of the pool, you randomly sample all adult members, to learn their ages and frequency of pool visits. Finding a strong positive product-moment correlation (r) between these two variables, you use a regression formula to predict how many days present or new members will use the pool, with age serving as the "predictor" variable and pool use referred to as the "criterion" variable.

The square of the correlation (r^2) between the predictor and criterion variables has significance to regression analysis. This value, known as the coefficient of determination, is the proportion of change in the criterion variable which can be explained by the predictor variable. For example, if we know the correlation between age and pool use is $r = 0.80$, then the coefficient of determination is $(0.80)^2$ or 0.64, which means 64 percent (moving the decimal point two places) of the difference in members' use of the pool can be explained by knowing their age. The coefficient of determination is commonly presented in the literature because it provides some indication of the usefulness of the regression equation. In the above example, one would indicate that age is a good predictor of pool use because a value of 0.64 is a relatively high coefficient in the behavioral and social sciences.

Bivariate regression analysis must meet all the assumptions for parametric procedures, and the variables involved must be at least at the interval level of measurement. However, as in product-moment correlation procedures, ordinal data may be assumed to meet the criterion for interval data when a Likert-type instrument has been used.

MULTIPLE REGRESSION

To predict behavior based on more than one predictor variable, multiple regression is used. This is an extension of bivariate regression, in which an overall coefficient of determination (R^2) is determined, as well as individual regression coefficients for each of the predictor variables. It makes it possible to determine the relative contribution of each predictor variable to the prediction of the criterion variable. This procedure is often used in recreation research when investigators seek to predict future recreation behavior.

OTHER STATISTICAL PROCEDURES

Thus far we have generally focused on procedures involving one independent variable in relation to one dependent variable. However, there are several statistical procedures which are used to examine the influence of several independent variables on one or more dependent variables. These are usually referred to as multivariate procedures. Some of the most common ones used in recreation research include: multiple regression, factor analysis, cluster analysis, canonical correlation, and discriminant analysis. Brief explanations of each of these follow; for a more detailed description the reader should consult an advanced textbook on statistical procedures.[5]

FACTOR ANALYSIS

Factor analysis should be thought of as a reduction technique, in which many items are reduced to fewer items based on their underlying dimensions or factors. The interrelationships of a multitude of items are analyzed, and subgroups of variables which reveal a high degree of interrelationship are combined into a single dimension or factor. This process is repeated until all potential relationships have been explored, and one has established the commonalities among related items.

As an example of the use of factor analysis in recreation-related research, Allen used it to group fifty-one leisure activities based upon respondents' stated level of interest in each activity.[6] The analysis resulted in grouping the activities under nine basic headings, according to the common elements within each such subgroup. The nine headings, or factors, were: outdoor activities, sports, hobby-domestic, social interaction, mechanics, cultural-intellectual, swimming, nature, and chance. Activities such as canoeing, motorboating, snow skiing, or tobogganing were most highly related to the "outdoor active" factor. The "social-interaction" factor included activities such as dancing, parties, social drinking, and visiting friends. The analysis found that interests in leisure activities were highly interrelated and generally such activities could be grouped into nine areas. To enrich the understanding of these factors, one might then explore the common elements in the activities within each factor, beyond the superficial analysis which was conducted to identify and label the factors.

CLUSTER ANALYSIS

This procedure is used to establish groups of highly similar entities. In this sense, it is similar to factor analysis. However, while factor analysis is usually employed to examine the interrelationship among variables, cluster analysis is normally used to classify or group sets of individuals that have a high degree of interrelationship.

Cluster analysis normally begins by gathering a data set of information on a sample of subjects. From this information, the researcher seeks to establish homogeneous groups (clusters) of individuals, in which those within each cluster have a higher level of similarity to each other than they do to those in other clusters. The most important step in conducting cluster analysis is the selection of variables that best represent the theoretical base of the study. Cluster analysis has been used extensively in market segmentation studies which group individuals into homogeneous subgroups according to their consumer behavior or preference. In the tourism literature, a number of studies have grouped participants according to the types of experiences they are seeking. To illustrate, Mazanea used cluster analysis to segment vacation travelers according to the benefits they sought.[7] He found three clusters: *(a)* one that exhibited interest in all the varied attractions in a vacation spot, *(b)* one that had a high interest in swimming and other aquatic activities, and *(c)* one that was most interested in the natural environment and beautiful landscapes. Once such homogeneous clusters have been established, it is possible to examine the demographic characteristics of each cluster, and thus to promote specific vacation destinations to appropriate segments of the potential tourist population.

DISCRIMINANT ANALYSIS

While cluster analysis is used to identify homogeneous groups of individuals, discriminant analysis is a method of studying the differences between two or more groups of subjects or objects in terms of several variables simultaneously. ANOVA or *t*-tests may be used to look at differences between groups with respect to a single variable or two or more variables independently. However, these techniques do not take into account the interrelationship among the variables, as discriminant analysis does.

Discriminant analysis is frequently used in recreation research today. For example, Rossman conducted a study which examined differences among five groups of participants, using eight leisure satisfaction dimensions as the discriminating variables.[8] Recreation participants were categorized into one of five groups, based upon the type of program format in which they participated most frequently. These formats were: *(a)* leader-directed groups, *(b)* leagues and tournaments, *(c)* instructional classes, *(d)* open facilities, and *(e)* special events. The eight leisure satisfaction dimensions were: achievement, autonomy, environment, family escape, fun, physical fitness, risk, and social enjoyment. Rossman found that there were significant differences among the five format groups, in terms of the leisure satisfaction dimensions, with achievement, family escape, environment, and social enjoyment being the most influential elements.

As with other multivariate procedures, an advanced understanding of statistical methods is necessary to conduct and interpret discriminant analysis. However, because of its increasing use and the availability of computerized statistical packages, it is becoming more readily accessible to those with limited statistical skills.

CANONICAL CORRELATIONS

Canonical correlation can be viewed as an extension of multiple regression analysis, where there is a set of criterion variables rather than a single one. It is possible to investigate a combination of criterion variables in relation to a set of predictor variables. The procedure is quite useful in recreation research since leisure phenomena are rarely related to each other on a one-to-one basis, without other influences playing a part.

For example, Buchanan used canonical-correlation analysis to identify the relationship between "secondary" recreation activities and the satisfaction derived from fishing trips.[9] Secondary activities, the nonfishing experiences encountered on a fishing trip, were investigated for a group of fishermen, along with twenty scores of leisure satisfaction. The extent to which each fisherman participated in a group of secondary activities served as the set of predictor variables, while the twenty leisure satisfaction scores constituted the set of criterion variables. Buchanan found a number of significant relationships between predictor and criterion variables. For example, the first such relationship (referred to as a canonical variate) showed that the secondary activities of visiting with others, going for a walk, and sitting around a campfire were highly related to the satisfactions of meeting new people, being with friends, and showing off equipment. He found three remaining canonical variates revealing relationships between different sets of secondary activities and leisure satisfactions. This method of analysis is extremely helpful to recreation researchers and planners because it closely approximates human behaviors in which a variety of satisfactions may be sought from different leisure experiences. Canonical-correlation analysis takes into account the interrelationships within each set of information as well as relationships across sets of information.

LIMITS OF QUANTIFICATION

It is worth repeating, in concluding this chapter, that statistics are only as useful as the data provided them. We tend to have an inordinate respect for quantification, as shown in the statement, "If it can't be expressed in figures, it is not science; it is opinion." As a society, we have respected numbers because they are very recognizable and appear to deal with hard, measurable facts as opposed to nonquantifiable elements. However, too often numbers themselves may be carelessly gathered and meaningless.

Therefore, it must be stressed that even the most sophisticated forms of statistical analysis cannot compensate for sloppy research work, and that quantification is not the *only* form of useful research. Other types of qualitative research, involving historical, philosophical, or other conceptual or model-building but nonempirical studies can also contribute greatly to our knowledge. At the same time, the fact that we can carry out complex statistical analyses using the methods described in this chapter means that we are able today to gather a wealth of useful information and to understand much more about the nature of leisure motivations and experiences than in the past.

SUMMARY

This chapter describes a number of important principles and methods used in inferential statistics, ranging from sampling distribution and the central limit theorem to hypothesis testing, ANOVA, and several multivariate procedures. It should be stressed again that the descriptions provided here are not intended to *teach* readers to carry out the procedures, but rather to familiarize them with the purposes and general approach of each procedure. Normally, those who seek to become more advanced researchers must take at least two or three courses in statistics—and sometimes several more, to become expert in a variety of specialized methods.

The chapter concludes with a warning about the uncritical acceptance of quantification and statistical analysis as the basis for scholarly research. Other forms of analysis can provide valuable insights to complement those derived from quantitative and statistical investigations.

ENDNOTES

1. John W. Best, *Research in Education* (Englewood Cliffs, N.J.: Prentice-Hall, Inc., 1981): 269.
2. Sidney M. Stahl and James D. Hennes, *Reading and Understanding Applied Statistics* (St. Louis, Mo.: C. V. Mosby Co., 1980): 148.
3. Schuyler W. Huck, William H. Cormier, and William G. Burch, Jr., *Readings in Statistics and Research* (New York: Harper and Row, 1974).
4. Neil Cheek, Jr., "Toward a Sociology of Not-Work," *Pacific Sociological Review* (July 1971): 245–258.
5. William W. Cooley and Paul R. Lohnes, *Multivariate Data Analysis* (New York: John Wiley and Sons, 1971); and Richard H. Lindeman, Peter F. Merenda, and Ruth Z. Gold, *Introduction to Bivariate and Multivariate Analysis* (Glenview, Ill.: Scott, Foresman and Co., 1980).

6. Lawrence R. Allen, "The Relationship Between Murray's Personality Needs and Leisure Interests," *Journal of Leisure Research* (1st Quarter 1982): 63–76.
7. Josef A. Mazanea, "How to Select Travel Market Segments: A Clustering Approach," *Journal of Travel Research* (Summer 1984): 17–21.
8. J. Robert Rossman, "The Influence of Program Format Choice on Participant Satisfaction," *Journal of Park and Recreation Administration* (January 1984): 39–51.
9. Thomas Buchanan, "Toward an Understanding of Variability in Satisfactions Within Activities," *Journal of Leisure Research* (1st Quarter 1983): 39–51.

WORKSHOP ACTIVITIES
TO BE CARRIED OUT IN CLASS

The material covered in this chapter is too advanced for most basic courses in research and evaluation in recreation, parks, and leisure-studies department—as far as mastery of the processes is concerned. Unless the students have taken appropriate outside courses in statistics, emphasis should therefore be placed on having students understand the basic concepts that are covered, and the *use* of different statistical procedures, rather than how to actually apply them.

Therefore, the most appropriate type of assignment or workshop activity would be in-class clarification of the different procedures, followed by student reviews of articles in research journals which make use of the procedures. Using these as illustrations and with the instructor's help, they may then show how each procedure is used to handle different types of data, or with different research designs. The findings of the statistical analyses may also be reviewed and interpreted.

However, the instructor should also feel free *not* to go into detail regarding these procedures, and to consider the methods presented in Chapter 8 as sufficient statistical orientation for an introductory course.

10

PREPARING THE RESEARCH REPORT

The research task is not completed until the report has been written. The most brilliant hypothesis, the most carefully designed and
conducted study, the most striking findings, are of little import
unless they are communicated to others. Many social scientists seem
to regard the writing of a report as an unpleasant chore tacked on to
the end of the research process but not really an inherent part of
it . . . Nevertheless, communication of the results so that they
become part of the general store of knowledge is an essential part of
investigators' responsibilities; such communication should receive
the same careful attention that earlier stages do.[1]

INTRODUCTION

The full value of any piece of research or evaluation has not been
achieved until its results have been carefully compiled and
interpreted, and made available to all appropriate audiences. This
chapter examines the process of preparing research reports of various types, ranging from full scholarly dissertations or theses to
brief summaries of research addressed to professional or lay readers. It outlines the content of typical research reports and presents
guidelines with respect to organizing and developing materials, as
well as other elements of style or format.

The obligation of the researcher to present full, accurate, and
honest findings is stressed; in many cases, published reports of
research tend to emphasize only favorable findings, or to distort

results in unacceptable ways. In keeping with sound scientific principles, this chapter suggests principles underlying the publication of findings that will contribute to scholarship and improved practices in the field, and to the professional career of the researcher.

THE ROLE OF RESEARCH REPORTS

Chapter 5 points out that the final stage of the research process involves preparing a research report that sums up the entire investigation and presents a detailed account of its findings. Why is such a report necessary?

The obvious answer is that research may be carried out for many reasons—but that none of them are likely to be fulfilled unless study findings are carefully compiled and made available to appropriate audiences. If a graduate student has undertaken a research study to meet degree requirements, he or she must write a thesis or dissertation report that is defended before a graduate faculty examining committee. Beyond this, there is the obligation to submit what has been learned to the scrutiny of one's academic peers, and to contribute new knowledge to the body of scholarship that supports the professional field of parks, recreation, and leisure services.

When research or evaluation studies are carried out to test the effectiveness of a form of professional service, or the work of a leisure-service agency, it is obviously important for the findings to be precisely reported and communicated to appropriate audiences.

For the individual researcher, particularly if he or she is a university professor or holds a high administrative post in a large organization, government agency, or professional society, publishing research is a useful way of advancing one's career and developing a reputation for outstanding scholarship. For generations, the saying, "Publish or perish" described the need for university faculty members to publish in order to obtain academic tenure. In some Catholic universities, the saying was changed slightly to "Publish or parish."

In any case, it is essential that research reports be prepared at the conclusion of a study, and addressed to one or more of the following audiences: (a) the scholarly community, including both faculty members responsible for supervising studies, and the broader group of one's academic peers; (b) professionals within the field who may be interested in the subject of the research; (c) the public at large, assuming that the topic is meaningful to them; and (*d*) whatever organizations may have assisted in the conduct of the study, or that may have commissioned or supported it financially.

TYPES OF RESEARCH REPORTS

Too often, it is assumed that the only kind of research report that is meaningful is the typical blackbound thesis or dissertation report or the shorter version of it that appears in scholarly research journals. To reach varied audiences, however, one can identify a much fuller range of possibilities for disseminating research findings:

TRADITIONAL ACADEMIC RESEARCH REPORT

This is the formal academic thesis or dissertation, often hundreds of pages long, which is normally read by members of the student's committee and then filed in the university library, although it may then become available through interlibrary loan or microfilm or microfiche exchange.

INDEPENDENT PUBLICATION

Many nonacademic studies, particularly planning reports or those funded by foundation grants or other sponsors, are summed up in separately published monographs. Often they are attractively produced and illustrated and may be widely distributed. Customarily, they are less technical and scholarly and designed for a broader audience than academic reports.

ARTICLE IN SCHOLARLY JOURNAL

Many academic research studies are summed up in articles in refereed journals (meaning that they must be reviewed by a jury of qualified scholars before they can be accepted for publication). These studies tend to be similar to theses or dissertations, although they are necessarily much briefer.

ARTICLE IN PROFESSIONAL/POPULAR MAGAZINES

Research studies which have a more applied focus may be reported in articles in magazines published by professional societies or even in appropriate popular publications. They may also be summarized in research "briefs," or concise statements of findings, in such magazines.

PRESENTATIONS TO SPONSORING ORGANIZATIONS

Sponsored study findings frequently are summarized directly in presentations to trustees, boards, membership meetings, town councils, and similar groups. The verbal presentation may be accompanied by printed summaries of findings.

PRESENTATIONS AT PROFESSIONAL MEETINGS

Recreation and leisure-studies research is frequently presented at professional society meetings in two forms: (a) technical reports focusing solely on research, at research symposia, and (b) part of the content at educational sessions dealing with current issues and trends.

In addition to these forms of publication, some research studies may also reach the public broadly through news reports or special programs on network or local television, on radio "talk shows," or through newspaper articles. Particularly if a research study deals with a timely or controversial theme, it may be picked up by the wire services or the news media and receive widespread dissemination, usually in a simplified form.

The researcher who is interested in reaching as broad an audience as possible may use more than one of these channels for disseminating study findings. Obviously, reports or articles intended for a scholarly audience are likely to be more theoretical in nature and to present more technical analyses of data than those directed to a professional or popular audience. Applied studies usually have less complex statistical analyses, fewer tables, and more obvious summaries of findings and recommendations for action.

CONTENT OF SCHOLARLY RESEARCH REPORTS

There is no single prescribed format which all research reports are expected to follow.

In academic research reports, however, a typical pattern is to require a thesis or dissertation to include five chapters. The first three are essentially an extension of the study proposal, with Chapter One being the *introduction, statement of the problem, and the purposes or hypotheses* of the study, Chapter Two being the *literature review,* and Chapter Three being a *report of the methodology* as it actually occurred. In each case, the chapter is likely to be expanded from the version found in the proposal. The literature review should be a full-scale survey of the relevant research on the problem, with the purpose not only to set the stage for the research study itself, but also to demonstrate the author's scholarly capability and worthiness of holding an advanced degree. The chapter on methodology should go beyond the initial plan that was advanced at the time the proposal was approved, and should describe what actually occurred. Often, studies are not fully crystallized at the time the study plan is approved.

> During the course of the investigation, a more nearly adequate statement of the problem itself may be developed, new hypotheses may emerge, unforeseen relationships may appear. Therefore, while the original formulation provides the basic point of reference for the report, there must also be room to include subsequent developments.[2]

Following the first three chapters, Chapter Four customarily gives a detailed presentation of the actual *findings of the study*. If the study involved a survey, each of the major sections of the questionnaire returns should be reported, with the key topics assembled in sequential sections of the chapter. Normally, data are summarized in tables, followed by interpretation or explanations of their meaning. If the study was an experimental one, customarily the data would be reported as they relate to the study hypotheses, with statistical treatment indicating whether there were significant findings accepting or rejecting the hypotheses.

While it is essential to include all important details in this chapter, the author may choose to be selective by presenting the most critical findings directly, and including other sections of materials in the appendix of the report. However, this must *not* distort the actual findings or implications of the research, which must be presented fully and clearly. Since data may be presented in varied ways, this text will not attempt to present any single model; instead, the reader is advised to examine a number of theses, dissertations, or other scholarly reports, to see how findings are typically analyzed and summarized.

The final chapter *summarizes the conclusions* reached by the study. Without repeating the data and their meaning at length, it draws out and presents the highlights of the research. It also interprets them in the light of the theoretical or conceptual framework presented in the first two chapters, and shows how they may support or challenge the findings of other studies. If findings are surprising in any way, the author may give his or her interpretation of why they occurred as they did, and what their implications are. Finally, Chapter Five should conclude with a statement of the meaning of the overall study for the field. The researcher may suggest recommendations for future research that will extend the boundaries of knowledge in the problem area. He or she may also suggest direct applications for professional practice, particularly if the study itself was of an applied nature.

GUIDELINES FOR PREPARING THE RESEARCH REPORT

The researcher should not wait until the full investigative process has been completed before beginning to write the report. Instead, it is advisable to think in terms of organizing and writing the final report from the very beginning. Isaac and Michael urge that the researcher keep notes on all processes and events, and prepare draft copies of major sections of the report at an early point—while his or her memory of the data-gathering process is fresh.[3] Similarly, Simon writes:

> To fail to make detailed plans is unwittingly to make important decisions by postponing or ignoring them . . . Specify as much as you can in advance. Draw up the tables for which you wish to collect data. . . . When possible, it is wise to write up the research report prior to collecting data as an aid to good design planning.[4]

He urges that jottings throughout the course of the study will help to explain methodological decisions that were made, and explain the background of all findings. In other ways, it is essential to keep all materials, files, forms, and administrative actions or summaries carefully organized and filed so they are accessible at the time of report writing. Other guidelines include the following:

WORK FROM OUTLINE

It is helpful to prepare a detailed outline of each chapter of the report in advance, with a clear indication of topics, subtopics, and other subdivisions of content. This makes it possible to determine that all important points are being covered, that duplication is avoided, that elements are introduced in the proper order, and it helps to reduce the anxiety that often makes it difficult for researchers to *begin* the final task of writing the report.

WRITING STYLE

The writing style should be clear and accurate. Although the material may be scholarly and technical, every effort should be made to have all passages understandable, with a minimum of jargon, convoluted writing, or excessively pretentious words. Typically, shorter sentences are more effective than long, "run-on" sentences. It is helpful to have fairly brief paragraphs, with a liberal use of headings to set off major sections of each chapter. In general, writing should be impersonal and written in the third person. While humor may be permissible at points, a scholarly work should be fairly reserved, and should avoid the use of slang or extremely informal writing.

FOLLOW MANUAL FOR STYLE AND FORMAT

Most dissertation committees require the use of a recognized manual which describes or presents an approved format for each section of the report, and which is the source for authoritative treatment of such details as punctuation, spelling, capitalizations, italics, abbreviations, use of quotations, design of tables and figures, and footnotes and bibliographic references.

As an example, the *Publication Manual of the American Psychological Association* gives detailed directions for the preparation of papers for publication, which defines different types of articles and describes in detail each of the elements that go into them.[5] It gives helpful suggestions with respect to writing style and other key elements of the report. Many universities rely on this and similar manuals for authoritative rules for the preparation of research reports.

EVALUATE REPORT CAREFULLY

When a first draft of the research report has been written, it is advisable to review it carefully. Of primary concern is the actual content of the report; such questions must be asked as:

Is the research question significant, and is the work original and relevant to scholarly or professional concerns?

Have the instruments been shown to have adequate reliability and validity?

Does the research design fully test the stated hypotheses or meet the other purposes of the investigation?

Are the study subjects representative of the larger population about which generalizations are made?

Were ethical standards observed in the treatment of human subjects?[6]

While such questions should have been asked at earlier stages of the investigation, they must again be raised at the point of preparing the final report. If any weaknesses are disclosed at this stage, they must be forthrightly discussed in the report itself. In addition, other questions must be raised regarding the quality of the presentation itself. For example, the American Psychological Association's *Publication Manual* asks the following questions with respect to research reports that are submitted to scholarly journals:

Is the topic appropriate for the publication to which the article is being submitted?

Is the paper's introduction clear and complete, and does its statement of purpose fully orient the leader to the thrust of the research?

Is the literature adequately reviewed, with appropriate and complete citations?

Are the conceptualization and rationale of the research clearly presented?

Is the methodology adequately described; could the study be replicated from the description given in the paper?

Are the data analysis techniques appropriate, with sound assumptions underlying the statistical procedures which were chosen?

Are the study results and conclusions unambiguous and meaningful?

Does the manuscript meet the style and format criteria of the APA, as outlined in the Manual's checklist?[7]

PREPARATION OF NONSCHOLARLY RESEARCH REPORTS

Research reports which are published in the form of independent, nonacademic publications, or in professional magazines addressed to practitioners, are likely to be much more flexible in their format and writing style. Typically, planning reports published by government agencies tend to avoid formal hypotheses and complex statistical analyses. Instead, they are likely to stress the applied purpose of the research, and to present findings in simple clear language, with a generous use of tables, diagrams, and other illustrative materials.

Often such reports, when published by professional societies, represent factual presentations describing current practices in the field, or analyses of trends or problems relating to professional development. They have relatively little conceptual content and do not usually present a detailed literature review as background. However, assuming that their methodology has been sound, they do provide an important body of information helpful to practitioners in advancing the work in their field.

ARTICLES IN PROFESSIONAL OR GENERAL MAGAZINES

Most magazines of a professional or general nature, like *Parks and Recreation, Journal of Physical Education, Recreation and Dance,* or *Recreation Canada,* do not normally include reports of recreation research in full-fledged articles. However, they frequently include articles dealing with problems or trends in research and evaluation, and may also accept articles dealing with issues of professional concern that are based heavily on research studies.

The researcher who seeks to prepare such articles for publication should carefully study the magazine to which he or she intends to submit material. Probably he or she will find that it is necessary to key the research findings to an issue or problem of important professional concern. While many articles in the publication are likely to represent "thought pieces" (meaning simply the point of view or opinion of the authors) others use research findings as a basis for their conclusions or analyses. In preparing the article, one normally would *not* include an abstract, a literature review, a detailed statement of hypotheses and purposes, or the study's data-gathering procedures and statistical analysis techniques. Instead, the study's focus and findings are of primary importance, presented at a level of sophistication and with a lively writing style keyed to the typical reader of the publication.

Often it is helpful to write the editor of the magazine *before* submitting an article and perhaps even before writing it. The purpose of such an inquiry is to solicit the editor's interest in the topic of the proposed article, hopefully to gain his or her encouragement in advance, and possibly also to get suggestions about the content that might be helpful in preparing the article. Not infrequently, the editor may point out that a special issue of the magazine is being planned and that this article would fit well into it, if it were given a certain emphasis and written at a given length. In any case, it is extremely helpful to know in advance that the editor has encouraged submission of the article and that, if it has been carefully prepared, it has a good chance of being accepted.

Unlike scholarly research reports that are sent to academic journals, which frequently have a lengthy waiting period during which they are being reviewed and which also may require extensive revisions, most articles sent to more general publications receive a prompt reading and may not require any significant rewriting.

PRESENTATIONS AT PROFESSIONAL AND SCHOLARLY MEETINGS

Often, in addition to writing full research reports or submitting brief articles to journals, investigators also make presentations at research symposia or other sessions of professional societies. Customarily these take two forms: (a) an individual presentation, often lasting about 20 minutes to half an hour, as part of a series of research presentations by other scholars; and (b) a general educational session, presented to a broader professional audience, not particularly interested in research, but open to its inclusion as part of a discussion of a significant current issue or trend.

While the presentation itself is a verbal one, often making use of audio-visual materials, it may also involve giving copies of an abstract or research summary to the audience. Sometimes these may appear in printed proceedings of conference presentations, or in annually published collections of presentations at research symposia.[8]

By taking advantage of all such opportunities for disseminating research findings, the investigator will have made certain that the original reasons for undertaking the study have been achieved. Instead of gathering dust on a library's shelves, his or her research will have reached one or more appropriate audiences and may, in fact, provide direction for future investigations. As pointed out in Chapter 3, research is often circular, with successive waves of scholars contributing new theories, testing hypotheses, and building on each others' contribution. This can happen best when there is a substantial body of sound research entering the literature each year.

NEED FOR HIGH STANDARDS OF ACCURACY

A final important consideration is the need for all published research reports to maintain the highest possible degree of scientific accuracy. Selltiz and associates point out that a cardinal rule of scientific reporting is to give all the evidence relevant to the research questions asked; scientific authors are not free to choose what they will include and exclude in terms of the effects they wish to create.[9]

Beyond this, it is important to recognize that scientific research is carried on by human beings, who are subject to the same temptations that people in other professions face. An individual researcher may have a stake in exaggerating or suppressing data because a particular outcome may confirm his or her theory, be consistent with his or her ideological biases, or may make him or her famous and successful. Simon cites a number of outstanding examples of scientific dishonesty, some resulting in frauds and mistaken beliefs in the scholarly world that lasted for long periods of time.[10] Anthropologists, medical researchers, chemists, and sociologists have all been guilty of significantly distorting research findings and in some cases perpetuating major, dishonest claims that ultimately destroyed their careers. Simon gives advice to the young researcher:

> Doctoring the data can ruin your reputation and it can cause you great suffering from pangs of conscience. On the positive side, some of the world's great discoveries have come from researchers who took apparently conflicting data seriously and pursued the discrepancy, rather than sweeping it under the rug, thereby leading to great new findings.[11]

It is important to recognize that even a study that achieves negative results, or that fails to confirm a researcher's pet hypothesis, makes a contribution to knowledge. All knowledge is valuable and part of the growing tide of scholarship that provides validity to the recreation and leisure-studies field—whether or not it provides dramatic new insights or proofs of valuable outcomes.

ETHICAL RESPONSIBILITY

It is critical that every research report be prepared according to a high standard of honesty and accuracy. Beyond this, researchers must be cautious in working with human subjects, carefully following the agreed-on plan for working with them and maintaining confidentiality in the report. Another ethical concern has to do with acknowledging and sharing credit fairly with individuals who assisted in the research effort. Authorship of published works, which is a key element in promoting academic careers, should be properly apportioned to those responsible for the work. Finally, researchers must keep careful records of all their analytical and investigative procedures and data files, both to share with other researchers as necessary and to meet possible challenges to their work.

SUMMARY

Preparing detailed, accurate research reports is a final critical step in the research process. This may take a number of different forms, ranging from scholarly theses or dissertations to articles in professional magazines or presentations at research symposia.

This chapter describes the task of writing research reports, including the typical content of scholarly publications and a number of guidelines related to writing style, using respected manuals to ensure correct usages, and similar functions. It gives suggestions to assist researchers in finding outlets for reports of their findings on different levels, and concludes with a reminder of the need for highly ethical behavior in conducting studies and reporting outcomes. Suppression of negative findings and unwelcome data or exaggeration of research successes occur in many fields, and researchers must be aware of the need to maintain rigorous standards of personal honesty and scientific accuracy.

ENDNOTES

1. Claire Selltiz, Lawrence S. Wrightsman, and Stuart W. Cook, *Research Methods in Social Relations* (New York: Holt, Rinehart and Winston, 1976): 500.
2. Ibid., 504.
3. Stephen Isaac and William B. Michael, *Handbook in Research and Evaluation* (San Diego, Cal.: EdITS Publishers, 1971, 1980): 10.
4. Julian L. Simon, *Basic Research Methods in Social Sciences: The Art of Empirical Investigation* (New York: Random House, 1978): 25.
5. *Publication Manual of the American Psychological Association* (Washington, D.C.: American Psychological Association, 1983): 21–22.

6. Adapted from APA Manual, 19–20.
7. Ibid., 29.
8. *Abstracts from Leisure Research Symposium* (Alexandria, Va.: National Recreation and Park Association, published annually following National Congress for Recreation and Parks).
9. Selltiz et al, op. cit., 504.
10. Simon, op. cit., 26
11. Ibid., 27.

INDIVIDUAL OR SMALL-GROUP ASSIGNMENTS TO BE PREPARED AND PRESENTED IN CLASS

30. Students may be asked to become familiar with the presentation of scholarly research studies to the academic community by:
    a. Attending a professional society meeting, and sitting in on research presentations; preparing summaries of these sessions and reporting on them in class.
    b. Reviewing annual collections of presentations at research symposiums published by the National Recreation and Park Association, and classifying reports according to subjects, methods or designs, and types (applied, pure, etc.).

31. Students may also examine research reports which are published by government agencies, nonprofit organizations, or similar groups, which are *not* academic in nature, and which are designed to provide information to a general professional or public audience. They should be contrasted in terms of both style and content to more academic reports.

32. Students may review several issues of general newspapers (*U.S.A. Today* is a useful example), or weekly news magazines, trade publications, etc., to identify summary reports of research in the social sciences, business field, etc. They should be summarized and reported to the class.

11

EVALUATION AS A PROFESSIONAL FUNCTION

The evaluator is looking at value, quality control, impact, and effects of performance at all stages of program development. Evaluation occurs at the point of input or start-up; during the process of delivery; and at outcome, result, or follow-up stages. It is conducted by boards, administrators, programmers, leaders, and participants, but the responsibility for its conduct is a function of management.[1]

INTRODUCTION

Evaluation may be regarded both as a specific type of research and as a professional function concerned with measuring the quality and effectiveness of leisure-service agencies and programs.

In the first context, evaluative research consists of studies designed to examine recreation agencies, programs, and methods, in order to contribute to the knowledge base of the recreation and leisure-service field. It may also constitute a step in other types of studies, such as experiments or action research projects. In such situations, it must be carried out with the same degree of rigor and systematic documentation that other forms of research possess.

In the second context, evaluation is regarded as an ongoing professional responsibility and an important element in the "control" function of park and recreation managers. It is intended both to assess outcomes and to validate programs, and to provide useful information to assist in program planning and overall agency operations. This chapter describes seven distinct models of evaluation and outlines the steps that are typically followed in applying these models in leisure-service programs. It concludes with a discussion of the benefits and risks involved in conducting evaluation from a human-relations perspective.

PURPOSES OF EVALUATION

Earlier in this text, evaluation is defined as the process of determining the adequacy of a product, objective, process, procedure, program, approach, function, or functionary. In simpler terms, it may be summed up with the questions, "Is an agency accomplishing its goals? How effective and productive is it?"

These questions may be expanded, to identify four major purposes of evaluation today:

1. To measure the overall quality of any leisure-service agency or program, in order to document its worth for the public, boards or commissions, trustees, owners, or other funding agencies.

2. To determine how effective it is, or has been, in terms of meeting its goals and objectives—either with respect to total, long-range goals, or the narrower and more short-term objectives of specific programs.

3. To assist agency managers and supervisory personnel in decision making, planning, problem solving, development of policies and procedures, or other ongoing operational tasks.

4. To ensure that public or membership needs and priorities are being met as fully as possible.

While evaluation is usually referred to as "program evaluation," it actually may encompass a much more varied range of subjects. Entire agencies or departments may be evaluated with respect to their structure and operations. Programs need to be carefully evaluated. A major task of supervisors is to evaluate the work of subordinate personnel. Facilities should be evaluated and, as Chapter 13 shows in detail, evaluation may also encompass the assessment of patients, clients, or other participants, and may measure their functional abilities, needs and interests, and behavioral change.

EVALUATION APPROACHES

Evaluation in recreation, parks, and leisure services may be carried out through several types of approaches, including the following:

PROFESSIONAL JUDGMENT

This model makes use of a critical review process and the application of professional judgment by one or more experts or authorities, who examine an agency or program. They examine records, manuals, and reports; interview board members, employees on various levels, and participants; observe programs and tour facilities; and gather other needed data. Based on the information they have gathered and their own judgment of the agency's practices in terms of approved professional guidelines, they prepare an evaluation report that identifies its strengths and weaknesses. In some cases, this report may be used to indicate whether the agency and/or program represents acceptable professional practice.

STANDARDS AND CRITERIA

A second approach is based on the use of a comprehensive evaluation or rating form that includes a number of approved standards for professional practice, each with its own set of supporting criteria. Customarily, the agency or institution is required to carry out a detailed self-study and prepare a report, using the standards and criteria as an outline of areas or practices to be covered. Typically, a team of outside evaluators comes in and, armed with the self-study report, examines varied aspects of the agency to determine whether the standards and criteria have been met. This method is commonly used in the accreditation of agencies and institutions.

GOAL ACHIEVEMENT

This approach is based solely on an agency or program's success in achieving specific objectives which have been precisely defined and which have measurable, quantitative outcomes or accomplishments. Such objectives may be stated in terms of populations served, behavioral or affective changes among participants, benefits derived by the community or the sponsoring organization, or similar measures.

A term that has sometimes been applied to this approach to evaluation is the "discrepancy" model. It refers to the possible discrepancy, or gap, between the objectives of the agency and what was actually accomplished.

PARTICIPATION/ATTENDANCE/INCOME

This represents a more limited approach to evaluation which is based on statistical reports of participation in an agency's programs, attendance totals, income derived, or similar measures of performance over a given period of time. It is concerned chiefly with profitability and popularity as measures of agency success, and does not seek to assess the actual quality of the program, or other social or personal benefits that may have been achieved.

STAFF RATINGS OR PARTICIPANT SATISFACTION

Frequently evaluation makes use of rating sheets filled out by staff members themselves, who may appraise the success of programs, workshops, or other events, based on a set of guidelines used to judge the quality of programs. Similarly, program participants may also be asked to appraise programs from a user perspective, or to rate the effectiveness of leaders or other program arrangements. In addition to using structured evaluation instruments like rating scales, this model may also solicit subjective statements, anecdotal accounts, or similar documentation as a basis for judging program success.

SYSTEMS-BASED EVALUATION

In this approach, evaluation represents a stage in the systems-based program planning process, in which evaluation is used to gather feedback during the course of program implementation. It may be used to modify goals and strategies, revise program plans, reallocate resources, or initiate fresh planning.

The essential elements of the program system, such as input, process, and outcomes, as well as the environment in which the agency operates, are reviewed. Each element is analyzed, including time and money costs, personnel functions, barriers to successful performance, and policy-making and planning functions. This approach is often based on computer analysis and may use complex formulas to carry out the overall assessment.

TRANSACTION/OBSERVATION MODEL

Like the fifth model presented, this approach uses ratings by staff members or program participants who indicate their judgment of program effectiveness. However, it is much more diverse in its documentation, making use of interviews, systematic observation, case studies, or other sources of data. In addition, it tends to focus heavily on the element of human resource management, the use of interpersonal or group dynamics theory, and similar materials that contribute to an integrated case analysis that identifies both strengths and weaknesses of an agency or program.

OTHER TYPES OF EVALUATION

In addition to these seven methods, evaluation may also be categorized in several other ways. For example, evaluation approaches may be divided into two major types: process and preordinate models.

PROCESS MODELS

These models make use of evaluation methods that are not firmly fixed or structured in advance, in terms of the procedures that are to be followed, the instruments, the standards that are applied, or similar elements. Instead, the group responsible for carrying out the evaluation may go through a process of determining the need for doing it, its purposes or goals, the methods to be followed, and ways of assigning responsibility—in a continuing, evolving way.

An example of a process model might be a therapeutic recreation program or department in a large psychiatric hospital, in which the staff members agree that they wish to review their operation systematically. To accomplish this, they start from the very beginning in reviewing their goals and objectives, and establishing the guidelines or standards through which the program is to be evaluated. In so doing, they must necessarily examine the program based on a fresh outlook and develop a dynamic approach to meeting contemporary needs and conditions.

PREORDINATE MODELS

Most agency evaluations are of this type. They use standards and criteria and other evaluative methods that are structured in advance and that are used to examine or accredit institutions or programs in a uniform way, with similar, objective rating systems.

An example of a preordinate model is found in the evaluation process used by the National Youth Sports Camps (see pg. 237). Evaluation teams are sent out all over the United States to observe and assess summer sports programs operated by urban colleges and universities for inner-city youth. The procedures, guidelines, and instruments are all uniformly determined in advance, and evaluation teams are carefully trained to apply them correctly.

Another important distinction must be made between *summative* and *formative* approaches to evaluation.

SUMMATIVE EVALUATION

This is the most widely used form of evaluation, and generally is applied at the *end* of a project, program, or work period. Although it obviously cannot then be used to improve an existing program (which has already been carried out), it *can* be used to plan effectively for the future.

FORMATIVE EVALUATION

Formative evaluation is carried on *throughout* a program or project, including its early stages of planning and implementation. Since it provides a constant review and assessment of the effectiveness of what is being done, it yields instant feedback that can be used to develop new strategies or program approaches as necessary.

ALTERNATIVE APPROACHES TO EVALUATION

Evaluation may take several different forms, and may be applied to any of the following elements:

1. *Overall agencies* and their administrative subdivisions, including such special units as divisions of maintenance and operations, personnel management, or specific service departments.

2. *Programs,* including total, year-round programs, seasonal programs, special-interest areas, single continuing activities (such as leagues or classes), and special events.

3. *Personnel* on all levels, including full-time supervisors, leaders, specialists or maintenance employees, and also part-time, session employees and volunteers.

4. *Facilities,* both in terms of overall areas and facilities belonging to a department, and also the adequacy of individual structures or areas for specialized purposes.

5. *Participants,* with respect to assessment of their needs and how effectively these are being met, as well as to participation patterns and outcomes.

LEVELS OF APPLICATION

In addition to these differences, evaluation may also be applied at a number of different levels and for varying administrative purposes. For example, it may be: (*a*) a periodic function, through which an agency carries out a self-study of its total operation every three to five years, as in the case of institutions which apply for renewed certification or accreditation; (*b*) a regular function, to be carried out at the end of each indoor or outdoor season and after each major activity or program unit; (*c*) an ongoing daily process, in which leaders and supervisors regularly evaluate program activities and events, staff performance, and other elements; and (*d*) a critical element in an organization's administrative process, which regularly feeds information into its management information system and into data bases, statistical summaries, and similar records and reports.

Evaluation may be voluntarily undertaken, required to meet Civil Service or union contract stipulations, or carried out at the request of a commission, board, or other supervising body. It may also be required as part of a subcontracting arrangement or grant, in which an agency is funded to conduct a given program and must then have the program systematically evaluated. Evaluation may be designed as a routine function, carried on without additional staff or funding assistance. However, when it is done on an agency-wide basis, and particularly when it is connected with a large-scale planning effort or with accreditation or certification, it may require a special authorization and funding approval.

It should be stressed that the key purpose of evaluation is *not* simply to provide a rating or score. Instead, it is to provide an accurate picture of strengths and weaknesses that can be used to bring about improvement. To the extent that specific standards or objectives are not being met, sound evaluation identifies actions that must be taken to improve procedures, change policies, or upgrade professional performance.

STEPS OF EVALUATION

Within any leisure-service agency, the following steps must be carried out if evaluation is to provide meaningful input to the management process:

ASSIGN RESPONSIBILITY

There is an old cliché that "everybody's business is nobody's business." This implies that saying that everyone is responsible for carrying out agency evaluation is tantamount to accepting that it will not be done in a purposeful and well-coordinated way.

Instead, it is advisable to put the chief responsibility for directing evaluation efforts in the hands of a single individual or—in the case of a larger organization—a small committee or work team that will have this as a direct responsibility. These individuals may then call on others to assist them in planning evaluation processes throughout the agency.

DEFINE AGENCY NEEDS

The second step is to determine exactly what needs to be evaluated and when. For example, in a therapeutic recreation agency, evaluation may include: (a) assessments of patient/client needs and functional abilities, (b) measurement of program outcomes, (c) assessment of staff performance, and (d) adherence of the program to professional standards or guidelines.

ASSIGN EVALUATION RESPONSIBILITIES

Who actually carries out evaluation in its varied forms? Often, routine observations and ratings are done by regular employees. However, when a large-scale or special agency self-study is to be done, or when an evaluation requires special expertise, one must make the choice of using internal or external evaluators or both.

Internal evaluators are regular employees of an organization, who may be used to gather data, make judgments, or critically analyze programs. Their *advantages* are that they are generally familiar with the situation, have ready access to the facts without being specially briefed, and are available without having to make special arrangements, or be paid special fees. Their *disadvantages* are that they may be too close to the situation to be able to view it accurately, or may be self-protective or biased in one direction or another. In addition, they may not be fully aware of current trends or standards in the field and may lack the high level of expertise that an outside evaluator might bring.

External evaluators are usually consultants who are regarded as being highly authoritative; they may be assigned by a professional society or accrediting body in a volunteer capacity, or may be working for a fee as paid consultants. Their *advantages* are that they may have a high level of knowledge or professional judgment and that they are able to carry out a fully impartial and objective analysis of an agency or program. Their *disadvantages* are that they may need considerable time to get all the needed information and even then may get a partial or distorted picture because of limited evidence and familiarity with the program. In addition, they may be quite costly, both in terms of a professional fee and personal expenses.

DESIGN INSTRUMENTS AND PROCEDURES

Evaluation should make use of systematic, carefully applied data-gathering procedures, just as other forms of research do. Therefore it is necessary to design appropriate questionnaires, observation and rating forms, and similar instruments, and to develop precise guidelines for carrying out the investigative process.

In some cases, it is possible to use forms developed by national organizations or accrediting bodies (see pgs. 233–239), or to modify them for use. However, since agencies vary so greatly in their goals and objectives, regional or community characteristics, and other factors, it is often necessary to develop instruments and procedures that are appropriate for an organization's special needs.

ANALYSIS AND CONCLUSIONS

When observations have been made, interviews carried out, records reviewed, and other data gathered, it is necessary to assemble and analyze the evidence. Some evaluation systems use a quantitative approach to delineate all areas of strength and weakness. An agency or program may be required to achieve a number of points to be regarded as passing, in order to justify future funding or continuing accreditation. In some cases, a profile is drawn, with the stipulation that the agency must meet a minimal standard of performance within each of several categories, such as health practices, public relations, and staffing procedures. In other evaluation models, there is little attempt to quantify the findings. Instead, anecdotal records, narratives, and summaries are used to describe a program or staff member's performance, with emphasis on human relations or group dynamics aspects of program experiences.

It is usually advisable to hold a preliminary conference with those being evaluated—particularly in the case of a program or agency that is being examined by outside consultants. Often, staff members may wish to challenge findings, correct misconceptions, or provide fuller understanding of what has occurred, and they should have the opportunity to do so. In any case, the final step of the process is to prepare a report which includes the actual findings of the evaluation and which presents conclusions and recommendations. Frequently, such recommendations may consist of specific suggestions for steps to be taken to improve agency or staff performance. In the case of programs, they may identify those which should be continued or expanded, as well as those which might well be reduced or terminated.

EVALUATION AS A STAFF PROCESS: HUMAN-RELATIONS IMPLICATIONS

In planning and carrying out evaluation procedures, it is essential to realize that it represents much more than a cut-and-dried, mechanical process that will result in a printed report destined for someone's file cabinet. Instead, evaluation has considerable potential for contributing to the effective functioning of organizations—but also may present a serious threat to many agency personnel.

When evaluation is properly approached, agency managers, supervisors, and leadership personnel in many job categories may join together in a cooperative staff process of developing goals and objectives, setting work or program standards and criteria, and reviewing performance on a continuous basis. Evaluation should be regarded as a process of constructive analysis, intended to improve present and future performance. On a broad scale, entire agencies or consortiums of social-service or health-related organizations may join together to identify community or regional needs, assess present programs, and develop short- and long-range goals and objectives and plans for action.

THREATS AND RISKS

However, evaluation may also represent an area of considerable sensitivity or even fear when it involves threats to job security, promotion, tenure, or the possibility of demotion or dismissal. When negative evaluation ratings are submitted, an organization's weaknesses have been exposed and its funding may be undercut.

Therefore, many professionals are reluctant to be evaluated. When they are placed in a position of responsibility where they must assess the work of others, research indicates that they may hesitate to be critical or judge others harshly even when the evidence may call for it. There is a tendency to "whitewash" other employees or programs, postpone evaluations, carry them out superficially, or sabotage them by making meaningless or mechanical judgments. In bureaucratic organizations, evaluation forms are often very simple and thus provide no basis for real discrimination, and no serious attempt is made to judge the worth of programs or people. In large cities, labor unions frequently resist serious efforts at personnel evaluation.

It is therefore necessary to recognize the human-relations aspect of evaluation. To develop a positive emotional climate, it is often desirable to separate evaluation from decision-making processes which involve funding decisions or personnel recommendations and to have at least part of the process concerned solely with the goal of improving future performance. Whenever possible, evaluation should involve a two-way sharing of views, rather than consist solely of authoritarian judgments made from above.

TODAY'S CLIMATE FOR SCIENTIFIC EVALUATION

Summing up, it should be stressed that evaluation has become an increasingly important aspect of leisure-service agency operations. There is a general trend toward providing fuller scientific documentation and accountability within all human-service fields, including both government and nonprofit organizations. Particularly in social-service or health-related agencies, this trend has been underlined by the fiscal austerity practices of the 1970s and 1980s, and the need for organizations to demonstrate their own worth, in order to compete successfully for funding support.

In all types of organizations, however, there is much greater use today of systems analysis, computer-based planning methods, and management information systems. Evaluation is an essential element in such processes, as Chapter 1 points out, and is clearly part of a scientific management approach—as compared to "fly-by-the-seat-of-your-pants" approaches. As a result, within each area of leisure-service program management, professional organizations have developed comprehensive standards and guidelines which are used in evaluation. A number of these approaches are described in Chapter 12.

SUMMARY

This chapter provides an overview of the role of evaluation in leisure-service agencies, beginning with a discussion of its purposes and seven common approaches to evaluation. It should be stressed that many organizations may use more than one approach, sometimes blending several of them in different evaluative processes.

Both summative and formative approaches to evaluation are also discussed, as are process and preordinate models of program assessment. Evaluation may be directed to several aspects of agency management, including programs, personnel, facilities, and participants. It may also be applied at different levels of program operations. Five steps of the evaluation process are identified, and the chapter concludes by discussing the degree to which evaluation is often perceived as a serious threat by practitioners.

ENDNOTE

1. Herberta M. Lundegren and Patricia Farrell, *Evaluation for Leisure Service Managers: A Dynamic Approach* (Philadelphia: Saunders College Publishing, 1984); 1.

QUESTIONS FOR CLASS REVIEW AND DISCUSSION

33. What forms does evaluation generally take in our lives—in other words, in what situations are we typically evaluated, or do we typically evaluate other people or processes?

34. What are the important purposes of evaluation for recreation, parks, and leisure-services departments?

WORKSHOP ACTIVITIES TO BE CARRIED OUT WITHIN THE CLASS

35. Have students divide into small groups, and identify a different type of recreation agency or situation for each group. Then have each group select three different approaches to evaluation, using the illustrations

given in this chapter. Have them show how these approaches might be used in the agency they were assigned, either to evaluate the overall agency and/or its program, or other specific elements of it. Make this a brief, preliminary plan; do not develop actual instruments or procedures.

36. Have members of the class plan a comprehensive use of evaluation procedures in a recreation and park curriculum, including the following: (*a*) evaluation of students by teachers; (*b*) evaluation of teachers by students; (*c*) evaluation of courses by students; (*d*) evaluation of teachers by teachers; (*e*) evaluation of the overall curriculum by students; (*f*) evaluation of the entire department by an outside accrediting body; or (*g*) evaluation of any other aspect of the program, such as student services or job placement, by current or past students. Consider the use of formal models (such as actual accreditation manuals) in this process.

12

PROGRAM-CENTERED EVALUATION

... there are several practical reasons for program evaluation. Services must be improved; resources must be allocated or reallocated based on rational decision making; the support of the grass roots consumer must be expanded; the ethic and value of a meaningful recreational lifestyle must be instilled; two-way communication between agencies and their public must be fostered; and a sensitivity to the impact of the leisure experience upon the individual must be maintained. What all this means is that we must use evaluation to critically examine our effectiveness.[1]

INTRODUCTION

Most references to evaluation in the literature describe its role in measuring the effectiveness of recreation programs. As Chapter 11 stressed, the true role of evaluation in recreation, parks, and leisure services is much broader, including the assessment of both the quality and effectiveness of agencies and their component elements. This chapter examines the application of the evaluation models described earlier, in several specific types of leisure-service settings. Thus, it presents the reader with a picture of evaluation in action.

THE MEANING OF "AGENCIES" AND "PROGRAMS"

The two terms "agencies" and "programs" are often used synonymously to refer to the overall operation of recreation and park organizations. One might comment colloquially about a given public or voluntary recreation agency with the phrase, "That's an excellent program."

More precisely defined, the term "agency" refers to the organization itself as an operating entity, including its legal status and governing boards or commissions, its managers on various levels, its structural units and physical resources, and—beyond all these—its essential character or identity as a social institution.

In contrast, the term "program" refers to the work of the agency in terms of service delivery. While it involves the organization's resources and operational procedures, it is *chiefly* concerned with goals, objectives, activities, services, and outcomes.

This chapter outlines contemporary approaches to evaluating both agencies and their programs, recognizing that in practice the structure and management approaches of an organization are closely intertwined with its program practices and may indeed be evaluated at the same time.

COMPREHENSIVE AGENCY/PROGRAM EVALUATION PLAN

A comprehensive evaluation plan may include three elements or phases: (1) administrative evaluation plan, (2) public assessment of program impact, and (3) use of external evaluation team.[2]

ADMINISTRATIVE PLAN

The agency's director and key management personnel work with members of a staff advisory team and possibly community representatives and/or advisory council members to lay the groundwork for carrying out the evaluation. They must:

a. Make decisions regarding the form of the evaluation:
   1. Who needs it?
   2. What purposes will it serve? What decisions must be made?
   3. What questions must be asked? What information will be needed to answer these?
   4. At what stage of agency operations or program implementation should questions be asked?
   5. What resources are available to do the evaluation?
   6. How are results to be reported, and to whom?
   7. Who should do the evaluation?

b. Determine what areas are to be reviewed, including the following:
1. Philosophy and goals.
2. Long-range planning process.
3. Agency resources: areas, facilities, and equipment.
4. Program effectiveness.
5. Personnel performance.
6. Community relations and input in policy development and program planning.
7. Effectiveness of interagency planning and utilization of existing community resources.

PUBLIC ASSESSMENT OF PROGRAM IMPACT

The staff team develops a questionnaire to be used with different groups of citizens: participants, parents, representatives of schools and other community agencies, and other professionals. Administered internally (by agency staff members), this survey examines:
1. Program variety and breadth.
2. Scheduling factors and suitability to different community needs.
3. Leadership effectiveness, including use of volunteers.
4. Use of available facilities, and varying locations in terms of needs of special populations in community.
5. Program costs and revenues, possibly using a cost/benefit analysis.
6. Public relations practices and community relations.
7. Community relations efforts, including cosponsorship with other community agencies.

EXTERNAL EVALUATION PROCESS

As an option, the overall evaluation may include a site visit and study by an external evaluation team. Composed of representatives of a professional society, other government agencies, or consultants, this team might have two emphases: product evaluation and process evaluation.

a. Product evaluation focuses on the program's effectiveness, utilizing:

1. Review of documents and reports developed by internal review team.

2. Examination of goals statements and evidence of their accomplishment.
3. Interviews with staff members and participants.
4. Application of professional standards and criteria, as basis for judgments.

 b. Process evaluation examines the "how" of program operations:

1. Review of agency program-planning process.
2. Examination of staff reports for major program elements.
3. Review of operations manuals, including leadership, maintenance, and programming for special populations.
4. Records dealing with community participation, interagency cooperation, and volunteer involvement.

This three-phase plan provides a framework in which each agency can develop its own approach to evaluation, depending on its special needs and resources. Typically, many leisure-service organizations are likely to rely heavily on a combination of the professional judgment and standards-and-criteria approaches described in Chapter 11. Often, the evaluation team makes use of self-study rating forms which contain recommended standards for practice.

THE NATURE OF STANDARDS

Standards represent desirable guidelines or descriptions of recommended professional practices, which have been formulated by respected professionals in the field. They provide a means of measuring the quality of programs—not as optimal or maximal goals, but rather minimal levels of quality or performance that are to be met. As an example, the National Institute of Senior Centers developed detailed standards over a five-year period based on the following assumptions:

Quality is best achieved from *within* a field through standards—guidelines to operating a successful program—rather than from outside through licensure and government regulations.

Standards should be realistic and flexible, adaptable to centers with a wide variety of structures, resources, and settings; they are *not* a list of components making up a model program.

Standards are not "cast in concrete," but should be continually monitored to respond to changing needs, resources and knowledge.[3]

Three examples of the use of standards in recreation agency evaluation follow.

NRPA COMMUNITY RECREATION EVALUATION MANUAL

In the early 1970s, the National Recreation and Park Association published a manual, *Evaluation and Self-Study of Public Recreation and Park Agencies: A Guide with Standards and Evaluative Criteria.* This instrument was the revised and updated version of an earlier manual which had been developed by the Great Lakes Standards Committee, based on numerous evaluation guidelines used by professional associations and voluntary organizations.

The primary use of the NRPA evaluation and self-study manual was to assist departments or local public agencies in examining and improving their own programs, by providing a systematic instrument through which their practices could be compared with statements of recommended practices. Specifically, it was recommended that the standards be used in four approaches to evaluation:

1. Self-appraisal conducted systematically by department personnel, making use of consultants if desired.
2. Utilization of the standards as guidelines for carrying out a major organization or reorganization of a public recreation and parks department.
3. Application of the standards by advisory or policy-making citizen boards, in periodic evaluation of recreation and park operations.
4. Providing assistance to civic organizations, such as the League of Women Voters or councils of social agencies, in examining municipal recreation programs and services.

The NRPA self-study manual has thirty-five standards in the following categories: (1) philosophy and goals; (2) administration; (3) programming; (4) personnel; (5) areas, facilities, and equipment; and (6) evaluation. Each standard is followed by one or more criteria, which represent a specific statement of recommended procedures or operational practice and thus a means of judging whether or not the actual standard has been met. An example of one standard, under the heading of Administration, follows:

Standard 3. Administration: Organizational Structure
The department's structure should reflect its purpose, its methods

of operation in relation to its resources, and its relationship to the community.

Criteria

a. The source of authority of and powers for the public recreation and park managing authority should be clearly set forth by legal document.

b. The organizational structure should provide for one public authority responsible for legislative (policy-making) functions.

c. There should be written and definitive guidelines for the relationships between the administrative and legislative (policy-making) functions.

d. There should be an administrator who is responsible to the managing authority for the entire operation and services based on established policies and procedures approved by the managing authority and the administrator.

e. The administrator should help the managing authority to become familiar with the areas of control and the individual responsibilities of the managing authority members, as well as the general operation of the department.

f. A specific distinction should be made among policies, rules and regulations, and operational procedures. It should be indicated how each is established and administered.

g. Where the legislative (policy-making) body is a citizen board, it should hold regular meetings monthly with the actions of the board and reports of the administrator officially recorded. Board members should be representative of the total community and serve with rotation of terms.[4]

In applying the manual, the self-study team must respond to the question, "Is criterion met?" by checking the appropriate box: "Yes," "Almost," "To some degree," "No," or "Does not apply." All replies are tabulated on a Standards Profile Computation Work Sheet. Scores are assigned for each criterion on the basis of 5 for a Yes, 3 for an Almost, 1 for To some degree, and 0 for No. Average scores of the criteria are compiled for each standard, and the results are plotted on a Standards Profile chart (see Fig. 12.1).

This approach makes it possible to assess the quality of an agency's professional performance. By identifying specific areas of strength and weakness, the administrative director or policy-making board can develop a statement of priorities, or identify both short- and long-range goals designed to upgrade its operation.

For each standard, plot the Standard Profile value as computed on the work sheet; then join the dots with a red line—shown as a broken line on this example—to give a graphic picture of the standards profile.

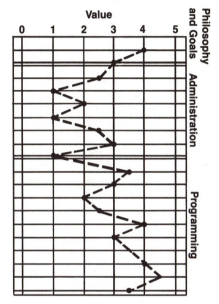

Standard		Value
1. Philosophy		Philosophy and Goals
2. Goals		
3. Organizational structure		
4. Administrative manual		Administration
5. Cooperative community planning		
6. Cooperative operations agreements		
7. Financial administration		
8. Public relations		
9. Service statistics		
10. Objectives		
11. Actionable experiences		
12. Types of opportunities		Programming
13. Varied participant requirements		
14. Scope of opportunities		
15. Total community programming		
16. Education for leisure		
17. Demonstration projects and research		
18. Selection of program content		
19. Participant involvement		

Note: This illustrates the first three categories of standards.

Figure 12.1 *Standards profile for NRPA community recreation evaluation manual.*[5]

NTRS STANDARDS OF PRACTICE

Similar manuals have been developed in other specialized areas of practice in the leisure-service field. For example, the National Therapeutic Recreation Society approved a comprehensive set of standards in the early 1980s, which outlines approved approaches to practice. It reflects changes in the therapeutic recreation field, and particularly an increased emphasis on a highly clinical approach to providing treatment services.

The NTRS manual is not designed specifically to be an evaluation instrument. However, each of its six major standards (covering the *Scope of Services, Agency or Department Objectives, Individual*

Treatment/Program Plans, Documentation, Scheduling of Services and *Ethical Practices)* may be used as the basis for examining and rating a therapeutic recreation program.[6] Figure 12.2 illustrates two of these standards.

Standard III. Individual Treatment/Program Plan[7]

The therapeutic recreation staff develop an individualized treatment/program plan for each client referred to the unit/agency/department.

CRITERIA

A. The plan is based on complete and relevant diagnostic/assessment data.
 1. The plan reflects the client's physical, social, mental, and emotional aptitudes and skills and current level of leisure functioning.
 2. The plan indicates precautions, restrictions, or limitations related to an individual's participation as determined by the diagnosis/assessment.
B. The plan is stated in behavioral terms that permit the progress of the individual to be assessed.
C. The plan is periodically reviewed, evaluated and modified as necessary to meet the changing needs of the client.
D. The plan differentiates among short-term, long-term and discharge/transition goals.
E. The plan is documented in the personal record of the client.
F. The plan reflects an integrated approach.
 1. The plan is consistent with interdisciplinary treatment goals for the client.
 2. When feasible, the client and/or his/her family assist in developing and implementing the therapeutic recreation treatment plan.
 3. The plan reflects the client's goals and expectation of benefits to be derived from the therapeutic recreation program.

Standard IV. Documentation

Therapeutic recreation personnel record specific information on assigned clients for the client/participant's record on a regular basis in accordance with the policies and procedures of the agency.

CRITERIA

A. The individualized therapeutic recreation treatment/program plan is recorded in the client/participant's record. It should include:
 1. The referral document or reason for referral.
 2. Assessment data.
 3. Identification of client's problem and needs.
 4. Treatment objectives.
 5. Methods and plans for implementation of the therapeutic recreation program.
 6. Methods and plans for evaluation of the objectives.

B. Progress of the individual and his/her reactions to the therapeutic recreation program are systematically recorded in the client/participant's record and reported to all appropriate parties (e.g., interdisciplinary team, parents, etc.)

   1. Subjective interpretation of client progress is supported with concise behavioral observations.

   2. Documentation of progress is directly related to the treatment goals.

C. A discharge/transition plan is included in the personal record and should include:

   1. A summary of the treatment/program implemented and the client's progress.

   2. An assessment of the client's current level of leisure function.

   3. Recommendations for post-discharge/transition planning.

   4. Information regarding appropriate community recreation resources and referral information as indicated.

D. Client records are reviewed regularly by therapeutic recreation staff in accordance with standards of regulatory agencies and documentation of such review is entered in the personal record.

Figure 12.2
NTRS standards of practice.

PROGRAM EVALUATION IN NATIONAL YOUTH SPORTS CAMP

A third example of agency/program evaluation that utilizes a combination of the professional judgment and standards-and-criteria approach may be found in the evaluation process used by the National Youth Sports Camp. This program is funded by the United States Congress and administered by the National Collegiate Athletic Association. Through it, many urban colleges and universities sponsor summer day camp programs which emphasize sports, and which are designed primarily for disadvantaged children and youth living in inner-city neighborhoods.

Each camp must have its program evaluated through a site visit by qualified evaluators who visit sponsoring colleges and universities, observe activities and facilities, interview staff members and participants, and examine records. Using a manual with 106 standards, they must rate the program in terms of whether or not each standard is fully or partially met. The standards fall under the following headings: *Institution, Participants, Activities, Enrichment Program, Project Schedule, Nutrition, Medical Services, Staff, Project Organization,* and *Coordination.* Several of these are illustrated in Figure 12.3.

A maximum number of 180 points may be awarded to any program. Depending on its total score, an institution may be approved fully for Youth Sports Camp funding in the following year, approved conditionally (with required actions that must be taken to improve the program), or disapproved.

Institution:	Points	Item	
	2	[1].	Institutional facilities are provided for an effective project
	1	2.	Cooperation afforded by several departments in the University or College
Total—13	1-2	3.	Lockers used daily by each participant
	1-2	4.	Playing fields are marked off and equipped to accommodate all field activities offered
	1-2	5.	Court areas are marked off and equipped to accommodate all court activities offered
	2	[6].	Adequate equipment was readily available for each activity
	2	[7].	NYSP shirts provided to participants
Participants:	2	[1].	Roster available
	2	[2].	Project meets minimum of 90% disadvantaged participants
	1-2	3.	If actual enrollment equals or exceeds projected enrollment
Total—23	2	[4].	If average daily attendance equals at least 80% projected enrollment
	1	5.	If average daily attendance equals at least 90% projected enrollment
	1-2	6.	Daily attendance recorded by name and filed
	2	[7].	Evidence of efforts made to maintain high average daily attendance
	1-3	8.	Data collected on (1) physical fitness, (2) performance records, and (3) behavior inventories
	1-2	9.	Observable evidence that participants are enjoying the experiences
	2	10.	At least 50 per cent of enrollees are returnees
	1	11.	Returnees exceed 60 per cent of enrollees
	2	[12].	All participants are within the age range of 10-18
Project Schedule:	2	[1].	Meets minimum: 5 weeks, 5 days per week; or 6 weeks, 4 days per week

_____	1	2.	Exceeds number of funded days
Total-11	2	[3].	Provides minimum of two hours of sports activity per day
	1	4.	Provides three hours of sports activity per day
	1	5.	Provides four hours of sports activity per day
	2	[6].	Majority of enrollment before summer project begins
	2	[7].	Staff orientation and briefing before summer project begins

Note: This table includes three of the form's ten sections.

FIGURE 12.3
NYSP evaluation form.

Evaluators must be carefully prepared to carry out the site visit. To assist them, the NYSP national organization has prepared a detailed set of instructions, including interpretations of each item and suggestions for applying them. These instructions also include guidelines for carrying out the site visits, with step-by-step procedures of the points to be covered by the study team (see Fig. 12.4).

EXAMPLES OF GOAL-ACHIEVEMENT MODEL IN PROGRAM EVALUATION

A second widely found approach to evaluating leisure-service agencies and programs consists of the goal-achievement model (see pg. 217). When the goals of an organization are extremely subjective or global in nature, it is difficult to evaluate them objectively. For example, the National Board of the Young Women's Christian Association has identified a number of major social goals related to the elimination of racism; promoting the legal, social, and economic rights of girls and women; and other priorities of this type. Clearly, it is almost impossible to determine whether an individual YWCA has achieved such goals satisfactorily.

Instead, a more practical approach to evaluation is to identify a number of more immediate, concrete, and short-term objectives. For example, a large urban YWCA might list the following objectives to be accomplished during the coming year: (a) raising the

1. Determine who is involved in the cooperative process of project development, i.e., staff, enrollees, advisory committee, etc.
2. See proof of lesson planning, i.e., written daily plans for each activity.
3. Copy of guide should be available for review.
4. Check letters and memorandums to ascertain if the Project Administrator performs the duties as directed by the guidelines.
5. Determine by observation and discussions with staff and Activity Director.
6. Determine by observation, discussion with Activity Director, and a check of the guidelines.
7. Check minutes of the meetings.
8. Planned procedures are published concerning the standards of conduct expected of the participants. Score additional point if standards are being upheld.
9. Check to make sure that purposes of the NYSP have been distributed to the parent.
10. Check the written invitations to parents.
11. One evidence of organizational planning is that no participants are wandering around.
12. Determine attainment of objectives—variable points.
13. Visitation Form must be correct and complete—variable points.

FIGURE 12.4 Steps involved in evaluating project organization (National Youth Sports Camp).[9]

proportion of minority-group membership and participation totals by a given percentage; (b) sponsoring a number of symposia on changing economic or family roles for women; or (c) serving the victims of sexual harassment or family or child abuse, through the provision of counseling or shelter services. This approach to goal-achievement evaluation may be closely tied to program budgeting, in which an agency outlines its specific goals for the coming budget year as a way of illustrating and justifying budget requests.

IDENTIFICATION OF SPECIFIC PERFORMANCE MEASURES

When program objectives are defined in proposed budgets for the coming year or in contractual agreements with funding or cooperating agencies, they are often spelled out in terms of specific performance measures. For example, Fig. 12.5 shows a number of objectives and related performance measures as stated in the annual budget of the Kansas City, Missouri Department of Parks and Recreation, in the section dealing with special programs serving the handicapped and elderly.

Key Objectives

1. Provide social and recreational activities to 5.5% of Kansas Citians 65 years of age or over
2. Plan and coordinate monthly meetings for the various Golden Age clubs
3. Conduct special city-wide events for older adults
4. Arrange and conduct a travel program for Golden Agers
5. Provide weekly instruction, competition, physical recreation and social activities for 200 handicapped children and adults

Performance Measures

1. Percent of target population being served	5.5%
2. Number of clubs	13
Number of monthly meetings	32
Average attendance per meeting	69
3. Number of special events	13
Average attendance per meeting	902
4. Number of trips	59
5. Weekly handicapped participation	132
Number of special handicapped events	1
Average attendance per event	125

FIGURE 12.5.
Program objectives and performance measures in Kansas City.[10]

A second approach to evaluating programs by measuring success in achieving objectives consists of assessing change in participants. While this may be done in a variety of settings, it is most frequently applied in therapeutic recreation programs, where it is customary to identify precise treatment goals for patients and/or clients. It is described more fully in Chapter 13, which deals with the evaluation of participants and personnel. The method also would apply to demonstration projects or socially oriented programs which seek to reduce juvenile delinquency, improve neighborhood morale, encourage positive relationships among different ethnic or racial groups, and similar efforts.

OTHER APPROACHES TO PROGRAM EVALUATION

Other approaches to program evaluation in recreation, parks, and leisure services include: (1) the participation/attendance/

income model, (2) staff ratings or participant-satisfaction questionnaires, (3) systems-based evaluation, and (4) the transaction-
observation approach.

PARTICIPATION/ATTENDANCE/INCOME MODEL

This represents one of the most common ways of evaluating program success. Typically, public, voluntary-agency, armed forces,
and other types of recreation sponsors tend to set attendance or
registration goals for programs. If these are met, and if the
number of those involved continues to grow, it is assumed that the
program is meeting the needs of the public or the organization's
membership. In addition, healthy attendance levels usually mean
that programs are yielding needed income. While commercial recreation businesses are the only type of sponsor with the primary
aim of making a financial profit, all types of agencies today rely on
fees and charges to some degree to pay for operational costs.

Cost-Benefit Analysis

Statistics of attendance and income from recreation facilities
and programs may also be used in cost-benefit analysis. This is a
method of measuring the relative costs and positive outcomes of
programs to determine those that are most successful and worthy
of continued support. It involves identifying all program costs, in
terms of direct charges for space, leadership, equipment and similar elements, and also taking into account a portion of the over-
head costs of the organization. It is also to assess the benefits, in
terms of the numbers served and their level of recreational need,
as well as other kinds of criteria which may be used to judge the
value of a program activity. Often this represents a complex calculation, in terms of balancing the goals and objectives of the organization and its priorities against the element of sheer numbers.

For example, should a sports program that serves 200 children
at a total cost of $1,000 be given a higher priority than one that
serves 50 senior citizens at a similar cost? Is a creative arts program more valuable than an environmental studies workshop?
Such issues must be considered in developing a cost-benefit
approach. Beyond this, it should be recognized that many of the
benefits of recreation are very difficult to measure quantitatively,
and that program impacts often extend over a period of time into
the future. Posavac and Carey write:

> A sophisticated cost analysis will include benefits occurring at times
> in the future. Successful rehabilitation or therapy will enable a per-

son to live with less need of special services in future years. Improvements in work skills, psychological adjustment, and physical health may well have benefits for the children of people served or cared for. The worth of these long-term benefits is, not surprisingly, hard to estimate.[11]

Attendance/Income Quotas

In some cases, attendance and income may be used to develop a productivity formula covering all the specialized facilities or programs within a large agency. In one YWCA which was evaluated by a coauthor of this text, the practice was to assign each of the different areas of the agency's building (including auditoriums, multipurpose or exercise rooms, arts and crafts rooms, pool, and gymnasiums) an actual quota which stated the revenue it was required to "earn." This was defined as an average hourly income during the period of active programming throughout the week. Each area or specialized facility was programmed to achieve its target income with a variety of revenue-producing activities. As an example, a large multipurpose room featured aerobics, yoga classes, gymnastics, La Maze natural childbirth classes, dance, toddler exercise classes, and similar activities. Attendance and income were used directly to assess the success of programming in this Y.

STAFF RATINGS AND PARTICIPANT-SATISFACTION APPROACH

Particularly in terms of evaluating specific program activities and events, this is one of the most common evaluation techniques. Staff members often are required to submit evaluation reports of programs they have directed. Their supervisors may also carry out evaluations of activities led by subordinates. Similarly, participants may be asked to fill out evaluation sheets about programs they have taken part in, dealing with such questions as the level of the activity, the adequacy of the facility, the leadership, the fee or charge, the schedule, and similar information. Often, such evaluations may be combined with questions about the future, asking whether they would enroll in a similar activity if it were offered again, or asking them to indicate their preferences for new programs that might be offered by the agency.

Evaluation of past or current program activities may be linked with needs assessments in this way, to provide guidance for future programming. This approach to evaluation is dealt with more fully as part of recreation planning and marketing strategy, in Chapter 14.

SYSTEMS-BASED EVALUATION

Evaluation is part of a systematic approach to recreation program planning, either as the final step in the process, or as a continuing source of feedback while the program is being carried on. This may lead to continuing activities as planned, or to redesign of goals, objectives, and program elements at any point. Russell presents a familiar sequence of steps involved in the program-planning process (see Fig. 12.6).

Organizing for Planning

Step One: Specifying the Problem
or Area of Need

Defining the Planning Task

Step Two: Identifying Program Objectives

Written Objectives Statement

Step Three: Generating Program Solutions

Brainstorming List of
Creative Program Ideas

Step Four: Selecting the Program Design

Program Proposal

Step Five: Implementing the Program Design

Action

Step Six: Evaluating the Program

Evaluation Results

FIGURE 12.6.
Program planning process.[13]

While evaluation appears to be emphasized only in the final stage of this process, in reality it may occur throughout the full sequence, with "feedback" loops from one stage to preceding ones. These may lead to changing goals and objectives, and rethinking program priorities and strategies.

In such systems-based planning approaches as planning-program-budgeting systems (PPBS), program evaluation review technique (PERT), critical path method (CPM), and management by objectives (MBO), both formative and summative evaluation must be used to assist in the planning process and help shape program and budget strategies (see pg. 288).

TRANSACTION-OBSERVATION MODEL

This final type of program evaluation measures the effectiveness or quality of a program, based primarily on direct observation, interviews, and a narrative type of account which documents the nature of staff performance and participant involvement. Olson has developed detailed procedures for carrying out such evaluations, and suggests such possible observational tools as photographs, videotapes and other recording devices.[14] In terms of its application to the ongoing process of program evaluation, this approach requires far more evaluator time and special expertise than other procedures like the professional judgment/standards-and-criteria method. In addition, its findings are more subjective and complex and therefore more difficult to present to a governing board or membership meeting, or to sum up in an annual report.

The strength of the transaction-observation model lies in its ability to explore problem situations where problems of staff or participant relationships are undermining the agency's effectiveness. In addition, it may be a source of generating theory that can lead to valuable research in agency management or program development.

SUMMARY

This chapter illustrates the application of the seven models of agency and program evaluation that were introduced in Chapter 11, with a number of examples drawn from specific agencies and programs. It begins with examples of the professional judgment and standards-and-criteria approach, as shown in the NRPA Community Recreation Evaluation Manual, the NTRS Standards of Practice Manual, and the program evaluation method used by the National Youth Sports Camp organization.

It then illustrates the use of the goal-achievement model, including examples of objectives and performance measures. It concludes with a discussion of: (a) the participation/attendance/income model, (b) the staff ratings and participant-satisfaction method; (c) systems-based evaluation; and (d) the transaction-observation approach. In actual practice, an agency may use several of these approaches at different times or in combination, depending on the benefits that it hopes to gain from systematic evaluation.

ENDNOTES

1. Christine Z. Howe, "Evaluation of Leisure Programs," *Journal of Physical Education, Recreation and Dance* (October 1980): 25.
2. Based on a model by David Santellanes, modified by Lawrence Allen, Univ. of Wyoming, 1983.
3. *Senior Center Standards: Guidelines for Practice* (Washington, D.C.: National Council on the Aging and National Institute of Senior Centers, 1978): 13.
4. Betty van der Smissen, *Evaluation and Self-Study of Public Recreation and Park Agencies: A Guide with Standards and Evaluative Criteria* (Arlington, Va.: National Recreation and Park Association, 1972).
5. Ibid., 57.
6. For a description of the process that evolved these standards, see Glen E. Van Andel, "Professional Standards: Improving the Quality of Services," *Therapeutic Recreation Journal,* (2nd Quarter 1981): 23–26.
7. For the complete guidelines, see Carol Ann Peterson and Scout Lee Gunn, *Therapeutic Recreation Program Design: Principles and Procedures* (Englewood Cliffs, N.J.: Prentice-Hall, 1984): 325–329.
8. *National Youth Sports Program: Manual of Directions for Project Evaluators* (Washington, D.C.: National Collegiate Athletic Association, 1984).
9. Ibid.
10. *Program Budget Form* (Kansas City, Mo.: Department of Parks and Recreation, 1978–1979).
11. Emil J. Posavac and Raymond G. Carey: *Program Evaluation: Methods and Case Studies* (Englewood Cliffs, N.J.: Prentice-Hall, 1980, 1985): 268.
12. Adapted from Richard Kraus, *Recreation Program Planning Today* (Glenview, Ill.: Scott, Foresman and Co., 1985): 291–292.
13. Ruth V. Russell, *Planning Programs in Recreation* (St. Louis: C.V. Mosby, 1982): 283–322.
14. See Ernest G. Olson, "Program Portrayal: A Qualitative Approach to Recreation Program Evaluation," *Leisure Today/JOPER* (October 1980): 41.

WORKSHOP ACTIVITIES TO BE CARRIED OUT WITHIN THE CLASS

37. Obtain the full evaluation or accreditation instrument used by any of the organizations cited in this chapter (National Recreation and Park Association, National Therapeutic Recreation Society, National Youth Sports Program, or National Council on Accreditation), or any similar manual.

    In class, have students review it for comprehensiveness, appropriateness of the items, usefulness of the rating system, effectiveness of the instructions, and similar elements. Have them prepare specific recommendations for updating or improving the manual.

38. Have students return to Assignments Nos. 3 or 4 (Chapter 11) and develop more detailed instruments and procedures for carrying out evaluations in settings or situations that were identified in these processes. For example, have them develop an evaluation instrument for evaluating a specific course, or a more detailed plan for evaluating a recreation agency.

    Have these instruments and procedures reviewed and analyzed in class and identify their strengths and weaknesses.

13

PEOPLE-CENTERED EVALUATION: PARTICIPANTS AND PERSONNEL

As therapeutic recreators become more actively concerned with issues such as accountability and quality assurance, and as accreditation standards . . . become more refined, the topic of assessment becomes a more critical concern in the field. Assessment is seen as a means to improve the quality of therapeutic recreation services to clients and to effectively individualize therapeutic recreation program planning for a particular client.[1]

Performance appraisal is a formal structured system of measuring and evaluating an employee's job-related behavior and outcomes to discover how and why the employee is presently performing on the job and how the employee can perform more effectively in the future so that the employee, the organization, and society all benefit.[2]

INTRODUCTION

This chapter is concerned with two special aspects of evaluation in leisure-service agencies, both of which focus on *people*. They involve: (*a*) the evaluation of participants and (*b*) the evaluation of personnel.

The evaluation of participants is frequently referred to as "assessment," and occurs at three stages of involvement: (*a*) the beginning stage, when there is a need to determine participants' recreational needs and interests; (b) the period of actual involvement, when behavior patterns may be monitored; and (c) at the conclusion of the program, when activity outcomes may be assessed. This is best illustrated in therapeutic recreation programs, which place the greatest emphasis on determining the leisure-related needs of patients and clients and on developing specific objectives as part of an overall treatment plan. However, participant assessment is also an important part of the overall evaluation plan in other types of agencies. For example, in public, voluntary, commercial, or other types of programs, evaluation should measure the degree of satisfaction of participants and their overall levels of involvement. In addition, in a YMCA or company-sponsored fitness program, success may be measured in physiological terms or with respect to improved health, lowered job absenteeism, and higher productivity. Thus, all types of recreation agencies should seek to develop objectives which can be used to measure program success in terms of participant outcomes.

Similarly, the evaluation of leisure-service personnel is carried on in all types of recreation agencies, both to measure the past performance of individual staff members and to improve future involvement. A number of approaches used to appraise personnel performance are presented in the second half of this chapter.

PARTICIPANT-CENTERED ASSESSMENT

While the term "evaluation" is generally used to describe the overall process of determining agency or program quality and effectiveness, the term "assessment" is usually applied to the measurement of participants' needs, interests, and behavioral outcomes. Typically, an important stage in recreation program planning has been to identify the leisure-related needs and interests of participants or potential participants as a basis for making program choices. For example, in many community recreation surveys, it has been the practice to list a wide range of recreational activities suitable for different age groups and to ask respondents to indicate their level of interest in these activities.

RECREATION NEEDS AND INTERESTS SURVEYS

Such surveys have usually sought the following kinds of information from potential participants (community residents, organization members, company employees, or other "target" groups):

1. The individual's age, sex, marital or family status, residence, and other appropriate socio-demographic information.

2. Past or current recreational involvements, usually identified through a comprehensive checklist of activities grouped by major categories.

3. Using a similar activity list, assessment of activities they would like to take part in, and the skill level or program format (class, competitive league, workshop/clinic, or other special event) they would prefer. The participant's ability or willingness to serve as a program leader may also be determined at this stage.

4. Other details, such as the extent of fees the individual might be willing to pay, preferred times or locations for participation, or possible barriers that prevent or limit participation.

Such surveys may be carried out at the beginning of a new program or school year in community agencies, or as part of a special self-study effort. Often they combine the individual's evaluation of programs that he or she has recently taken part in, with a projection of future interests or recommended program activities or needed facilities. An example of such a community survey appears in the Appendix.

CLINICAL ASSESSMENT IN THERAPEUTIC RECREATION

Over the past fifteen years, much fuller attention has been paid to the process of gathering information about the needs, interests, and functional abilities of patients and clients in therapeutic recreation. Dunn writes:

> Gathering information about an individual is the basic focus of assessment. Individuals have been tested, evaluated, and measured in such areas as physical functioning, overall health, mental status, personality, social development, educational achievement, intellectual abilities, and vocational potential. Aspects of interests, beliefs, attitudes, preferences, and motivation have been measured and classified according to a number of variables. Representative standards of performance (norms) have been generated. . . . The process of gathering information to formulate these descriptions is referred to as assessment.[3]

To illustrate, Kinney describes the process of assessing newly admitted clients in mental health settings.[4] This involves far more than having the individual fill out a questionnaire. Instead, it may include a series of interviews and observations of the individual's performance in both structured and unstructured individual and group settings.

INITIAL PATIENT/CLIENT ASSESSMENT

The initial assessment provides a detailed clinical picture of the patient or client at the time of admission to a treatment program or institution, including:

Personal presentation: appearance, physical mannerisms, eye contact, quality of speech, reality orientation, motor behavior, impulse control, affect, insight, and similar elements.

Task Performance: the ability to follow directions, organize his/her own resources, solve problems or make decisions, set realistic goals, maintain a reasonable attention span, and deal concretely with tasks.

Interpersonal Skills: relating effectively with peers and authority figures in competitive or cooperative situations; playing constructive group roles showing both dependence and independence, and assuming responsibility.

As part of this process, the recreation therapist examines the client's leisure attitudes and behavior:

History: What is the leisure history of the client? What kinds of activities has he/she engaged in, e.g., active or passive, group or individual, participative or observant?

Interests: What are the expressed interests of the client? In what kinds of activities does he/she currently participate?

Motivation: What is the client's level of leisure motivation? Does he/she engage voluntarily or require prompting from others? Does he/she seek structured or unstructured activity, and with what apparent goals?

Lifestyle/Organization: What is the client's overall lifestyle like? How does recreation fit into it, in terms of organization of time and daily life activities?[4]

Based on such an assessment, the recreation therapist develops an individual treatment plan for the client, often in collaboration with other members of the treatment team. This plan should include activities designed to strengthen and reinforce areas of positive functioning, and to encourage improvement in areas of present dysfunction or skill deficit. For example, Kanfer and

Grimm describe the process of identifying target behaviors suitable for intervention:

> Clients at various levels of intellectual and social functioning may reveal "pockets" of deficits in self-care behaviors, physical skills, or other motor behaviors that may be essential for adequate functioning. Extreme examples are seen with retardates or chronic institutional residents who may be unable to dress or feed themselves. However, with higher functioning individuals, deficits in relatively simple skills such as driving, use of cosmetics, cooking, and habits of personal hygiene can have a substantial effect on the person's life.[5]

The client's deficits may include both *information* deficits, which are based on the lack of knowledge about appropriate behaviors, and *skill* deficits, which consist of the lack of a repertoire of needed abilities. To remedy them, the therapist may use not only recreation activities as such, but also varied behavior modification techniques, such as prompting, reinforcing, shaping, modeling, and behavior rehearsal.

ASSESSING RECREATIVE BEHAVIOR

Following the initial intake process and development of a treatment plan, the second stage of participant assessment consists of a formative approach, carried on while the individual engages in program activity. The recreation therapist observes the nature of the participants involvement, his or her ability to adapt to challenges of the situation, and the degree of success achieved. Based on such observations, the therapist may provide special assistance or modify program activities by simplifying them, changing the rules, or in other ways helping the patient or client achieve success. The therapist may also revise the treatment plan or change program objectives based on the behavioral assessment. At this stage, many of the areas that were initially observed during the intake process are now appraised in fuller detail, including:

1. *Areas of Knowledge.* The assessment may measure the individual's demonstrated knowledge of the skills, strategies, or rules involved in a given activity. For example, understanding the purpose of a table game, being able to move a marble or checker into the correct place, rolling dice and interpreting them correctly, would fall under this heading.

2. *Attitudes.* A related area of patient/client involvement consists of measuring his or her attitudes toward participation, in

terms of readiness and enthusiasm in taking part, as opposed to having to be persuaded to take part.

3. *Social Behavior.* The participant's involvement in the group, and with other participants, is assessed, with respect to obeying rules and respecting group norms, showing consideration for others, accepting their leadership, cooperating with others, demonstrating awareness of their needs, and, at a higher level, assuming a leadership role.

4. *Skills Mastery.* This refers to the ability to perform appropriate activity skills at designed developmental levels. It may include the specific physical skills involved in such activities as swimming, bowling, skating, dancing, or arts and crafts, or may also extend to skills of self-care or daily living, in areas such as dressing and clothing care, cooking and cleaning, shopping, the ability to use means of transportation, and similar activities.

Often, the assessment may be based on a sequential analysis of skill development, with the participant's initial performance determining the starting point, and with step-by-step progress noted after that point to determine the impact of the program. For example, ongoing evaluation of a multiple handicapped individual's ability in learning to swim might include such elements as partially immersing hands or feet in the water, lowering the lower portion of the body in the water, walking in the water, getting the upper part of the body wet, immersing the face and blowing bubbles, and similar step-by-step tasks.

Progress in such areas may be extremely slow and painstaking, since severely disabled people often lack a wide range of earlier experiences and previously acquired skills on which to build. Thus, performance appraisal must seek to measure even small gains and progress that is uneven or inconsistent.

Contingency Contracting

A form of evaluation used in settings that use behavior-modification techniques is called *contingency contracting*. The client and therapist identify behavioral deficits that need to be improved, and agree on specific goals or target behaviors to be achieved during the activity program. In the case of deviant youth with behavioral problems related to alcohol or drug abuse, high-impulse aggressive behavior with poor self-control mechanisms, frequent lateness or absenteeism, or similar deficits, they may agree to reduce certain negative behaviors over a specified period of time, with a given reward if this is accomplished successfully. In one such project, for example, a young man who had been enrolled in a behavioral treatment program for deviant youth contracted with his activity therapist to reduce his temper outbursts and cursing episodes to no more than three a day, over a period of several weeks.[6] Both the activity therapist and other treatment personnel at the agency were responsible for overseeing his behavior and recording such episodes systematically. With feedback to the client and discussion of the causes and outcomes of his behavior, his aggressive outbursts were gradually reduced to the point that he became a reasonably cooperative member of the group.

In such programs, evaluation provides a continuous stream of feedback to the client and his or her therapist, which can be used in several ways: (a) to help motivate the client and encourage efforts toward improvement; (b) to force the client to face his/her negative behavior and its results realistically; and (c) to be used as the basis for therapeutic discussions, work sessions, or group activities within the agency.

ASSESSMENT OF OUTCOMES

The third stage of patient/client assessment comes at the conclusion of the recreational experience, when it is time to measure the extent to which program objectives have been accomplished. This may include specific measures of behavioral change, in terms of improved skills, knowledge, attitudes, group involvement, or social adjustment. It may include the patient's or client's perception of the activity and its value, or the level of satisfaction he or she has derived from it. It may also be based on the judgments of third parties, such as parents or relatives of disabled participants who may not be able to make objective judgments themselves. Wehman and Schleien stress that parents should be included in the assessment process where feasible, since the law mandates their right to participate in Individualized Education Plans (IEP):

Assuming that the recreation specialist knows *how* and *what* to ask parents, the information gained through structured interviews can be extremely enlightening. The parents . . . see the child as a whole person and not only as someone with a hearing problem, a motor deficiency, or language limitation. They are able to observe how the child uses his or her leisure for long periods of time in a natural context at home; furthermore, they will best understand family dynamics or a neighborhood situation which may be placing undue emotional stress on the child.[7]

BEHAVIORAL ASSESSMENT METHODS

Throughout the entire process of patient/client assessment that has just been described, it is essential that valid observational techniques be used within the program setting. For example, in measuring whether program objectives have been reached, the following guidelines are helpful:

1. It is desirable to use a formal instrument which defines the objectives within appropriate categories of performance. A good measurable objective should be as concrete and specific as possible; it should state: (a) who is going to exhibit the behavior; (b) what behavior will be counted, verified, or measured; (c) conditions under which the behavior will occur; and (d) the minimum level of performance.

2. The participant should be aware of the performance objectives, and should accept them as desirable goals and be willing to work toward them. They should be relevant to his/her overall development, part of normal functioning, and appropriate to the program. Obviously, they should be attainable at a level suited to his/her realistic potential.

3. The program situation should permit the therapist or leader to observe individuals closely enough to be able to record behavior, knowledge, and attitudes correctly and efficiently—in terms of staff-participant ratio, physical proximity, or similar factors. If it were a research situation, it might be necessary to employ other observers to make such judgments, both to ensure their rigor and accuracy, and also to avoid the possible bias that might come from the therapist's being asked to judge client behavior that reflects on his or her own success. However, in most situations, leaders themselves are in a good position to carry out such assessments accurately.

OBSERVER TECHNIQUES

Levy identifies several methods through which trained observers use valid measures to record behavior over time, including: (a) continuous recording in which the observer makes an effort to write down everything as it happens, or in which automatic photographic equipment or videotaping are used to record actions; (b) frequency counts or event recording, which use checklists or rating scales to record behaviors; (c) duration recording, which tells how long a particular behavior lasts; (d) latency recording, which measures the time elapsing between cues or instructional acts and patient/client responses; and (e) interval recording, time sampling, and other special methods.[8] Obviously, those methods that demand constant attention and making notes or filling out charts do not permit an therapist or leader to carry out leadership functions at the same time, and thus require additional trained observers.

INSTRUMENTS USED IN ASSESSMENT

At all three stages of the assessment process, it is essential to use appropriate instruments to ensure that systematic and objective data are gathered. These may include: (a) standardized instruments that measure aspects of personality; (b) comprehensive instruments that measure general aspects of participation in the program; and (c) specially designed instruments that measure specific skills performance or success in achieving behavioral goals within the program.

Standardized Psychological Instruments

One common means of evaluating the outcome of therapeutic recreation experiences is to use standardized instruments that measure such elements as the subject's self-concept. For example, Wright describes the use of the Tennessee Self-Concept Scale in measuring the effectiveness of an experimental Outward Bound program involving forty-seven adjudicated (delinquent) youth in Pennsylvania.[9] Other instruments, such as the Minnesota Multiphasic Personality Inventory or the Devereux Child Behavior Rating Scale, have been used in such projects to measure changes in behavior that may have occurred during the program.

In some cases, instruments that have been developed for broader purposes have been adapted to meet the special needs of evaluative research in therapeutic recreation service. For example, Crewe and others report the use of Goal Attainment Scaling (GAS), an instrument originally designed for use in mental health programs, as a means of measuring the degree to which the goals of physically handicapped adolescents and adults were met in a recreational summer camp program.[10] The setting was Camp Courage, located near the Minneapolis-St. Paul metropolitan area. Four groups of subjects, including both first-time and returning campers, were interviewed to determine the extent to which they had achieved personal goals in four areas: socializing, self-care, emotional well-being, and an optional area related chiefly to participation in specific recreational activities. Figure 13.1 shows the primary goals selected by campers in three of these areas. The overall GAS scores confirmed that the goals which were set were realistic, since the outcomes fell predominately within the *expected* category.

GOALS	CAMPER GROUP			
	Adults		Adolescents	
	1st Time (N = 4)	Returning (N = 13)	1st Time (N = 5)	Returning (N = 10)
Social				
Making new friends	2	5	3	6
Renewing acquaintance with old friends	—	4	—	2
Initiating conversations	2	2	—	—
Spending time socializing	—	1	—	—
Getting to know names of cabin-mates	—	1	—	—
Meeting female campers	—	—	1	—
None	—	—	1	2
Self-Care				
Improved hair-grooming	—	2	—	—
Brushing teeth	—	1	—	—
Losing weight	—	2	—	—
Washing self in shower	—	1	—	—
Improved self-feeding and drinking	1	1	—	1
Refusing unnecessary help	—	—	1	—
Doing transfers	—	—	1	1
Getting enough sleep	—	—	—	1
Improving dressing skills	—	—	1	2
None	3	6	2	5
Emotional Well-Being				
Talking with people	2	—	—	—
Making new friends/acquaintances	—	1	—	—
Meeting members of opposite sex	—	1	—	—
Positive self-talk regarding disability	—	1	—	—
Doing nice things for people	—	1	—	—
Getting good feelings from playing piano	1	—	—	—
Accepting group decisions	—	—	1	—
Losing weight	—	—	—	1
Not feeling homesick	—	—	—	1
None	1	9	4	8

FIGURE 13.1
Goals selected by disabled campers.[10]

Another example of an instrument designed to measure behavior was originally prepared for use in sensory training programs, a technique used in working with disoriented elderly residents in nursing homes (see Fig. 13.2). This instrument is applied by having the recreation therapist or other activity leader who is conducting the sensory training session rate the participants at its end, using the instrument.

CERT Scale

Another example is the Comprehensive Evaluation in Recreational Therapy Scale (CERT Scale), designed by Parker and associates for use in short-term acute-care psychiatric settings. This instrument, which has been presented to the profession in journals and textbooks,[12] provides a rating scale useful for measuring patient/client behavior under the following headings:

I. *General:* attendance, appearance, attitude toward recreational therapy, coordination of gait, and posture.

II. *Individual Performance:* response to therapist's structure: one-to-one; decision-making ability; judgment ability; ability to form individual relationships; expression of hostility; performance in organized activites; performance in free activities; attention span; frustration tolerance levels; and strength/endurance.

III. *Group Performance:* memory for group activities; response to group structure; leadership ability in groups; group conversation; and display of sexual role in the group.

Selected sections of the CERT Scale are shown in Fig. 13.3. It will be seen that a number of rating items are presented in ambiguous enough terms so that different raters might score the same behavior quite differently.

For example, in the first two items, raters might have difficulty in distinguishing between "intense dislike" and "hostility," or between "hesitant" and "superficial," or "distant" and "rejecting." While these choices are apparently intended to be *ordinal* in nature, they sometimes tend to be *nominal*, in that they simply describe different kinds of behavior, rather than behavior in a clearly defined order or ranking (see pg. 140). The third item, having to do with "display of sexual role," illustrates another problem in instrument development. It suggests a strong bias toward heterosexual behavior as the only healthy form of sexual identification, and relies on stereotypical views of appropriate gender-related behavior which might be challenged in some treatment settings or communities. The very phrase, "meets society's norms," poses a difficulty in that society's norms are often ambiguous or rapidly changing in such areas.

Interest   **Comments**
  Refused to come to meeting 0
  Attended, but showed minimal interest 1
  Showed some interest 2
  Interested 3
  Interested and appreciative 4

Awareness
  Unaware of what went on 0
  Distracted by "voices" 1
  At times was unaware of what went on 2
  Generally aware of proceedings 3
  Extremely aware of proceedings 4

Participation
  Did not talk 0
  Answered some direct questions 1
  Would echo answers of others 1
  Answered most direct questions 2
  Volunteered some answers and comments 3
  Volunteered many answers and comments 4
  Talked too much 3

Speech
  Difficult to understand 1
  At times difficult to understand 2
  Fair speech 3
  Good speech 4

Awareness
  Can neither name nor locate body parts 0
  Can name, but can't locate body parts 1
  Can locate, but can't name body parts 2
  Can name and locate some body parts 3
  Can name and locate all body parts 4

Physical Exercise
  Refused to do exercises 0
  Imitated gestures 1
  Needed assistance 2
  Tried, but physically unable 3
  Did all exercises independently 4

Physical Contact
  Hostile withdrawal 0
  Withdraws 1
  Non-committed 2
  Reacts positively 3
  Initiates contact 4

FIGURE 13.2.
Sensory training client-analysis rating scale.[11]

I. C. Attitude Toward Recreational Therapy   (Date)

    (0) Enthusiastic   _____
    (1) Interested   _____
    (2) Indifferent   _____
    (3) Intense Dislike   _____
    (4) Hostile   _____

II. D. Ability to Form Individual Relationships

    (0) Relates Readily   _____
    (1) Hesitant   _____
    (2) Superficial   _____
    (3) Distant   _____
    (4) Rejecting   _____

III. E. Display of Sexual Role in the Group (Male–a; Female–b)

  a. (0) Meets Society's Norms   _____
      (1) Needs to prove (strength, courage)   _____
      (2) Effeminate in Some Mannerisms/Dress   _____
      (3) Effeminate in Most Mannerisms/Dress   _____
      (4) Seductive with Other Males   _____

  b. (0) Meets Society's Norms   _____
      (1) Seductive   _____
      (2) Masculine in Some Mannerisms/Dress   _____
      (3) Masculine in Most Mannerisms/Dress   _____
      (4) Castrating   _____

FIGURE 13.3.
Selected items from CERT scale.[13]

Because of such difficulties, relatively few standardized instruments designed to measure recreational behavior have been developed. Dunn comments:

> Client assessment procedures are the major tool used to individualize program planning, thus contributing to accountability. Because therapeutic recreation is in the early stage of assessment use, few procedures exist. Many of the existing procedures are problematic due to inappropriate development and utilization.[14]

Clearly, an important step for therapeutic recreation specialists and educators in the years ahead will continue to be the development of more-effective instruments and procedures for patient/client assessment, as part of the overall evaluation process.

PERSONNEL EVALUATION

The evaluation of personnel performance represents another key area of administrative responsibility in leisure-service agencies. Frequently it is mandated by Civil Service regulations, or the procedures for carrying it out may be stipulated by labor union contracts. Typically, there is an agreement that all regular employees within the bargaining unit below the level of administrator or division head be evaluated by their immediate supervisors, using a uniform procedure and report form, each year or each six months.

Culkin and Kirsch describe this process as "performance appraisal" and offer the following definition of it:

> Performance appraisal is a formal structured system of measuring and evaluating an employee's job-related behavior and outcomes to discover how and why the employee is presently performing on the job and how the employee can perform more effectively in the future so that the employee, the organization, and society all benefit.[15]

PURPOSES OF PERSONNEL EVALUATION

There are essentially three purposes for carrying out personnel evaluations:

1. To provide an objective and documented basis for personnel decisions and actions related to approval or regular job status (after a probationary period), transfer to another position, promotion eligibility, bonuses, job upgrading, or similar actions. This may include records of both positive and negative examples of the employee's performance, including warnings, disciplinary actions, or citations for superior on-the-job performance.

2. To provide a systematic method for gathering information about the employee's work, and for assessing it in order to help the individual recognize his or her strengths and weaknesses and upgrade future performance. A key purpose of evaluation must be not simply to appraise or rate what has happened in the past, but to provide direction to the employee by recognizing past successes and identifying areas in which improvement is needed.

3. Personnel evaluation may also be used to obtain an accurate picture of the utilization of staff members within the organization. In this sense it may include an analysis of work assignments and schedules, problems of work commitment and motivation, or other factors in the job situation that encourage or inhibit fully productive staff functioning.

Personnel evaluation must be examined within the context of the philosophy of supervision that prevails within an organization. If the management approach is an old-line, authoritarian approach to having a clearly defined chain of command, with orders passed down in an autocratic way from supervisors to subordinates, and with sharply defined and rigidly enforced work assignments, evaluation must be designed to enforce this approach. Its purpose essentially will be to measure whether staff members are adhering to agency policy and performing as required, with resultant rewards or punishments part of a "carrot-or-stick" supervisory process.

If, however, the management philosophy is marked by open communication, shared decision making, and delegation of authority within a participative management approach, staff evaluation must assume a different style. It becomes more of a two-way process, with an open, trust-based effort to analyze the work situation and the individual's performance in it. Performance standards are more flexible, with creativity being encouraged and a readiness to accept temporary failures as part of a larger effort to enrich and strengthen agency productivity.

EVALUATION METHODS AND INSTRUMENTS

Personnel may be evaluated in a number of ways, including: (a) casual daily or weekly observation by supervisors, with informal feedback; (b) staff meetings that review program activities and staff performance; (c) supervisory coaching or counseling sessions with staff members; or (d) program reports submitted at the end of events or seasons.

A common procedure is to require a formal, written evaluation report, frequently linked to a supervisor-subordinate conference that is held at regular intervals. Typically, such reports are based on a detailed evaluation of the employee's work, which he or she is required to read and sign. The employee may enter his or her own statement in the form, which may include a response to criticism or justification for actions taken. The forms that are used vary greatly, ranging from extremely simple, impersonal assessments of the individual's work to a much more complex and probing analysis.

There are three kinds of information that may be assessed to judge an employee. These are: (1) the personal traits or qualities of the individual that are relevant to his or her job; (2) specific work performance and on-the-job behaviors; and (3) outcomes or results, as measured by the accomplishment of predetermined objectives.

While measurement of personal traits and qualities used to receive considerable emphasis in personnel evaluation, today they tend to be considered too subjective a basis for accurate judgments. In addition, they are not as relevant to job performance as a more objective measure of the individual's actual behavior and accomplishments. In measuring the latter, various techniques may be used, including scales used to rate employees on various job functions; recording of critical incidents or specific actions; the use of descriptive essays or anecdotal descriptions of work performance; and comparison of actual results with predetermined objectives. Information can be gained from various sources, including ratings by the employee's immediate supervisor, fellow-workers, participants, or even the individual himself or herself.

Examples of Instruments

Several examples of personnel evaluation instruments follow, drawn from those used in a number of public recreation and park departments. They vary in quality, beginning with an extremely simple and crude form, and moving to more complex and detailed procedures.

The form shown in Fig. 13.4 is taken from a large Eastern city, which will not be identified here. It is notable not only for its brevity, but also for its exclusive emphasis on the staff member's poor performance—which suggests that its chief purpose is to document disciplinary personnel actions. Most employee evaluation instruments seek to give a fuller picture of the staff member's personal qualities and on-the-job performance. A fairly typical exam-

---

Name _____ Title _____ Borough _____

Areas of Performance:
  1. Absenteeism (Specify Dates)
  2. Lateness (Specify Dates)
  3. Other Job Problems (Specify Incidents/Dates)

Evaluator: _____ (Use other side if necessary)

Signature: _____ Title: _____

Office Address: _____ Telephone: _____ Date: _____

(Confidential)

FIGURE 13.4.
Example of personnel rating form in City X.

ple is shown in Fig. 13.5. While brief, it seeks to measure a number of the most important traits related to job performance.

Montclair, New Jersey, Recreation and Parks Department

Name: _____

Position: _____

Location: _____

Date: _____ 19 _____

Outstanding Above Standard Satisfactory Below Standard Unsatisfactory Overall Evaluation:

Factors Evaluated

1. *Personality:* appearance, dress, poise, and tact.
2. *Cooperation:* cordial relations with staff and public.
3. *Initiative:* works effectively without detailed instruction.
4. *Organization:* plans and implements program according to needs and objectives.
5. *Leadership:* rounded leadership ability.
6. *Promotion:* submits timely, well-written publicity.
7. *Dependability:* punctual, carries out assignments.
8. *Emotional Stability:* can objectively accept suggestions and criticism.
9. *Enthusiasm:* interested in work and reflects interest to others.
10. *Reports:* submits reports correctly and promptly.
11. *Skills:* knowledge and ability in varied activities.
12. *Safety Hazards:* recognizes and eliminates them.
13. *Facility Upkeep:* bulletin, play equipment, supplies and apparatus.

Evaluated By: _____ Employee Signature: _____

FIGURE 13.5.
Example of leadership evaluation rating form.[16]

One problem with such forms is that their items are rather subjective and may be interpreted differently by different supervisors. Some forms avoid this problem by providing a range of descriptive statements that characterize behavior in specific terms. This is illustrated in Fig. 13.6, which shows the rating system used by the Nassau County, New York, Department of Recreation and Parks. It is to be filled out by the employee's direct supervisor.

PLEASE PRINT:

Employee _____

Civil Service Title _____

Duties (working title) _____

Park or Unit _____ Division _____

Period of Supervision From _____ to _____

Reason for Report _____

Last Name _____   First Name _____

1. JOB CAPABILITY				
☐ Not observed.	☐ Has gaps in fundamental knowledge and skills of his job.	☐ Has a satisfactory knowledge and skill for the routine phases of his job.	☐ Has excellent knowledge and is well skilled on all phases of his job.	☐ Has an exceptional understanding and skill on all phases of his job.

2. PLANNING ABILITY				
☐ Not observed.	☐ Relies on others to bring problems to his attention. Often fails to see ahead.	☐ Plans ahead just enough to get by in his present job.	☐ Is a careful effective planner. Anticipates and takes action to solve problems.	☐ Capable of planning beyond requirements of the present job. Sees the big picture.

3. LEADERSHIP				
☐ Not observed.	☐ Often weak in command situations. At times unable to exert control.	☐ Normally develops fairly adequate control and teamwork.	☐ Consistently a good leader. Commands respect of his subordinates.	☐ Exceptional skill in directing others to great effort.

4. EXECUTIVE JUDGMENT

☐ Not observed.	☐ Decisions and recommendations are sometimes unsound or ineffective.	☐ His judgment is usually sound and reasonable, with occasional errors.	☐ Displays good judgment, resulting from sound evaluation. He is effective.	☐ An exceptionally sound, logical thinker in situations which occur on his job.	☐ Has a knack for arriving at the right decision, even on highly complex matters.

5. HUMAN RELATIONS

☐ Not observed.	☐ Does not get along well with people. Definitely hinders his effectiveness.	☐ He has difficulty in getting along with his associates.	☐ Gets along with people adequately. Has average skill at maintaining good human relations.	☐ His above average skills in human relations are an asset.	☐ Outstanding skills in human relations increases his effectiveness.

6. JOB ACCOMPLISHMENT

☐ Not observed.	☐ Quality or quantity of his work does not always meet job requirements.	☐ Performance is barely adequate to meet job requirements.	☐ Quality and quantity of his work are very satisfactory.	☐ Performance is above normal expectations for meeting job requirements.	☐ Quality and quantity of his work are clearly superior.

FIGURE 13.6.

Selected items in performance evaluation rating form, Nassau County, New York.[17]

The second page of the Nassau County form calls for an overall evaluation of the staff member, with documentation required if he or she is rated in an extremely high or low category. It also asks for a recommendation with respect to "promotion potential."

EMPHASIS ON IMPROVING PERFORMANCE

Some agencies stress the need to make concrete recommendations for improving the individual's work. For example, in the Long Beach, California, Recreation Department, each employee is asked to identify several challenging, specific objectives to be accomplished during the next rating period. Such objectives should involve both regularly assigned job responsibilities and new projects to be undertaken. When feasible, estimated dates of completion should be given with detailed measures of successful performance. Examples of possible objectives are cited in the department's appraisal report form:

"Develop effective demonstration materials to aid teaching of new craft skills."
"Organize a soccer team in the fall."
"Contact fifty families in the area within the next six months."
"Eliminate a safety hazard."

Two-Way Rating Process

An interesting feature of the Long Beach evaluation approach is that employers are asked to evaluate their supervisors anonymously and to forward the confidential statements to the supervisors for their personal use. Questions such as the following are asked:

"In your opinion, what kind of job is this supervisor doing? Consider both his or her good points and weaknesses needing improvement."
"Were you in his or her position, what would you do to improve and to bring about improvement in your employees?"

Detailed Job Analysis Methods

A last example of personnel appraisal methods is found in the Edmonton, Alberta, Canada Parks and Recreation Department. Here, both leaders and supervisors play an active role.

Leaders are required to analyze their job responsibilities and to identify all significant functions, estimating the amount of time given to each responsibility during the week. They must then describe their work in detail, including: (a) statements about those who supervise them and with whom they work in the department; (b) responsibility for management functions; (c) policy-related functions; (d) personal schedule and role in supervising other employees; and (e) difficult or abnormal working conditions and similar information.

In turn, supervisors must list each leader's key responsibilities and analyze how well they are carrying them out, with specific statements regarding planning, organizing, communicating, problem solving, and other areas of performance. Supervisors must then suggest ways to improve performance in each of these areas, suggesting a priority order for each method and providing a timetable for carrying them out. These include such methods as:

1. Directed self-development (reading, self-study, and so on).
2. Formal training program in in-service courses within department.
3. Outside educational programs, such as courses or seminars.
4. Counseling or coaching assistance by the supervisor.
5. Other on-the-job training.

The plan must be discussed and signed by both the supervisor and the subordinate employee. In addition to a systematic appraisal of the employee's personal qualities, a final confidential section describes the "promotional potential" of the employee, and the supervisor's recommendation as to the best ways in which he or she can be used in the department.

PERSONNEL EVALUATION AND AGENCY PRODUCTIVITY

In addition to improving the performance of individual employees, personnel evaluation may also be used to upgrade the overall productivity of the leisure-service agency.

Glen Alexander, manager of Canyonlands National Park, illustrates this function in describing a review procedure designed to document the weekly activities of each employee within each district. Weekly work schedules showing each employee's daily patrols, programs, or projects were reviewed, along with a comparison of projected versus completed services. By tabulating total employee days spent on projects, Alexander was able to reorganize work assignments to obtain a higher level of employee productivity, resulting in an increase of as much as 100 days in a single district devoted to program coverage—without any increase in staffing costs. He concludes:

The increase in available days came when this district manager found more days were spent in the contact station than were needed to serve visitors. Hence, he let contact station personnel handle administrative duties when no visitors were present; he got rid of pet projects of marginal value when he found they were absorbing large numbers of man days; and he more closely controlled patrol activities to curtail excessive patrols in "favorite" areas.[18]

While such methods are useful chiefly in assessing output in a quantitative way, they may also be used systematically to appraise qualitative performance. Thus, personnel evaluation provides a helpful tool not only in working with individual employees, but also in upgrading the entire process of staff development and work assignments. Tedrick suggests several possible measures that might be used to evaluate the effectiveness of staff performance as a whole.

... (1) a cost-effectiveness ratio between staff required and hours open or numbers served; (2) accident statistics showing low rates per participant; or (3) praise or a lack of complaints by attenders or parents of attenders. Rather than focus on a negative standard ... managers may find it helpful to develop measures of performance oriented toward positive situations. . . .[19]

SUMMARY

This chapter presents two aspects of people-centered evaluation, beginning with the assessment of participants in therapeutic recreation settings. It describes three stages of such assessments: (a) the intake or diagnostic stage, leading to the development of a treatment plan; (b) the formative stage, which observes the patient or client while taking part in activity programming; and (c) the summative stage, which examines the outcomes of recreational programming, with emphasis on the participant's behavioral change or success in achieving other program objectives. It describes several types of instruments used in patient/client assessment, concluding that there is a continuing need to develop new, valid forms and procedures.

The concluding section of the chapter describes the purposes and steps of personnel evaluation. It illustrates several different approaches, all geared to improving the employee's future performance, rather than simply grading him or her on past work.

ENDNOTES

1. Nancy Navar, "A Rationale for Leisure Skill Assessment with Handicapped Adults," *Therapeutic Recreation Journal* (4th Quarter 1980): 21.
2. Randall S. Schuler, cited in David E. Culkin and Sondra L. Kirsch, *Managing Human Resources in Recreation, Parks, and Leisure Services* (New York: Macmillan, 1986): 166.
3. Julia Kennon Dunn, "Assessment," in Carol Ann Peterson and Scout Lee Gunn, *Therapeutic Recreation Program Design: Principles and Procedures* (Englewood Cliffs, N.J.: Prentice-Hall, 1984): 267.
4. W. B. Kinney, "Clinical Assessment in Mental Health Settings," *Therapeutic Recreation Journal* (4th Quarter 1980): 42–44.
5. Frederick H. Kanfer and Lawrence G. Grimm, "Behavioral Analysis," *Behavior Modification* (January 1977): 17.
6. Enid Chasanoff, *Contingency Contracting in a Behavior Modification Program* (New York: Herbert H. Lehman College, Unpublished Master's Thesis, 1978).
7. Paul Wehman and Stuart J. Schleien, "Relevant Assessment in Leisure Skill Training Programs," *Therapeutic Recreation Journal* (4th Quarter 1980): 11–12.
8. Joseph Levy, "Behavioral Observation Techniques in Assessing Change in Therapeutic Recreation/Play Settings," *Therapeutic Recreation Journal* (1st Quarter 1982): 25–32.
9. Alan N. Wright, "Therapeutic Potential of the Outward Bound Process: An Evaluation of a Treatment Program for Juvenile Delinquents," *Therapeutic Recreation Journal* (2nd Quarter 1983): 33–41.
10. Nancy M. Crewe, Diane Garetz, David J. McCaffrey, and Jeffrey P. Prince, "A Pilot Examination of the Use of Goal Attainment Scaling with a Physically Disabled Summer Camp Population," *Therapeutic Recreation Journal* (3rd Quarter 1982): 17–24.
11. Rating form developed by Leona Richman, Patricia Nolan and Matthew Gold, Bronx, N.Y. Psychiatric Center, 1974.
12. Robert A. Parker, C. H. Ellison, T. F. Kirby and M. J. Short, "The Comprehensive Evaluation in Recreation Therapy Scale: A Tool for Patient Evaluation," *Therapeutic Recreation Journal* (4th Quarter 1975): 143–152.
13. *Ibid.* See also Peterson and Gunn, op. cit., 305–308.
14. Dunn, op. cit., 318.
15. David F. Culkin and Sondra L. Kirsch, *Managing Human Resources in Recreation, Parks and Leisure Services* (New York: Macmillan Co., 1986): 166.
16. *Personnel Evaluation Form,* Montclair, N.J., Recreation and Parks Dept., n.d.

17. *Performance Evaluation Rating Form,* Nassau County, N.Y. Department of Parks and Recreation, n.d.
18. Glen D. Alexander, "Evaluate Your Personnel Services for Greater Productivity," *Parks and Recreation* (October 1978): 31.
19. Ted Tedrick, "Personnel Evaluation: In Search of Valid Performance Standards," *Journal of Park and Recreation Administration* (July 1983): 38–39.

QUESTIONS FOR CLASS REVIEW
AND DISCUSSION

39. What is the role of clinical assessment within the overall process of program planning and implementation in therapeutic recreation service? At what stages does it occur and how does it contribute to the treatment process?

40. Contrast the traditional approach to personnel evaluation in recreation and park agencies, with the newer approaches that are based on current participative-management theories. In your discussion, deal with the issue of the human-relations aspect of personnel evaluation and the threats that it may pose for employees.

INDIVIDUAL OR SMALL-GROUP
ASSIGNMENTS TO BE PREPARED AND
PRESENTED TO CLASS

41. Form small groups to search for several standardized instruments which may be used to evaluate behavioral change, self-concept, or other aspects of participants in recreation programs. These may be identified in research journals or dissertations but may require time to obtain. When they have been gathered, duplicate and review them in class.

42. Have individuals or small groups develop personnel evaluation forms specifically designed for use in armed forces, voluntary agency, campus recreation, or other types of recreation agencies. Review and critically analyze them in class.

14

ROLE OF RESEARCH IN PLANNING AND MARKETING

A fundamental skill of a professional parks and recreation administrator is the ability to prepare a community parks and recreation master plan. However, many parks and recreation professionals have not received specific instruction in the development of a master plan, and they may not have been required to learn this skill as functioning professionals. With the tide of budget justification and program evaluation, the master plan concept emerges as a mandatory . . . administrator skill.[1]

Market research is applied research and is directed toward helping owners and managers of business gain information regarding the market to which they want to sell their products and services. Market research is involved with such topics as the size of the market, consumer preferences (and changes in same), information about competition, price changes, conditions related to supply, and other economic or political variables that might affect a business's operations.[2]

INTRODUCTION

In the past, many leisure-service managers operated on the basis of personal conviction, subjective judgments, or rule-of-thumb appraisals. Today, there is a critical need for full documentation of program values and outcomes, and for systematic use of empirical data in all recreation and park planning and decision-making processes. Thus, many agencies have developed management information systems which gather, analyze, and record such data for use in varied management functions.

Two of the most important of these functions are planning and marketing. In the past, it was assumed that such businesslike approaches were suitable chiefly for profit-oriented companies in the recreation field. Today, it is recognized that every type of leisure-service agency *must* employ efficient and up-to-date planning and marketing techniques if it is to be successful.

MANAGEMENT INFORMATION SYSTEMS

One might ask—why does a textbook on research and evaluation also include a chapter on planning and marketing methods? One answer is that research in these areas may yield new insights or conceptual approaches to successful practice. A second answer is that organizations are relying increasingly on systematically gathered data amassed through the use of research and evaluation. Such facts and figures comprise what is today known as "management information systems." Perlman writes:

> The term Management Information System (MIS) refers to the processes and procedures by which raw data are organized into information useful for administrative decision making. Management information systems are commonly computer-based since the repetitive task of tabulating and aggregating large quantities of detailed information can be handled most efficiently by data-processing machines. . . . [3]

What characterizes a true management information system is the quality, accessibility, compatibility, and comprehensive nature of the data, and the way in which they have been organized to serve important management needs. He concludes, "An integrated management information system is necessary to implement other new administrative techniques and strategies."[4]

In large organizations, the task of developing effective information systems is carried out by a combined team of systems analysts or data-management specialists, working together with representatives of the agency who are familiar with its programs, maintenance operations, personnel practices, and fiscal structure. Together, they determine exactly what kinds of information must be gathered, and the uses to which it will be put.

Program codes are developed and software acquired to permit efficient processing of the data, using programs that are compatible with the computer hardware being used. Such a system makes it possible to analyze costs and conduct inventories with much greater speed and specificity than is possible under other approaches. For example, Lange and Mescher describe a new management information system developed for the Pittsburgh, Pennsylvania, Department of Parks and Recreation and housed within the department itself, rather than in a centralized office of city government:

> Department managers now have the ability to compare actual program costs against planned program costs. Facilities were inventoried, and facility codes were developed so that cost information can be retrieved by operating division, primary site, or by a sublocation. . . . An additional benefit of the system is a "computer mystique" which has encouraged compliance with program and facility coding. . . . Historical information is produced for code account, subaccount, facility, and program codes for up to three years on-line, and for as many years as needed through batch reporting.[5]

RECREATION AND PARK PLANNING

While management information systems may be used for a variety of operational functions, one of their most important contributions is to the planning process. Planning has traditionally been recognized as an important managerial responsibility in recreation and park agencies.

A dictionary definition of the term "planning" describes it as "a method or scheme of action; a way proposed to carry out a design; project; as, a plan of campaign."[6] Within the recreation and parks field, it is usually regarded as the process of defining agency goals and priorities; assessing present programs, resources, and capabilities; and laying out a course of action for the future.

In addition to identifying resource needs or developing land-use recommendations, planning may also focus on the general goals and purposes of an organization and may therefore deal heavily with its programs and services. It must rely heavily on economic and demographic analyses, and should deal realistically with political factors and with the role of the leisure-service organization within the total spectrum of other community agencies.

ORIENTATIONS OF RECREATION PLANNERS

Recreation planners may represent varied perspectives and disciplines. Some are trained in civil engineering or landscape architecture, and are therefore heavily concerned with a technological or resource-oriented approach to identifying needs and priorities. Others may have a background in sociology, political science, or urban planning, and are likely to be concerned with user behaviors and preferences, and the social impact of recreation facilities and programs.

Recreation and parks planning is usually concerned with the environment as a setting for leisure involvement. Gold refers to it as a process that relates the leisure time of people to space. He writes:

> In practice, recreation planning blends the knowledge and techniques of environmental design and the social sciences to develop alternatives for using leisure time, space, energy, and money to accommodate human needs.[7]

He goes on to contrast the traditional approach to recreation and park planning with a newer, more innovative approach. The traditional approach emphasized: (a) quantity over quality, (b) physical over social objectives, (c) form over function, (d) expansion of recreation areas despite possible negative effects on the environment, and (e) community needs rather than individual needs.

The newer approach, Gold writes, is heavily concerned with human benefits and outcomes, but also with costs and efficiency. It is:

> ... more quantitative in method and qualitative in its ends than the traditional approach. It relies on the use of sophisticated research methods, gaming simulation, systems analysis, program budgeting, and advocacy planning to develop policy alternatives that can be translated into action programs.[8]

THE PLANNING PROCESS

The planning process varies greatly according to the scale of the problem or the agency that is carrying it out. However, in general it involves the following steps:

DETERMINE BASIC PHILOSOPHY AND MISSION

At the outset, whether the purpose of the planning is to provide direction for an entire, large-scale recreation and park system over a period of time or to establish guidelines for a much more limited project, it is essential to develop or determine a basic philosophy that will govern the effort. This consists of a mission statement or overall statement of purpose that provides a framework for all agency efforts.

INVENTORY PRESENT FACILITIES, PROGRAM, AND RESOURCES

Next, it is essential to carry out a comprehensive analysis of the agency's present areas and facilities, programs, and services, and other resources, including personnel, fiscal support, and similar areas of information. In a fully detailed planning study, it might also be desirable to examine its current policies, the constraints under which it operates, and the levels of support it enjoys within the community.

NEEDS ASSESSMENT

This is a critical aspect of any planning study, since it defines the leisure needs and interests of community residents. Customarily, this is accomplished through a needs-assessment study, in which community residents fill out questionnaires that evaluate the present program activities and present their views or wishes regarding future program opportunities. This is a narrow approach to the problem, however. An effective needs assessment study should examine a *comprehensive* cross section of the community, in geographic, demographic, and generational terms. It should also take into account the opportunities provided by other agencies, through a thorough environmental scan that identifies the facilities and programs provided by public, private, commercial, and other types of recreation sponsors. It should forecast future needs by estimating probable shifts in public leisure demands and contrasting them with the existing supply of facilities and services.

DEVELOP GOALS AND PRIORITIES

Based on the preceding steps, it is now possible to develop a set of short- and long-range goals for the community or other sponsoring agency. These may relate to specific population groups, broad program purposes or social needs, property acquisition, or other types of desired outcomes. Some planning studies identify priorities on several levels of importance. For example, they may assign a high-priority level to youth gangs in the inner city, while placing other needs at a lower level of concern. Generally, long-range goals or priority statements are then broken down into intermediary objectives which constitute the actual tasks to be accomplished in achieving the study recommendations.

IDENTIFY ALTERNATIVE STRATEGIES

At this stage, the planning team identifies a number of possible strategies or courses of action. These may have to do with site acquisition and development, the initiation of new programs, or reallocation of the agency's resources.

They may present sharply different approaches to resource development or program planning, or may present essentially the same recommended course of action at several levels of support, ranging from an extremely high-level or ambitious approach to a more conservative and limited recommendation.

ANALYZE AND SELECT RECOMMENDED STRATEGIES

Each alternative strategy or course of action must be analyzed, in terms of: (a) its desirability or projected benefits; (b) its costs, in economic and other terms; (c) its probability of success, in terms of the obstacles that might limit it, or the kinds of support that it might gain; (d) its appropriateness in terms of the stated philosophy of the organization and the findings of the needs assessment; and (e) all other factors that would bear on its adoption and probable success.

Based on such considerations, the planning team prepares a set of recommended actions. These may consist of properties to be acquired, facilities to be rehabilitated, programs to be initiated, or other concrete suggestions. If the plan's primary focus is on land use and resource management, new maps may be developed which give detailed demographic information in relation to presently available facilities and programs in each sector or district of the community, as well as preliminary designs of sites to be developed.

PRESENT PLANNING REPORT

The final phase of the planning process is to develop and present a final report to the agency or board that has authorized the study. This often occurs in stages, with an initial presentation of preliminary study findings and recommendations, followed by possible revisions or rethinking of specific aspects of the proposal, and, finally, the finished report.

The report may include recommendations for implementation—for example, suggested sources for funding, special grants, initiating of new types of revenues or charges, and similar guidelines. It may also suggest ways of evaluating the progress and outcomes of the plan, both during the implementation process and at a later stage.

Throughout this process, it is obvious that planning represents a form of systematic investigation which has much in common with the more traditional types of research studies. For example, in the needs-assessment stage of planning, instrument development and data analysis methods are similar to those used in social research generally. If rigorous research standards are not applied throughout, the findings and recommendations of planning studies may have little worth.

OTHER PLANNING GUIDELINES

In carrying out this process, it is essential to ask the following kinds of questions:

What will be the scope of the planning effort and who should be involved in it? What outcomes are desired? What will be required to carry it out, and what specific objectives must be achieved to accomplish the overall goals?

What planning methods should be used, and what standards or criteria will provide a basis for making planning decisions? How can future trends best be identified, with respect to population, economic, or environmental changes?

In developing specific planning recommendations, it is essential that the fullest possible use be made of advisory councils, neighborhood associations, public hearings, or similar methods of gaining input from the community residents. In addition, cooperative or interagency planning sessions should seek to develop joint efforts with municipal departments or community organizations, to promote the maximum coordination of facilities and programs.

Finally, planning recommendations should be based not only on the accepted standards and social needs within the community, but also on its economic capability and the potential ability of new recreation facilities and programs to yield new sources of revenue. In an era of growing costs for energy, it is essential to take into account the continuing costs of utilities and maintenance in determining whether given facilities will be feasible.

RECREATION AND PARK MASTER PLANNING

One of the most common forms of planning for recreation and park agencies is the comprehensive master plan. Normally this is a long-range plan for parks and facilities development. It may include guidelines for acquisition of parklands, conceptual drawings of communitywide park systems, and preliminary layouts for specific facility development. It should also provide implementation plans which consist of specific recommendations for property acquisition and development, and estimated capital and operational costs, along with potential sources of special funding and estimates of projected revenues of facilities. It does not normally, however, include fully developed designs for parks or other facilities.

Elements related to programming or administrative functions are usually excluded from master planning reports for the following reasons: (1) physical development is regarded as more important than program planning; (2) public officials are oriented to activities which have visible and tangible results, as exemplified in land-use recommendations; (3) architectural or other planning firms which tend to conduct such studies rarely have expertise in recreation programming or administrative practice; and (4) many professionals believe that it is impractical to attempt to include programmatic concerns in long-range master planning because public interests tend to change so rapidly. However, it is the authors' view that a number of these arguments are unfounded, and that program and administrative functions *should* be included in well-conceived recreation and park master planning studies.

In terms of sponsorship, master planning on the local level is usually funded and authorized by municipal, county, or township governments and is usually assigned to outside planning firms, following a process of competitive bidding and submission of proposals for conducting the study. It may be carried out at regular intervals (such as every five or ten years), or to meet a special need, such as the consideration of a possible major acquisition of property. It may also be conducted to meet the requirements of state or federal authorities for local planning information, as in the development of state outdoor recreation plans.

ELEMENTS OF MASTER PLANNING

Contemporary master planning is basically quantitative in its reliance on the numerical analysis of facilities and acts of participation. It places heavy emphasis on basic econometric principles of supply and demand. Variations of this approach have been used extensively with the Statewide Comprehensive Outdoor Recreation Plans (SCORP) mandated by the federal government. It is recognized that this is not the only approach to master planning; some planners place heavy emphasis on political, social, and esthetic factors in the decision-making process, and it is possible to blend all such elements in comprehensive studies.

Establishment of Planning Direction or Mission

As stated previously, the first step in planning is to establish its purpose, outcomes, and limitations. It is important to differentiate between the goals *of* the planning study, and the goals that are likely to be identified *in the course of* the study. Usually, the goals of the planning study are determined by the sponsors themselves (the funding public authority), although they may be influenced by the regulations or requirements of outside bodies, such as state or federal agencies. In addition, the actual scope and procedural design of a master planning study is usually the prerogative of the agency commissioning the effort.

Clarification of Setting

It is essential to gather detailed background information related to the setting itself, including: (1) geographical boundaries and related topographical, climatic, and similar factors; (2) demographic analysis of the population; (3) economic conditions and trends; and similar elements. It is also important to identify anticipated changes in the social, economic, or other conditions of the area being studied, which may influence recreation and park needs and capabilities.

Assessing Present Adequacy

This stage requires a systematic inventory of the existing supply of recreation areas, facilities, and programs within the community. It is usually conducted by a team of agency staff members and community residents working cooperatively, although if an outside planning firm is carrying out the study, it may gather such information independently. Each park and recreation area and facility is mapped, examined, and systematically described, in terms of its location; the specific recreation resources it provides (sports fields, swimming pools, meeting rooms, and so on); the uses that are made of each facility on a year-round, season-by-season basis (including the specific activities that are carried on, and the volume of participation); the present condition and maintenance or rehabilitation needs of each facility; and its staffing levels. In addition, it is helpful to develop a statement of the operational costs of each facility, as well as a summary of the revenues it yields through fees and charges, assuming that they are in force.

The physical location and similar details should be recorded on maps, with locations, types, and actual recreation resources identified using a system of keys symbolizing each type of facility or available activity. In a large municipality or county program, they may be shown in separate districts or areas, and in a smaller community in a single map. In some cases, colored transparent overlays may be used to show different types of special facilities: green for parks, nature reserves, and open spaces; brown for indoor facilities and structures; red for athletic areas; and blue for lakes, pools, or other aquatic areas. Tables may be used to show summaries of staffing patterns, volumes of recreational use, or costs and income levels of areas and facilities.

Establishing Need

Planners often rely on widely accepted standards to measure the adequacy of present resources in meeting community recreation needs. These include: (a) space standards based on the "population ratio method" (acres of park land per 1,000 people); (b) recreation space based on area percentage; (c) availability of specific facilities by proximity to user groups; (d) needs determined by user characteristics or demand projections; or (e) carrying capacity of land or other recreation resources.[9]

For several decades, the United States and a number of other industrialized nations accepted a guideline applicable to urban communities, that there should be a minimum of 10 acres of park and recreation land for every 1,000 residents. In the mid-1960s, the National Recreation and Park Association developed a revised standard recommending that a minimum of 25 acres per 1,000 residents be provided by local government authorities and that 65 acres be provided by state agencies—a total of 90 acres in all. Recognizing that this standard could not possibly be met by many larger cities, the National Recreation and Park Association has more recently promulgated a recommendation that park systems, at a minimum, be composed of a "core" system of parkland, with a total of 6.25 to 10.5 acres of developed open space per 1,000 population. The availability of "adjunct" parklands, provided by county, park district, or state authorities must be taken into account when considering a total well-rounded system of park and recreation areas.[10]

It is generally recognized that such standards, as well as classification systems which recommend that a given percentage of all space within a community be assigned to park and recreation use, must serve as a *guide* to planning—not as an absolute blueprint. Cities vary so much in their capabilities and needs that it is impossible to define any single standard that will apply to all communities. In addition, the specific recreation interests of the population and the ways in which facilities are used will dictate the minimum standards that should be applied. Because of the great differences among communities, it is desirable that communities that wish to use a standards approach to needs identification develop their *own* set of standards, based on those that have been professionally promulgated. These standards should take into account the unique circumstances and characteristics of the community or surrounding region. For example, the State of Wyoming developed its own set of standards because it felt that the existing national standards were inappropriate for a basically rural, resource-oriented state.

Linked to the standards approach is a classification system which defines the specific number of persons that facilities of different types may be expected to serve, and which thus provides the basis for a set of standards for individual sports areas, as an example. To illustrate:

Ice hockey requires an area of 22,000 square feet, including support areas; one such indoor rink should be provided for each 100,000 in population, and may be expected to serve people within a ½ to 1 hour of travel time.

Tennis requires an area of 7,200 square feet for a singles court; one court should be provided for each 2,000 in population, and should serve people with a service radius of ¼ to ½ mile.

Football requires a minimum of 1.5 acres; a football field should be provided for each 20,000 in population, and should serve people with a service radius of ¼ to ½ hour of travel time.[11]

Similar standards have been developed and published recently for different categories of parks. For example:

Mini-parks of 1 acre or less should have a service area with a less than ¼ mile radius, to meet the needs of a concentrated population or special groups such as tots or senior citizens in close proximity to apartment complexes, townhouse developments, or housing for the elderly.

Neighborhood park/playground areas should consist of 15 or more acres, with service radiuses of ¼ to ½ miles to meet neighborhood needs for populations of up to 5,000.

Community parks, which may include varied athletic, aquatic or natural areas, should serve several neighborhoods, with a 1 to 2-mile service radius.[12]

Here too it must be recognized that any arbitrary standard which itemizes population-ratios guidelines or service-radius minimums is not likely to apply to all situations. Indeed, each type of activity may have different forms that dictate the number of people who can be served, or the distance they will travel to go to a particular type of facility. Lancaster writes:

> A family camping experience in the High Sierras is dramatically different from an organized camp-out with the Cub Scouts at a local park. A pick-up game of softball may have a service radius measured in minutes, while a championship tournament of competing leagues could require several hours of travel for participation. Activity classification may be similar, but the quality of the experience and the attraction capability of facilities can be substantially different.[13]

Supply-Demand Approach

Based on such factors, the Standards Revision Task Force of the National Recreation and Park Association has developed a model through which each community may measure its own needs for specific recreation and park facilities and acreage. This is a supply-demand model based on the following key concepts:

Participation Rate (PR): The percentage of a given population that will participate in a specific activity.

Participation Days (PD): The average number of times each individual user will participate in a recreation activity during a year.

Demand (D): The number of people who can reasonably be expected to attend or participate in a particular recreation activity during a year.

Design Day (DD): An average weekend day during a peak season of use for a particular activity.

Design Capacity (DC): The percentage of participation days that can be expected to occur in a specific activity on a design day.

Spatial Standards (SS): Reasonable capacities of recreation facilities or areas by spatial unit at any given time.

Turnover Rates (TR): The number of times a recreation activity spatial unit can be used during a single day.

Facility Need (FN): The number of spatial units required to accommodate a particular activity.[14]

To apply this model, it is necessary to gather scientifically valid information about the population to be served. Surveys are carried out to determine the preference or demand for each type of facility or activity. The participation rate multiplied by the base population and an estimate of the number of participation days yields the total number of preference days that will occur during a year, or "preference."[15]

The model then employs the following formula:

$$\frac{\text{Preference} \times \text{Design Capacity}}{\text{Spatial Standard} \times \text{Turnover Rate}} = \text{Facility Need}$$

Facility need is an expression of the activity preferences translated into specific facility requirements. In it, the spatial requirement for a given activity or facility use is multiplied by the turnover rate to establish the total number of participation events each unit can accommodate on a given day. Multiplying preference by design capacity determines the number of participation events accommodated for each activity. Dividing this number by the product of the standard and turnover rate results in the basic facility need, including both active and passive events. The facility need should be measured against the currently available supply of facilities in the community, in order to determine the number of new facilities that would be needed to accommodate projected demand. This is the approach most frequently used in SCORP and municipal master planning studies. It implies that, while the same set of space or facility standards will not apply to all communities, the same basic principles and methodology *do* apply. And, while many recreation and park managers may not elect to apply this planning system as a routine mathematical procedure, they will find its concepts and elements helpful.

Final Recommendations

Realistically the final recommendations of master planning studies are likely to be strongly influenced by political and other social factors. The conflicting demands of different neighborhoods or social groups, the battle between environmental and business interests, or even between different recreational interest groups, tends to make planning a highly controversial operation. In many large cities, for example, there is a tendency for members of the city council to fight to gain new facilities, such as swimming pools, recreation centers, or skating rinks, for the neighborhoods they represent, as tangible evidence of their ability to represent their constituents forcefully. At the same time, they tend *not* to fight as effectively for the continued budget support needed to operate such facilities, which is usually a citywide concern. Planners have the obligation to provide a rational, professional basis for making recommendations in such areas and wherever possible for removing the planning process from the partisan political arena.

OTHER TYPES OF PLANNING STUDIES

In addition to park and recreation master planning, there are a number of other types of planning studies used by leisure-service agencies. For example, many communities or professional organizations have conducted planning studies concerned with such elements as: (a) the development of policies and priorities; (b) personnel management; (c) the development of expanded revenue sources, including fees, charges, and concessions; (d) the maintenance and rehabilitation of deteriorating park resources; (e) problems such as crime and vandalism in recreation areas; (f) the use of volunteers; and similar specialized concerns.

Fairmount Park Master Plan

As an example, an extensive planning study was carried out of Philadelphia's historic Fairmount Park, which examined such elements as its vegetation; hydrology; historical and cultural resources; circulation, access, parking, and signage; engineering systems; archeological resources; fiscal support and operations; and user demands.

The study was conducted by an outside planning firm that used consultants who were specialists in each of the technical areas concerned, ranging from civil engineering to financial analysis. The final report presented a detailed picture of the park's overall operation, including its major strengths and weaknesses and the steps—

both immediate and long-range—needed to restore it to a state of vigorous health and attractiveness. To illustrate, several of the recommendations dealing with natural drainage basins in the park follow:

Recommendations

1. Undertake a program of construction for erosion control and stormwater management.

2. Cooperate with other agencies to produce and enforce development planning and regulations which reduce stormwater-related impacts.

3. Coordinate volunteer groups, such as watershed organizations, equestrian and hiking clubs, and environmental groups, to assist in repair and maintenance of trails.

4. Conduct aquatic habitat improvement project, including dredging of pools above dams in Fairmount Park streams.

5. Work with Pennsylvania Department of Environmental Resources, the U.S. Geological Survey, the Delaware River Basin Commission, and the Philadelphia Water Department to expand and coordinate ongoing water quality monitoring programs.

Priority Actions

1. Repair and prevent further erosion in gullies and on slopes in stream drainage basins within Fairmount Park.

2. Provide bank and channel stabilization in eroded streams. Methods would include . . . stabilization of large eroded areas in channels using gabions (wire mesh baskets filled with rocks) or rip-rap; and repair and fill of eroding and undercut retaining walls.

3. Repair and maintain storm sewer inlets, culverts, and drainageways.[16]

Policy Planning Studies

Other organizations may conduct studies on a national, regional, or state level to evaluate their current policies and establish new priorities based on changing social conditions. For example, the Jewish Welfare Board carried out a nationwide evaluation and planning study of Jewish community centers and YM-YWHA's during the mid-1970s.[17] Using a mixture of interviews, workshops, and survey techniques, the study team examined the health, physical education, and recreation programs of hundreds of centers throughout the United States. It also examined the social forces that were encouraging sedentary lifestyles, and the place of sports and fitness programs in the culture at large.

Based on input from hundreds of board members, center directors, and consultants, the study team prepared a report with recommendations concerned with: (*a*) clarification of agency goals and program objectives; (*b*) the conduct of competitive sports activities; (*c*) the operation of fitness centers and health clubs; and (*d*) the initiation of fitness, preventive, and rehabilitative services, including stress-testing and postcoronary programs. It also made recommendations regarding the role of the national body (Jewish Welfare Board) in formulating policies and coordinating the work of member units throughout the country.

Systems Planning Methods

Still other recreation and park agencies make use of systems-based planning methods that have been developed in industry or government, including the following:

PPBS: Planning-Program-Budgeting Systems (PPBS) was developed in the early 1960s by the U.S. Department of Defense, and has since been used by many organizations.[18] It involves a planning mechanism that integrates information of all kinds into a single, coherent management decision-making and controlling process, with emphasis on budgetary planning. Although PPBS represents a costly and complex process which requires sophisticated computer analysis and is rarely used by small organizations, many planners make use of its basic principles as a way of carrying out planning in a rational and efficient way.

PERT AND CPM: Program Evaluation Review Technique (PERT) and CPM Critical Path Method (CPM) are network models—a term used to describe planning methods that are carried out over a period of time, with a series of stages. These include the following: (1) identifying and/or planning a project's essential *events* and *activities* (the tasks that must be accomplished and the work necessary to do this) and arranging them in a logical sequence; (2) scheduling the *estimated period of time* it will take to accomplish each activity and cumulatively the entire project; and (3) *controlling* or *monitoring* the network of events, step by step, including possible delays, changes of plans, or modifications as they occur.[19]

Management by Objectives

This represents a popular planning strategy in which supervisors and subordinates are jointly involved in establishing agency objectives at several levels: department, divisional, unit, and staff.[20] Recognized as a useful means of encouraging employee input in the management process and carefully evaluating the success of program efforts, this systems-based approach leads to improved agency efficiency and organization.

In all three systems-based approaches, planning should involve the input of staff members on all levels and should be based on solid data with respect to the agency's goals, program needs, and resources. Clegg and Chambliss describe the process of using MBO in the Dallas Parks and Recreation Department; it requires sophisticated staff-training exercises in methods of writing objectives and action plans, evaluating program outcomes, and determining benefits to be derived from the system.[21] Perhaps more than any other approach, it shows how evaluation is an integral part of the planning process.

MARKETING IN LEISURE-SERVICE MANAGEMENT

A second key element of management responsibility in recreation and park agencies of all types today is marketing. Too often, this term is thought of primarily as *selling*—not infrequently with the implication that its sole concern is advertising or promoting a product with the use of flashy gimmickry or hucksterism.

This is far from the truth; instead, marketing represents the total process through which any organization or business designs and delivers products or services in an efficient and successful manner. Its key element is the idea of "exchange," in the sense that individuals or social units offer and exchange objects or services of value with each other on a voluntary basis. Thus, marketing may be defined as:

> . . . the analysis, planning, implementation, and control of carefully formulated programs designed to bring about voluntary exchanges of values with target markets for the purpose of achieving organizational objectives. It relies heavily on designing the organization's

offering in terms of the target markets' needs and desires, and on using effective pricing, communication, and distribution to inform, motivate, and service the market.[22]

Marketing represents a systematic approach to planning programs or services that will appeal to specific "target" populations, and then delivering these products in the most efficient way. Each stage of the marketing process must involve systematic and objective analysis. This often requires extensive market research to gather critical information on consumer attitudes, opinions, and reaction to product offerings.

Marketing is as important for nonprofit organizations as it is for commercial businesses. When properly done, it accomplishes two goals: (1) it ensures *improved satisfaction* on the part of clients or service consumers, since their needs will have been carefully studied in advance and programs and services designed to meet these effectively; and (2) it helps to guarantee a *successful operation,* in terms of products or services that reach a substantial segment of the potential market population and either make a profit or satisfy other objectives of the agency.

MARKETING ANALYSIS

Kotler points out that, if a marketing expert from the business world were asked to appraise a nonprofit organization, he or she would probably analyze three elements:

First, he would evaluate the marketing environment of the organization, specifically its markets, customers, competitors, and macroenvironment. Second, he would evaluate the marketing system within the organization, specifically (its) objectives, programs, implementation, and (structure). Third, he would evaluate the major marketing activities of the organization, specifically its products, pricing, distribution, personal contact, advertising, publicity, and sales promotion.[23]

This process is illustrated, step by step, in Fig. 14.1, which shows how a recreation and park agency may adopt a marketing strategy to ensure that its overall plan of action is as effective and successful as possible. Each of the steps of this approach is briefly discussed in the following section of this chapter.

AGENCY MISSION AND PRIORITIES

At the outset, it is essential that the sponsoring organization clearly define its basic philosophy and mission. Just as in the plan-

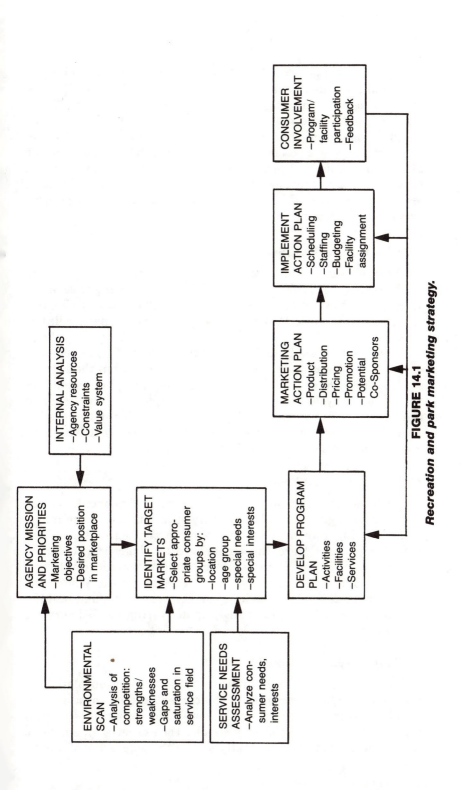

FIGURE 14.1
Recreation and park marketing strategy.

ning process (see pg. 276), this is necessary to provide a framework for the kinds of decisions and choices that must be made throughout the program planning and marketing sequence. In addition to identifying specific marketing objectives, this first stage may assign a high-level priority to providing certain types of facilities or programs, and a secondary priority to providing others. It may also define its desired place in the leisure-service marketplace in terms of a stated share of the public's participation, or in terms of a given percentage of generated revenues needed to support programs and facilities.

ENVIRONMENTAL SCAN

In evaluating the marketing environment, agency planners might ask, "What is our competition? Who is providing leisure services, and with what degree of success? What are their pricing policies, and how successful are they from a cost-benefit point of view?"

As part of this analysis, it is desirable to identify existing gaps or areas of saturation or excessive competition within the leisure-service field. Researchers have identified the phenomenon of "program life cycles" in recreation. In assessing current trends in the leisure-service field, it is important to identify possible activities that are on the "rise," rather than those that have been overdone or are on the decline in public interest.

INTERNAL ANALYSIS

In addition to examining the marketing environment, the leisure-service agency should carefully study its present management system, and develop appropriate strategies for future marketing efforts. Here, the agency's staff and physical resources, its ability to deliver services, its public or community relations processes, and its public image must all be examined. Where necessary, changes must be made to correct weaknesses and build in needed capabilities for creating and delivering needed services appropriately.

SERVICE NEEDS ASSESSMENT

The next step in developing the marketing action plan is to carry out a needs assessment of the current and potential recreational interests of the agency's clientele. Identifying the overall population should be relatively simple. For example, an employee recreation department normally serves the employees of a company and their families, just as a YWCA typically serves both its own members and other residents within the adjacent community, usually with emphasis on girls and women. In some cases, as in the situation of a theme park that draws visitors from the entire country and from other lands as well, it may be a more complex task.

In-depth marketing research or consumer studies may be carried out at the point of involvement or service-delivery, or at the source of potential participants. To illustrate, Walt Disney World does extensive market research with users, commissioning dozens of surveys each year involving many thousands of participants or potential visitors. These studies are done both at the theme parks themselves, and also in sample cities around the United States and Canada to gain detailed understanding of the perceptions and wishes of both "users" and "nonusers."

Motivations for Participation

Sophisticated marketing studies do not simply ask what people "want" to do. Instead, they seek to explore the reasons *why* people attend an event or take part in an activity. Understanding leisure motivations makes it possible both to design more attractive and satisfying activities or facilities and to package them appealingly, in order to draw the largest possible audience. To illustrate, if people go to a race track or major auto racing event, their reasons may include such elements as the desire to gamble, to share in the excitement of a high-risk activity, to be seen, or similar factors. Attending a rock concert would involve another set of motivations, and registering for a weaving class an entirely different group of reasons. Social interaction, a sense of accomplishment, the opportunity to express oneself creatively, illusion or escape, relaxation, or the admiration of others may all be potential outcomes that are part of the expectation of potential audiences. Programs and activities, Crompton writes, are simply vehicles for the outcomes or satisfactions that users hope to reach. To illustrate:

> Charles Revson, who was responsible for building Revson cosmetics into the thriving enterprise it is today, once said, "In the factory we make cosmetics. In the store we sell hope." He realized people use the product—cosmetics, but they do not buy them. They buy hope.[24]

Thus, it becomes necessary to determine not only what activities or services are to be provided, but how this is to be done in terms of the level of quality, the packaging of the product, the image it would have, and similar factors.

IDENTIFY TARGET MARKETS

Based on all that has gone before—including the review of the agency's mission and priorities, its competitive position within the marketplace, and a needs assessment of participants and potential participants—it is now possible to identify the specific target markets that the leisure-service agency will concentrate on.

The term "target market" is used to describe relatively homogeneous groups of people with similar service needs or preferences. Crompton writes:

> Target marketing is a key marketing concept. Every park and recreation agency has to decide *whose* needs should be served before deciding *what* needs to serve. The identification and selection of target market groups influences and often directly determines all the ensuing decisions regarding types of services and their distribution, pricing and communication.[25]

Within a community served by a public recreation and park department, this might include developing priorities as to which age groups are to be served, and in which locations programs are to be developed. The needs of special populations, such as different ethnic groups, the economically disadvantaged, or the physically and mentally disabled, should be taken into account.

The special interests of different population groups must also be considered. Here, both general surveys of recreational interests of the public at large, and specific market surveys of the population in question, should be utilized. The varying interests of sports enthusiasts, those involved in the arts, social activities, fitness, or outdoor recreation should all be represented in the selection of target populations. Within the overall marketing plan, certain activities may be designed like a rifle shot, in the sense that they are aimed to reach a small, readily identifiable audience, while others are like a shotgun, in that they are aimed at a broad, undifferentiated audience.

In considering potential audiences for their programs, recreation agencies obviously must consider not only their current or potential leisure interests, but also such factors as family status, ability or willingness to travel, and financial capability. Particularly in the case of target market groups that have limited ability to pay for the use of facilities or programs, it may be ncessary to determine whether it is possible to modify fees or to obtain special funding or other assistance from the business community, foundations, or other sources of grants. Such considerations are particularly important for public or nonprofit agencies with high-priority social-service goals. They are obviously less critical for commercial or private agencies.

DEVELOP PROGRAM PLAN

At this point, all of the earlier marketing study findings culminate in an overall plan for providing facilities, programs, and other types of leisure services to the target markets that have been selected. In some cases, these may represent simply traditional forms of recreational activity, such as sports, games, arts and crafts, music, drama, and dance—all placed within appropriate program formats and scheduled at convenient times and in readily accessible locations to serve the maximum numbers of participants.

In other cases, the program plan may focus on the development of a new facility, such as a large recreation center or a new ski complex. Here, it becomes necessary to analyze all the products, services, and auxiliary enterprises or functions that might be involved in the operations. In a theme park, for example, in addition to programmatic or entertainment features, the programming process would deal with the development of hotels, campsites, shops, restaurants, and other profit-oriented sites and services. In the case of a government agency or nonprofit organization, it may be that other considerations, such as esthetic or health-related benefits, would also be critical. For example, a comprehensive new senior center might involve health services like dental clinics or glaucoma screening sessions, legal aid, nutritional programs, transportation assistance, and special assistance to the homebound.

At this stage, it is essential to consider not only the activity that is to be offered, but exactly how it is to be delivered in terms of audiences served, the nature of instruction or involvement, timing and scheduling, the specific objectives that are attached to each program element, and similar factors. Targets might be established for desired attendance or registration totals over a period of time, as well as projected costs and revenues.

Quality Factors

The quality of the product or service is a critical consideration in marketing analysis. Any recreational pursuit may be offered at different levels of quality and expense. The size of the group, the attractiveness of the environment, the nature of the instruction provided, and even the social aura of the group itself may vary greatly. Parasuraman, Zeithami, and Berry argue that the perceived quality of any product or service contributes significantly to its ability to gain a projected share of the market and return on investment. They define the concept of service quality as a comparison of the consumer's expectations and the actual performance that takes place:

> Service quality is a measure of how well the service level delivered matches consumer expectations. Delivering quality service means conforming to customer expectations on a consistent basis.[26]

MARKETING ACTION PLAN

In a literal sense, this represents the key stage of the marketing process, for it is at this point that the agency *presents* its program to its intended public. In a business sense, the so-called mix of "product," "distribution," "pricing," and "promotion" must all be blended to reach target markets with the most appealing and attractive images that can be developed. *Distribution* refers to the location of different program elements to ensure that there is appropriate coverage of the community or region, as well as convenient accessibility for each subset of potential participants.

Pricing policies should be based not solely on "what the traffic will bear," but on a combination of factors, including the actual costs of the activities or services that are provided, as well as the assigned mission of the agency. *Promotion* includes a wide range of advertising methods, public relations outlets, special events, and other techniques designed to inform the public of available programs and services and to motivate them to become involved. A critical element in many recreation programs involves the recruitment of possible cosponsors who will assist in funding, staffing, publicizing, or otherwise helping to carry out major events, tournaments, leagues, cultural activities, or similar activities.

IMPLEMENT ACTION PLAN

This is the culminating stage of the entire marketing process. It involves putting the plan into action, in an appropriately timed sequence of announcements, events, registration periods, "open houses," tours, package deals, membership drives, news releases, and similar activities. Facilities are opened, classes, workshops, or leagues get under way, and the action plan is put into effect.

This represents a management process, in which all of the traditional elements of staffing, scheduling, activity leadership, supervision, health and safety practices, community relations activities, and facilities maintenance come into play.

Each such function must be carried out with full awareness of its important impact on the public's perception of the agency and its programs. Clean rest rooms; courteous office staff; colorful and attractive brochures; events that are carried out efficiently; the large-scale use of community volunteers; and sensitive, enthusiastic leadership all contribute to a positive view of the program. Without them, all the publicity in the world and all the careful preplanning that has been done will be of little avail.

CONSUMER INVOLVEMENT AND FEEDBACK

Participation by target market groups represents the final step in the model that has just been outlined. It is at this stage that feedback must be obtained from participants—both *during* the program itself and at its *conclusion*. As Chapter 12 makes clear, program evaluation may utilize a number of approaches, including the use of formal evaluation instruments that measure consumer satisfaction, as well as the recommendations of advisory groups, informal program appraisals, the measurement of attendance or registration, and similar methods.

Depending on the content of feedback, the program may continue as originally planned, or may undergo fresh planning at any point. By using a feedback "loop" to provide input at the earlier stages of the process (see *Fig. 14.1*), it may be necessary to redesign program elements; to substitute one target market for another; or to modify "distribution," "pricing," or "promotion" practices. By retaining successful program elements, facilities, or services, and by modifying and reshaping those that are less successful, it becomes possible to build a highly productive and cost-effective enterprise that consistently achieves its stated objectives.

Throughout the process that has just been described, it is obvious that effective marketing strategy must employ valid data-gathering methods and must analyze them using sound research and evaluation methods. These methods represent a blend of business-oriented analytical tools and other social-research techniques drawn from the social and behavioral sciences. In some cases, although the primary purpose of marketing research is clearly an *applied* one, it may also lead to the development of new *theoretical* models of consumer behavior or of leisure motivations. In conclusion, then, it is obvious that both planning and marketing functions in recreation management are closely linked to research and evaluation.

SUMMARY

Management information systems are becoming increasingly important today in many types of organizations, as a means of organizing data so that they are readily accessible and are designed to meet important management needs. Planning is usually thought of in terms of recreation and park master planning. This process extends from the point of developing an agency philosophy to a detailed inventory of present resources and programs and a needs assessment of varied community groups. It involves developing and selecting appropriate strategies to achieve stated objectives and usually includes both short- and long-range recommendations for land acquisition and facility development. Land and facility standards are frequently used in the master planning process, as well as formulas designed to analyze participation demand, turnover rates, and facility needs.

Other types of planning studies may examine specific aspects of management operations, or problem areas related to personnel, programming, maintenance, or vandalism. Systems-based planning methods have been particularly useful in developing budget and fiscal policies and initiating and monitoring various types of projects. The chapter concludes with an overview of marketing principles and methods in recreation and parks, including evaluation of the marketing environment, product and management analysis, and the use of research methods in the marketing plan.

ENDNOTES

1. Craig Kelsey and Howard Gray, *"Master Plan Process for Parks and Recreation,"* (Alexandria, Va.: American Association for Leisure and Recreation, 1985): 1.
2. John J. Bullaro and Christopher R. Edginton, *Commercial Leisure Services: Managing for Profit, Service, and Personal Satisfaction* (New York: Macmillan, 1986): 214.
3. Daniel H. Perlman, "New Tools and Techniques in University Administration," in Diane Borst and Patrick J. Montana, eds., *Managing Nonprofit Organizations* (New York: AMACON, American Management Association, 1979): 61.
4. Ibid., 62.
5. Alice M. Lange and Dolores M. Mescher, "Development of a Management Information System," *Journal of Park and Recreation Administration* (3rd Quarter 1985): 15–19.
6. *Webster's New International Dictionary* (Springfield, Mass.: G. and C. Merriam Co., 1956): 1881.

7. Seymour M. Gold, *Recreation Planning and Design* (New York: McGraw-Hill Book Co., 1980): 5.
8. Ibid., 26.
9. Roger A. Lancaster, ed., *Recreation, Park and Open Space Standards and Guidelines* (Alexandria, Va.: National Recreation and Park Association, 1983): 40–41.
10. For a fuller discussion of space standards, see William F. Theobald, *Evaluation of Recreation and Park Programs* (New York: John Wiley and Sons, 1979).
11. Adapted from Lancaster, Ibid., 60–61.
12. Ibid., 56.
13. Ibid., 48.
14. Ibid., 46.
15. Ibid., 47.
16. *Fairmount Park Master Plan Summary* (Philadelphia, Pa.: Wallace, Roberts and Todd, 1983): 14–15.
17. *JWB Health, Physical Education and Recreation Study Report* (New York: Jewish Welfare Board, 1976–1977).
18. See Richard Kraus and Joseph E. Curtis, *Creative Management in Recreation, Parks, and Leisure Services* (St. Louis, Mo.: C. V. Mosby Co., 1986): 47–50.
19. Ibid.
20. See Perlman, in Borst and Montana, op. cit., 65.
21. Charles C. Clegg and George Chambliss, "Management by Objectives: A Case Study," *Leisure Today, Journal of Physical Education, Recreation and Dance* (April 1982): 45.
22. Dennis Howard and John Crompton, *Financing, Managing and Marketing Recreation and Park Resources* (Dubuque, Iowa: Wm. C. Brown, 1980): 320.
23. Philip Kotler, *Marketing for Non-Profit Organizations* (Englewood Cliffs, N. J.: Prentice-Hall, Inc., 1975): 74.
24. John Crompton, "Beyond the Better Mousetrap," *Employee Services Management* (May/June 1984): 16.
25. John Crompton, "Selecting Target Markets—A Key to Effective Marketing," *Journal of Park and Recreation Administration* (January 1983): 8.
26. Robert C. Lewis and Bernard H. Booms, cited in A. Parasuraman, Valarie A. Zeithami and Leonard L. Berry, "A Conceptual Model of Service Quality and Its Implications for Future Research," *Journal of Marketing* (Fall 1985): 42.

QUESTIONS FOR CLASS REVIEW AND DISCUSSION

43. Why is there a need for management information systems in recreation and park agencies? Identify a number of key management functions in

such organizations, and then list the kinds of information that are required in order to carry out these functions effectively. How can evaluation and research techniques be used to gather such information?

44. In class discussion, select a particular type of leisure facility or program. In a logical sequence, determine what kind of marketing research plan you might develop for such a facility or program—including the kind of information you might need to know and then the methods you would use to gather it. Focus particularly on the planning or initiating stage of the process.

WORKSHOP ACTIVITY TO BE CARRIED OUT WITHIN THE CLASS

45. Obtain a master planning study that has been done by a public recreation and park agency. Analyze it, including the kinds of data it includes, the standards that are cited, and the recommendations or conclusions it reaches. How have the data-based findings of the report been used to justify the recommendations?

This may consist of a large-scale federal or state planning report, or a planning study done within a smaller city or county setting. As an alternative, examine a planning study done for a therapeutic, nonprofit, or other type of agency.

APPENDIX
An Example of a Community Survey

This community recreation survey was carried out for Lower Paxton Township, Pa. in 1985–1986. Diane Wilson directed the study, and Lawrence Allen served as consultant.

**LOWER PAXTON TOWNSHIP
BOARD OF SUPERVISORS**
FRANCIS R. MUMMERT MEMORIAL BUILDING
SUITE 206 — 75 SOUTH HOUCKS ROAD, HARRISBURG, PA 17109
Telephone (717) 657-5600

Chairman, Richard N. Koch
Vice Chairperson, Jane D. Martizo   Member, Carl "Dutch" Lentz
Member, James L. Snyder   Member, H. Michael Liptak
Township Supervisor, Jack F. Hurley

LOWER PAXTON TOWNSHIP COMMUNITY SURVEY

Dear Lower Paxton Township Resident,

The Lower Paxton Township Board of Supervisors, in its ongoing efforts to respond to residents' needs, is seeking your input regarding present and future public services including recreation and park facilities. This community survey allows you and other members of your household a means of direct communication with the Board. Please take the time to complete the enclosed questionnaires. Your responses enable us to obtain information from a true cross-section of Township residents and provide the best information upon which to base our future planning.

Two questionnaires have been provided, one for adult members of your household and the other for youth. We would like you to complete the adult questionnaire. Also, under the recreation activities section we are asking you as well as one other adult to respond to these questions.

On the youth questionnaire, space has been allotted for up to three individuals under the age of 18 to respond. Have the three oldest youth in your household complete this questionnaire. For younger children, please assist them with their responses. If no children reside in your household, disregard this questionnaire.

It is most important that we have your response to all the questions. The information collected will have a direct bearing on establishing priorities for programs, facilities, and improvements in the Township. All individual responses will be kept strictly confidential. If you have comments on issues not covered in the questionnaire, please feel free to write in your concerns and wishes.

If you have any questions about the study, feel free to call us. The telephone number is 657-5628. Please return the completed questionnaires in the enclosed self-addressed stamped envelope.

Again, thank you for your input.

Respectfully,

Richard Koch, Chairman
Board of Supervisors

301

INDIVIDUAL INFORMATION

To assist us in organizing the responses to this survey, we need some information about you and the members of your household. All of this information is STRICTLY CONFIDENTIAL and your name will not be associated with your answers.

1. How long have you lived in the township? _____ years.
2. What is your marital status?
   ☐ Single (never married)   ☐ Divorced/Widowed/Separated
   ☐ Married   ☐ Other
3. What is the age, sex, and completed schooling of each member of your household? All individuals 18 years and older are considered adults.

Highest Level of School Completed

	AGE	SEX Male	SEX Female	Elementary	Some High School	High School Graduate	2 Year College	4 Year College	Graduate School
Yourself (Adult #1)	_____	☐	☐	☐	☐	☐	☐	☐	☐
Adult #2	_____	☐	☐	☐	☐	☐	☐	☐	☐
Adult #3	_____	☐	☐	☐	☐	☐	☐	☐	☐
Youth #1	_____	☐	☐	☐	☐	☐	☐	☐	☐
Youth #2	_____	☐	☐	☐	☐	☐	☐	☐	☐
Youth #3	_____	☐	☐	☐	☐	☐	☐	☐	☐
Youth #4	_____	☐	☐	☐	☐	☐	☐	☐	☐

4. Are you presently (check one)
   ☐ Self-employed   ☐ Retired
   ☐ Full-time Employee   ☐ Unemployed
   ☐ Part-time Employee   ☐ Full-time Homemaker

RECREATION ACTIVITIES

We are interested in how often the adult members of your household participate in the following recreational activities. We would like you (Adult #1) and a second adult (Adult #2) in your household to complete this section. First, for yourself and the second adult, please check how often each of you participated in the activitites listed below. Second, indicate if you or Adult #2 would like to participate in the activities more in the future.

	Adult #1 (Yourself)						Adult #2 (second Adult in previous section)					
	Frequency of participation					Check if you would like to participate more	Frequency of participation					Check if you would like to participate more
Activity	Never	In-Frequently	Sometimes	Frequently	Very Frequently	Yes	Never	In-Frequently	Sometimes	Frequently	Very Frequently	Yes
Acting	☐	☐	☐	☐	☐	☐	☐	☐	☐	☐	☐	☐
Aerobics/Fitness Classes	☐	☐	☐	☐	☐	☐	☐	☐	☐	☐	☐	☐
Auto Repair	☐	☐	☐	☐	☐	☐	☐	☐	☐	☐	☐	☐
Baseball	☐	☐	☐	☐	☐	☐	☐	☐	☐	☐	☐	☐
Basketball	☐	☐	☐	☐	☐	☐	☐	☐	☐	☐	☐	☐
Bicycling	☐	☐	☐	☐	☐	☐	☐	☐	☐	☐	☐	☐
Bowling	☐	☐	☐	☐	☐	☐	☐	☐	☐	☐	☐	☐
Camping	☐	☐	☐	☐	☐	☐	☐	☐	☐	☐	☐	☐
Canoeing	☐	☐	☐	☐	☐	☐	☐	☐	☐	☐	☐	☐
Ceramics	☐	☐	☐	☐	☐	☐	☐	☐	☐	☐	☐	☐
Cultural Trips	☐	☐	☐	☐	☐	☐	☐	☐	☐	☐	☐	☐
Downhill Skiing	☐	☐	☐	☐	☐	☐	☐	☐	☐	☐	☐	☐
Drawing	☐	☐	☐	☐	☐	☐	☐	☐	☐	☐	☐	☐
Flower Arranging	☐	☐	☐	☐	☐	☐	☐	☐	☐	☐	☐	☐
Football	☐	☐	☐	☐	☐	☐	☐	☐	☐	☐	☐	☐
Gardening	☐	☐	☐	☐	☐	☐	☐	☐	☐	☐	☐	☐
Golf	☐	☐	☐	☐	☐	☐	☐	☐	☐	☐	☐	☐
Gourmet Cooking	☐	☐	☐	☐	☐	☐	☐	☐	☐	☐	☐	☐
Hiking	☐	☐	☐	☐	☐	☐	☐	☐	☐	☐	☐	☐
Home Repairs	☐	☐	☐	☐	☐	☐	☐	☐	☐	☐	☐	☐

	Adult #1 (Yourself)						Adult #2 (second Adult in previous section)					
Activity	Never	In- Frequently	Sometimes	Frequently	Very Frequently	Yes	Never	In- Frequently	Sometimes	Frequently	Very Frequently	Yes
Horseshoes	☐	☐	☐	☐	☐	☐	☐	☐	☐	☐	☐	☐
Horseback Riding	☐	☐	☐	☐	☐	☐	☐	☐	☐	☐	☐	☐
Knitting/Needlework	☐	☐	☐	☐	☐	☐	☐	☐	☐	☐	☐	☐
Leatherwork	☐	☐	☐	☐	☐	☐	☐	☐	☐	☐	☐	☐
Martial Arts	☐	☐	☐	☐	☐	☐	☐	☐	☐	☐	☐	☐
Microwave Cooking	☐	☐	☐	☐	☐	☐	☐	☐	☐	☐	☐	☐
Painting	☐	☐	☐	☐	☐	☐	☐	☐	☐	☐	☐	☐
Photography	☐	☐	☐	☐	☐	☐	☐	☐	☐	☐	☐	☐
Music Lessons	☐	☐	☐	☐	☐	☐	☐	☐	☐	☐	☐	☐
Running/Jogging	☐	☐	☐	☐	☐	☐	☐	☐	☐	☐	☐	☐
Sculpture	☐	☐	☐	☐	☐	☐	☐	☐	☐	☐	☐	☐
Sewing	☐	☐	☐	☐	☐	☐	☐	☐	☐	☐	☐	☐
Singing	☐	☐	☐	☐	☐	☐	☐	☐	☐	☐	☐	☐
Soccer	☐	☐	☐	☐	☐	☐	☐	☐	☐	☐	☐	☐
Social Dance	☐	☐	☐	☐	☐	☐	☐	☐	☐	☐	☐	☐
Softball	☐	☐	☐	☐	☐	☐	☐	☐	☐	☐	☐	☐
Stain Glass	☐	☐	☐	☐	☐	☐	☐	☐	☐	☐	☐	☐
Swimming	☐	☐	☐	☐	☐	☐	☐	☐	☐	☐	☐	☐
Tennis	☐	☐	☐	☐	☐	☐	☐	☐	☐	☐	☐	☐
Volleyball	☐	☐	☐	☐	☐	☐	☐	☐	☐	☐	☐	☐
Weight Training	☐	☐	☐	☐	☐	☐	☐	☐	☐	☐	☐	☐
Sightseeing	☐	☐	☐	☐	☐	☐	☐	☐	☐	☐	☐	☐
Going to Movies	☐	☐	☐	☐	☐	☐	☐	☐	☐	☐	☐	☐
Racquetball	☐	☐	☐	☐	☐	☐	☐	☐	☐	☐	☐	☐
Other _____ Specify	☐	☐	☐	☐	☐	☐	☐	☐	☐	☐	☐	☐

We are interested in your past/current involvement in programs and services sponsored by the Lower Paxton Parks and Recreation Department. Please check the appropriate box.

Has any family member participated in recreation program(s) offered by Lower Paxton Township?
☐ Yes ☐ No

If you answer NO to the above question, would you please explain the reasons why? _____

_____

_____

ELEMENTS OF COMMUNITY LIFE

We would like to find out how important the following elements of community life are to you and how satisfied you are with those elements in Lower Paxton Township. Please check the appropriate box for each item in set 1 (importance) and in set 2 (satisfaction).

IMPORTANCE TO COMMUNITY LIFE
How important is each of these elements in determining your overall satisfaction with community life? Please check the appropriate box.

SATISFACTION IN YOUR TOWNSHIP
How satisfied are you with the availability and quality of these elements of community life in your township? Please check the appropriate box.

	Very Important	Important	Neutral	Un- Important	Very Unimportant	Very Satisfied	Satisfied	Neutral	Dis- Satisfied	Very Dissatisfied
Shopping Facilities	☐	☐	☐	☐	☐	☐	☐	☐	☐	☐
Private/Commercial Recreation (health clubs, movies, bowling)	☐	☐	☐	☐	☐	☐	☐	☐	☐	☐
Fire Protection	☐	☐	☐	☐	☐	☐	☐	☐	☐	☐
Welfare and Social Services	☐	☐	☐	☐	☐	☐	☐	☐	☐	☐
Cost of Living	☐	☐	☐	☐	☐	☐	☐	☐	☐	☐

304

	IMPORTANCE TO COMMUNITY LIFE					SATISFACTION IN YOUR TOWNSHIP				
How important is each of these elements in determining your overall satisfaction with community life? Please check the appropriate box.						How satisfied are you with the availability and quality of these elements of community life in your township? Please check the appropriate box.				
	Very Important	Important	Neutral	Un-important	Very Unimportant	Very Satisfied	Satisfied	Neutral	Dis-Satisfied	Very Dissatisfied
Physical Geography or Terrain	☐	☐	☐	☐	☐	☐	☐	☐	☐	☐
Housing (cost and availability)	☐	☐	☐	☐	☐	☐	☐	☐	☐	☐
Public Transportation	☐	☐	☐	☐	☐	☐	☐	☐	☐	☐
Citizen Input into Community Decisions	☐	☐	☐	☐	☐	☐	☐	☐	☐	☐
Opportunities to be with Friends and Relatives	☐	☐	☐	☐	☐	☐	☐	☐	☐	☐
Environmental Cleanliness (air, water, soil)	☐	☐	☐	☐	☐	☐	☐	☐	☐	☐
Medical Facilities (clinic and/or hospital)	☐	☐	☐	☐	☐	☐	☐	☐	☐	☐
Publicly Funded Recreation (social, cultural, and sports/fitness programs for youth and adults)	☐	☐	☐	☐	☐	☐	☐	☐	☐	☐
Medical Doctors	☐	☐	☐	☐	☐	☐	☐	☐	☐	☐
Dentists	☐	☐	☐	☐	☐	☐	☐	☐	☐	☐
Climate and Weather	☐	☐	☐	☐	☐	☐	☐	☐	☐	☐
Utilities (water, gas, electric, and sewage)	☐	☐	☐	☐	☐	☐	☐	☐	☐	☐
Job Opportunities	☐	☐	☐	☐	☐	☐	☐	☐	☐	☐
College/University Courses (for credit)	☐	☐	☐	☐	☐	☐	☐	☐	☐	☐
Adult Education (non-credit classes)	☐	☐	☐	☐	☐	☐	☐	☐	☐	☐
Churches and Religious Opportunities	☐	☐	☐	☐	☐	☐	☐	☐	☐	☐
Opportunities for Civic and Fraternal Organizations	☐	☐	☐	☐	☐	☐	☐	☐	☐	☐
Police Protection	☐	☐	☐	☐	☐	☐	☐	☐	☐	☐
Public Schools (K through 12 programs)	☐	☐	☐	☐	☐	☐	☐	☐	☐	☐
Local Government	☐	☐	☐	☐	☐	☐	☐	☐	☐	☐
Roads and Highways	☐	☐	☐	☐	☐	☐	☐	☐	☐	☐
Parks and Open Spaces	☐	☐	☐	☐	☐	☐	☐	☐	☐	☐
General Appearance of your area of the Township	☐	☐	☐	☐	☐	☐	☐	☐	☐	☐
General Appearance of the Township	☐	☐	☐	☐	☐	☐	☐	☐	☐	☐
Public Health Services	☐	☐	☐	☐	☐	☐	☐	☐	☐	☐
Opportunities to Become Familiar with Other Residents	☐	☐	☐	☐	☐	☐	☐	☐	☐	☐
Technical and/or Vocational Training for Career Development	☐	☐	☐	☐	☐	☐	☐	☐	☐	☐
Emergency Services	☐	☐	☐	☐	☐	☐	☐	☐	☐	☐

COMMUNITY SATISFACTION

Please mark the response that BEST DESCRIBES YOUR FEELINGS about each of the following statements.

1. How satisfied are you with your township as a place to live?
   - ☐ Very Satisfied
   - ☐ Satisfied
   - ☐ Neutral
   - ☐ Dissatisfied
   - ☐ Very Dissatisfied

2. How satisfied are you with the quality of life in your township?
   - ☐ Very Satisfied
   - ☐ Satisfied
   - ☐ Neutral
   - ☐ Dissatisfied
   - ☐ Very Dissatisfied

3. This township is an ideal place to live.
   - ☐ Strongly Agree
   - ☐ Agree
   - ☐ Neutral
   - ☐ Disagree
   - ☐ Strongly Disagree

4. The future of this township looks bright.
   - ☐ Strongly Agree
   - ☐ Agree
   - ☐ Neutral
   - ☐ Disagree
   - ☐ Strongly Disagree

5. People won't work together to get things done for this township.
   - ☐ Strongly Agree
   - ☐ Agree
   - ☐ Neutral
   - ☐ Disagree
   - ☐ Strongly Disagree

6. This township has good leaders.
   - ☐ Strongly Agree
   - ☐ Agree
   - ☐ Neutral
   - ☐ Disagree
   - ☐ Strongly Disagree

7. Not much can be said in favor of this township.
   - ☐ Strongly Agree
   - ☐ Agree
   - ☐ Neutral
   - ☐ Disagree
   - ☐ Strongly Disagree

8. Residents of this township continually look for new solutions to programs rather than being satisfied with things as they are.
   - ☐ Strongly Agree
   - ☐ Agree
   - ☐ Neutral
   - ☐ Disagree
   - ☐ Strongly Disagree

9. Overall, how satisfied are you with community life in your township?
   - ☐ Very Satisfied
   - ☐ Satisfied
   - ☐ Neutral
   - ☐ Dissatisfied
   - ☐ Very Dissatisfied

Please write in your response

10. What are the two MOST SATISFYING aspects of living in Lower Paxton Township?
    1. _____
    2. _____

11. What are the two LEAST SATISFYING aspects of living in Lower Paxton Township?
    1. _____
    2. _____

BARRIERS TO PARTICIPATION

The following statements are frequently given as reasons why people do not participate as often as they would like to in the activities in which they are most interested. Please indicate whether you agree or disagree with each statement as it relates to participation in the recreational activities in which you are most interested.

	Strongly Disagree	Disagree	Neutral	Agree	Strongly Agree
1. It costs too much to participate in the recreational activities in which I am most interested.	☐	☐	☐	☐	☐
2. The facilities necessary to participate in the activities in which I am most interested are not available	☐	☐	☐	☐	☐
3. The available facilities are too far away	☐	☐	☐	☐	☐
4. I do not feel safe while participating in the activities in which I am most interested	☐	☐	☐	☐	☐
5. I don't know anyone with whom I can participate in the activities in which I am most interested	☐	☐	☐	☐	☐
6. I don't know where to go to participate in the activities in which I am most interested	☐	☐	☐	☐	☐
7. I don't have a way to get to the facilities and/or area where I can participate in the activities in which I am most interested.	☐	☐	☐	☐	☐

FACILITIES

Your answers to the following section will help us establish priorities for facility development and improvements. Please check the box that best describes how you feel about the number of facilities currently provided in Lower Paxton Township:

	Not enough: the township should provide more.	Not enough, but not worth spending public money to provide	ENOUGH	TOO MANY
Large Community Parks _____	☐	☐	☐	☐
Neighborhood Play Parks _____	☐	☐	☐	☐
Tennis Courts _____	☐	☐	☐	☐

	Not enough: the township should provide more.	Not enough, but not worth spending public money to provide.	ENOUGH	TOO MANY
Football Fields _____	☐	☐	☐	☐
Softball/Baseball Fields _____	☐	☐	☐	☐
Fitness Course _____	☐	☐	☐	☐
Soccer Fields_____	☐	☐	☐	☐
Meeting Rooms_____	☐	☐	☐	☐
Picnic Facilities _____	☐	☐	☐	☐
Outdoor Basketball _____	☐	☐	☐	☐
Open Park Space _____	☐	☐	☐	☐
Outdoor Volleyball Courts _____	☐	☐	☐	☐
Indoor Program Facilities (Lower Paxton Soccer Assoc.)	☐	☐	☐	☐

2. Please check if you think Lower Paxton Township Parks and Recreation Department should provide the following facilities:

Comprehensive Recreation Center .... ☐ Yes ☐ No
Indoor Pool .... ☐ Yes ☐ No
Outdoor Pool .... ☐ Yes ☐ No
Nature Study/Nature Center .... ☐ Yes ☐ No
Gymnasium (independent of a comprehensive
center) .... ☐ Yes ☐ No
Large Outdoor Sports Complex .... ☐ Yes ☐ No
Other (please list): _____
_____

3. Please check the box that best describes how well you think Lower Paxton facilities are maintained:

	Very Well Maintained	Adequately Maintained	Poorly Maintained	Don't Know
Large Community Parks....................	☐	☐	☐	☐
Neighborhood Play Parks..................	☐	☐	☐	☐
Tennis Courts..........................	☐	☐	☐	☐
Softball/Baseball Fields	☐	☐	☐	☐
Picnic Facilities	☐	☐	☐	☐
Outdoor Basketball/Volleyball Courts	☐	☐	☐	☐
Meeting Rooms	☐	☐	☐	☐
Soccer Fields	☐	☐	☐	☐
Football Fields	☐	☐	☐	☐
Open Park Space	☐	☐	☐	☐
Fitness Course	☐	☐	☐	☐
Indoor Program Facilities (Lower Paxton Soccer Asso.)	☐	☐	☐	☐

DEPARTMENT OVERALL

Please check the box that best describes how you feel about each of the statements below. If you would like to comment on the statements, please do so in the space provided.

	Strongly Agree	Agree	Don't Know	Disagree	Strongly Disagree
1. There is enough publicity to let you know about recreation services and programs in Lower Paxton Township .... Comments: _____	☐	☐	☐	☐	☐
2. Lower Paxton Township's parks are adequately maintained to provide safe and pleasant recreation experiences .... Comments: _____	☐	☐	☐	☐	☐
3. The equipment at Lower Paxton Township's parks meets your recreational needs .... Comments: _____	☐	☐	☐	☐	☐
4. Lower Paxton Township's indoor recreation facilities are adequately maintained to provide safe and pleasant experiences. .... Comments: _____	☐	☐	☐	☐	☐

	Strongly Agree	Agree	Don't Know	Disagree	Strongly Disagree
5. There is enough community input into the type of programs and services offered by the Township's Parks and Recreation Department . . . . Comments: _____	☐	☐	☐	☐	☐
6. Township parks are well marked and easily found . . . . Comments: _____	☐	☐	☐	☐	☐
7. Currently, there are adequate recreation programs in Lower Paxton Township . . . . Comments: _____	☐	☐	☐	☐	☐
8. Programs and services offered by Lower Paxton Township Parks and Recreation Department are well supervised and organized . . . . Comments: _____	☐	☐	☐	☐	☐
9. Registration for Lower Paxton's recreation programs and services is well organized . . . . Comments: _____	☐	☐	☐	☐	☐
10. Lower Paxton Township offers an adequate variety of recreation programs and services for all age groups. . Comments: _____	☐	☐	☐	☐	☐
11. The fees charged for Lower Paxton's recreation programs and services are fair . . . . Comments: _____	☐	☐	☐	☐	☐

THANKS

Thank you for responding to this questionnaire. If you have any comments regarding recreation and parks services in Lower Paxton Township, please use this space to convey your thoughts.

AUTHOR INDEX

310

Isaac, Stephen, 8, 11, 99-100, 206

Jackson, Edgar L., 22

Kelsey, Craig, 273
Kerlinger, Fred, 3, 31, 34, 39, 117
Kinney, W. B., 251-252
Kirby, T. F., 259
Kirsch, Sondra, 262
Kotler, Philip, 290
Krathwohl, David, 90

Lange, Alice M., 275
La Page, W. F., 19
Lancaster, Roger A., 282, 284
Levy, Joseph, 256-257
Locke, Lawrence, 89-90
Lundegren, Herberta, 215

Mason, Emanuel, 29, 31, 38, 41-42, 57
Mazanea, Josef A., 197
McCafferty, Margaret E., 17
Mescher, Dolores M., 275
Mescher, Michael, 129
Michael, William B., 8, 99-100, 206
Mihalik, Brian, 20
Mills, Allan S., 22
Mobley, Tony A., 8, 10
Moeller, George, 129
More, Thomas, 129
Myrdal, Gunnar, 6

Navar, Nancy, 249
Northrop, F. S. C., 81-82

Olson, Karen P., 17

Parker, Robert, 259

Perlman, Daniel, 274
Phillips, L. E., Jr., 19

Rogers, Nancy C., 17
Rossman, J. Robert, 197

Schleien, Stuart, 17, 255
Schroth, Richard J., 20
Schuler, Randall, 249
Sellitz, Claire, 9, 11, 40, 47, 201, 211
Shafer, Elwood, 129
Sharpless, Daniel R., 20
Short, M. J., 259
Siderelis, Chrystos D., 19
Simon, Julian, 61, 206, 211
Simpura, Jossi, 22
Spirduso, Waneen, 89-90
Snyder, Eldon E., 22
Spreitzer, Elmer, 22
Suchman, Edward, 10

Tedrick, Ted., 18, 270

van der Smissen, Betty, 234
Veblen, Thorstein, 6

Wankel, Leonard, 18
Warnick, Rodney B., 20
Weber, Max, 36
Wehman, Paul, 255
Weiner, Andrew, 65
Whitehead, Alfred North, 36
Witt, Peter A., 15
Wolf, C. P., 7
Wong, Robert A. G., 22
Woo, Judith, 15, 27
Wright, Alan, 257
Wrightsman, Lawrence, 9, 11, 40, 47, 201, 211

SUBJECT INDEX